The Moon in

M000083199

AN IMMIGRANT'S JOURNEY HOME

Kate Saller

University of Missouri Press
Columbia

Copyright © 2014 by
The Curators of the University of Missouri
University of Missouri Press, Columbia, Missouri 65201
Printed and bound in the United States of America
All rights reserved

5 4 3 2 1   18 17 16 15 14

Cataloging-in-Publication data available from the Library of
Congress
ISBN 978-0-8262-2030-1

∞ This paper meets the requirements of the
American National Standard for Permanence of Paper
for Printed Library Materials, Z39.48, 1984.

Cover design: Jennifer Cropp
Interior design and composition: Richard Farkas
Typefaces: Palatino Linotype, Expectation Std., Gotham Narrow

For
Annah Frances Emuge
with gratitude and admiration
for telling her story
with courage and grace

For
Esther, Christopher, and James,
whose spirits have nourished so many,
and for all of Annah's children

Contents

Photographs follow page 132

Preface

I had just finished speaking to the Rotary Club of St. Charles, Missouri, about my humanitarian work in Africa when a beautiful, statuesque black woman approached me. Without prelude she asked me, "Do you know how to get mosquito nets for fifty-four children in Uganda?" This was my introduction to Annah Frances Acam Emuge, the determined and courageous woman who is the subject of this book.

As I came to know Annah, I was amazed to learn about the joys and tribulations of her life. It seemed as if, every time she told me a story from her past, I was incredulous that one human being could have survived it, and yet that was just one part of her story. Annah was the third daughter born to a poor family in rural Uganda in 1959. I wrote her life entirely through her eyes, to give readers a full sense of growing up as a village child in a country being systematically decimated by its maniacal dictator, Idi Amin Dada. As a child and teenager, this remarkable young woman matured and set the course of her life while enduring the kinds of devastations and threats that we have read about in many such accounts of life in twentieth-century rural Africa. What set Annah's story apart for me was that it is not about an individual overcoming such an existence, coming to the United States, and finding a clear path back to her roots to improve the lives of those left behind; rather, it is the story of a woman who was faced with even tougher challenges here, and of her extraordinary and largely solitary triumph over all of them.

Entwined in Annah's tale of grace and strength is the sadder story of her husband, who came to this country filled with hopes and ambitions, only to find that they were all beyond his reach. The loss of his dreams, along with the realities of the life he found here, proved to be more than this talented and brilliant man could withstand.

To accurately portray Annah's life, I created an outline of the book and then had her tape-record her recollections from each period of her life, one section at a time. I took notes from each recording and then interviewed her to fill out my knowledge of that part of her life. After writing each chapter from my notes, I went over the material with Annah to ensure that she felt it was an accurate and complete picture of her life at that time. As this process progressed, Annah and I realized that I am unusual among her American acquaintances in that I understand and have observed firsthand the life she led in Uganda, sleeping in mud huts and working on the family's subsistence farm to survive. Through my affiliation with the service organization Rotary International, I have been to five African countries, traveling to and staying in rural areas to immunize children, distribute mosquito nets to orphans, and coordinate the placement of filtered wells in poor communities with no access to clean water. In spite of the unbelievable hardships suffered by the people I encountered there, all of them were warm and welcoming, finding joy in things like the simple act of offering me a crude, handmade stool to rest on in the shade as I worked. It was this same spirit that drew me to Annah when I met her.

Annah did get her fifty-four mosquito nets through Rotary connections, and St. Louis—area Rotarians donated the money needed to purchase them. She has now created a 501(c)(3) organization, the Atai Orphanage Fund (www.ataiorphanagefund.org), which collects donations to help support the children who live in the orphanage created by her mother. I am a member of the AOF's board, and we are proud to say that we were able to raise the funds to place a 240-foot bore-hole well on the orphanage's land in 2010. Although the children sleep in mud huts and live a simple, poor life that differs very little from Annah's childhood there, they proudly tell anyone who asks that they have a mama in America who loves them. All of the proceeds from sales of this book will be used to support Annah and the orphans of Atai.

All of the events presented in this book are Annah's personal memories of her life and her relationships to the people in her life. The names of some individuals have been changed.

I gratefully acknowledge the assistance and support of many individuals in creating this book. Foremost is Annah herself, who described her life fully and vividly, allowing me to write clearly about her and all of her joys and sorrows. My understanding of Annah, her village, and her family was enhanced by the opportunity I had to accompany her to her home village of Agu and the orphanage in December of 2009. There, through conversations with and observation of the orphans of Atai, I gained good insights into Annah's own childhood and early adulthood.

Grateful appreciation goes to the individuals in Annah's life who helped me to understand the depth of her character and love, especially her parents, Christopher and Esther; her sister Rosemary and her brother Charles; and her nephew George. Special thanks go to Annah's children, who demonstrated to me the nurturing and constant lifeline that Annah was, and is, to them.

I can't express the depth of my thanks to those who supported me untiringly throughout the creation of this book: my husband, Howard Schwadron; my children, Paul, Lydia, Luke, and Kelly; and my friend Julie Hereford. Their wisdom and understanding made the task of getting it all right seem possible and worthwhile. I thank my mentor, Dr. Diana Hume George, whose advice and support went way beyond her role as my teacher.

I also gratefully acknowledge my editor at the University of Missouri Press, Gary Kass, who patiently led me through the publication process and offered excellent advice. Thanks to all from the University of Missouri Press who brought this book to life: Clair Willcox, Sara Davis, Kristi Henson, Lyn Smith, and especially Gloria Thomas, whose keen eye and unlimited memory astound me.

The Moon in Your Sky

Prologue

ON NIGHTS WHEN THE VAST Ugandan sky poured moonlight into every corner of his family compound, Christopher liked to sit in the doorway of his hut, after Esther and the girls had gone to sleep, and look in at his son. He pictured all that he would teach little Francis: how to urge the goats and cows to the river with shouts and soft swats, how to cut the stunted trees into branched poles for the animal-pen fence, how to manage this patch of scratchy land that had been his family's possession for scores of generations. Sometimes when Esther turned in her sleep he was sure he could see the outline of his boy, forming strength and character inside her.

"It is a girl," Esther would say to him when she saw him glancing toward her belly in the daytime. "See how she lies curled on my side, just like Rosemary and Magdalene? She is Annah."

"It's a boy," he would mutter, never letting her see the doubt. "It's time you gave me a son, and this is Francis." After all, he knew when he married her that Esther was a good woman. She surely was capable of producing a male child. After the first girl, when his parents had urged him to take a second wife, he had been quick to defend her: "Esther Atai has good ancestors and she's named for one of the best—a mother to many sons and grandmother to village elders and wealthy men. Didn't Esther's own mother have three strong sons?"

When Esther had borne a second daughter, he let them bring in Lucy. But what good did a second wife do—she bore no sons either. Sometimes he worried that he had brought bad luck on himself by marrying Lucy, but surely now his luck was changing. His Esther, his first, true wife, would bear him a son this time.

Every look at her swollen belly reassured him. Sometimes the tiny creature inside would stretch out an arm or leg, poking a foot or hand at him from its fleshy cage. These were the long, strong limbs of a boy. And this was the impatience of a boy unable to leave the women behind and go with his father through the day's tasks.

1

Often now, when Christopher was out with the cows and goats at the river, he would speak softly to Francis, imagining how he would teach him.

"We never use sticks on the animals, Francis," he would say. "A swat or a shout is enough to move a goat or cow, and the meat is more tender when they haven't been beaten. Keep your eyes open wide, my son; if even one strays to the neighbor's field and eats his crops, we will be fined severely and embarrassed before the village."

He would look at the four mud huts in his compound—one for his parents, one for his family, one for cooking, and the one off in the back for Lucy—and he would picture how he and Francis would create bigger and better structures together. They would sketch their plans in the soft orange dirt and then begin the work. He would show Francis just how to cut the mud bricks from the river banks, lay them out to dry to just the right hardness, and then haul them to the site for the hut. As he grew taller and stronger, Francis would be the one doing most of the carrying and placing of the bricks into the precise, upright circle that would be the hut wall. They would cut the tall grass together and he would train Francis's supple young fingers to arrange the fronds into a thatch covering for the roof. His compound would be the envy of his neighbors.

As the time grew to less than a month, Christopher stayed busy in the fields, overseeing the women who were helping to harvest the year's grains. Sometimes, while he was working in the fields or tending the animals, Christopher was sure that he could hear Francis's little spirit calling to him.

"My angel, my boy," he would think. "It won't be long before I will sit at my own drum and proudly beat out the song that my son, my heir, is born."

It was around midmorning on a Friday when a woman from the village came to tell him that Esther was going to the hospital in town.

"It is too early and she has great pain," the woman said. "She must begin the journey now, before it is too late." Christopher looked out beyond the fields and watched his wife walk stiffly down the path that would take her the twelve miles to the midwife. Birthing children was no business for him, and he knew there would be women to help if she needed it. Someone had undoubtedly already run to alert Esther's mother that she must go to the hospital with food and supplies. Christopher sent a silent message to his son to persevere in spite of his early birth.

On Saturday, September 19, 1959, weighing less than six pounds, Annah became the smallest live baby ever to be born in the small mission medical facility called Fredika Hospital, near Ngora Township. She was named for the nun who had checked Esther's health each month during the pregnancy, and who now cared for the two of them for five days. The day after Annah's birth, the news of her arrival was relayed to Christopher. The birth of a daughter certainly wasn't enough reason for a man to travel twenty-four miles, so the introduction of the tiny girl to her father didn't occur until a week after he had watched his wife leave for her journey, expecting her to return with his son.

Christopher was told on Friday afternoon that his wife and baby had arrived home. Near nightfall, when he had finished his day's activities, he went to the doorway of his hut and looked in on Esther, who lay on her bedding with a small bundle at her breast. She rose and brought the child to him, a look of mingled fear and pride on her face. Christopher was a gentle man, so he offered no reproach, but merely leaned down from his height of well over six feet to get a look at the child.

"Your little Annah has a fighter's spirit, Christopher, and look at those long arms and legs. She'll be a good, strong girl." His mother spoke from behind him, where she had come to stand when she saw him striding toward the hut. He felt a stab of pride, in spite of himself, and then caught his breath when he glanced at the baby's eyes. Her dark eyes seemed to be regarding him with an even, direct look. Startled, he stared into her eyes for several moments, remembering the little boy he thought he had known all those months. His tiny daughter returned his gaze steadily.

"Annah Frances Acam," he said. He gave a curt nod to Esther and she turned, smiling, back into the hut to nurse the baby. That middle name meant that he loved his daughter, in spite of his wishes for a boy. And by giving her the ancestral name of Acam, Christopher had bestowed on Annah the name of a beloved and revered female family member.

1959 to 1973

IN THE LATE 1950s, the eastern African country of Uganda was a beautiful but contradictory land that contained the rushing headwaters of the Nile, mountainous rainforests filled with spectacular waterfalls, and the pristine waters of Lake Victoria on the south and Lake Alberta to the west. Yet only one-quarter of its land was sufficiently fertile to support the six and a half million inhabitants. In the semiarid northeastern region, families like Christopher's lived in compounds of mud huts and eked out their subsistence from small farm plots that they tended during the two rainy seasons. A British protectorate since the late nineteenth century, Uganda was granted home rule in 1961, and the country achieved independence and elected Prime Minister Milton Obote in 1962. Ugandans in even the smallest and most remote villages saw Obote as the architect of their independence and celebrated his presidency. As his tenure progressed, however, Obote seized more and more power, and he abolished the constitution in 1966. In 1971, the ambitious army commander Idi Amin Dada overthrew Obote and became president. Obote's corrupt presidency had left the citizens in poverty, and the early years of Idi Amin's cruel reign centered on the use of his soldiers, who were mostly from the favored tribes of the south, to dominate and terrorize the Ugandans who were from the less powerful tribes, especially those in the north: the Iteso, the Acholi, and the Langli.

Chapter 1

BY THE TIME ANNAH (AH-nah) was four years old, she was hard at work mastering her little world. For the most part it was joyful work: helping her mother and sisters with the chores, sharing family times, and playing in the maze of mud huts, animal pens, and vegetable fields that was their home in Agu Village in Teso District, Uganda. Annah was just becoming aware of a sense of yearning that she felt, especially when her father cast a disapproving glance her way. Sometimes her mother would notice his gaze and step quietly over to Annah and suggest that she go collect wood or help her sister. Other times, Annah simply returned his look, studying the face that was so familiar yet foreign to her. At those times she felt sad, as if her father expected something from her but she didn't know what it was.

On most mornings, Annah awoke to the cries of her two-year-old sister, Rebecca. At the age of six, her older sister, Magdalene, was expected to get Rebecca and Annah up and ready for the day before their mother, their "toto," came back from the fields, where she and her husband had been working since dawn. When there wasn't a drought, they would take a small pot of water from the storage basin and wash their faces. Toothbrushing was done with a stick from a special tree: the children chewed on the end of the stick until it was shredded into bristles and then used it to clean their teeth. Baby Rebecca didn't wear clothes because she hadn't learned to use the latrine yet, but the older girls were already being taught to emulate their mother's modesty. Each morning Annah wrapped a rectangle of ragged cloth around her torso, tying it under her arm to hold it in place. Real dresses were a rarity and used only for school or church.

"Come, come, girls. We can't take all day," Toto would call as she came from the near field where she always worked while the girls slept in the morning. Toto put porridge or leftover stew into bowls and then Papa joined them for a quick breakfast. As soon as the food was eaten, the family set out for the fields to continue the day's work there. Toto wrapped Rebecca in a shawl and tied it around herself so that the baby was held against her back. Rebecca spent almost all day there, watching the world and taking naps. Annah thought it looked really boring to be there all day. She didn't think she had liked it when she was as little as Rebecca.

In the field, the family spread out to weed or to harvest along the rows of the vegetables and grains that would sustain them. Annah's toto and papa took rows on the outside while the girls worked down their rows between the two parents. The grown-ups alternated between their own rows and the girls' rows so that the family stayed even. When Toto saw that the girls were tiring out, she would send them back to play near the huts for a while. Sometimes, Toto would have Annah sit under a tree on the edge of the field and hold her little sister, Rebecca. She loved sitting there, leaning against the cool bark of the tree trunk and watching the way the leaves and sky seemed to fight for her attention as she gazed upward. Papa worked the fields until midmorning, when he left to take the animals to the river to graze. On many afternoons, after the girls had been released to play and rest, Annah would look back toward the fields and watch Toto working the four rows they had begun, occasionally standing to adjust Rebecca's position on her back as she bent to her tasks. She couldn't have explained it then, but Annah knew that it was her graceful, patient mother who ensured the family's survival.

Her father usually returned with the cows and goats in early afternoon and herded them into the pen that he had created for them. It was a circular area surrounded by stubby trees that had been planted to form the perimeter. Papa cut the trees back frequently, so that the branches were thick, and the sharp twigs that protruded from them helped to keep the animals from going close enough to lean on them. Annah could see many little gaps between the branches near the ground, but apparently only she thought about squeezing through them: the animals never tried to escape from their pen. Sometimes, Papa just stayed in the compound then, sitting in the scant shade and drinking beer; but more often he went off to the village to drink and talk with the men from neighboring compounds, or he took longer trips on his bicycle to visit friends and cousins in other villages. Toto was usually still in the field finishing the work there, so Papa just called to her as he left and she waved a hand while she moved on among the plants.

While most of the elders in Agu had bicycles, this was strictly something used by men. Women were never taught to ride; they did all their traveling on foot. Each day, early in the morning and again in midafternoon, Annah's mother would gather the girls to walk with her to the river to fetch water in pots that they carried on their heads. Magdalene had a clay pot that was smaller than Toto's, but Annah wasn't ready for a pot that could break. She bore a small metal cooking pot that bounced as she walked, often forgetting to keep her back straight and her eyes ahead, as Toto had taught her. Each trip was a constant struggle for Annah to keep herself from breaking into a happy skip or bending over to inspect a bug on the ground.

"Careful, Annah. Think about what you are doing," her mother often said just as the pot slipped from its precarious perch and rolled across the ground. Annah laughed and chased the pot, put it back on her head, and marched forward, her lips pursed in concentration. Stifling a smile, Toto clucked at her and reminded her that women have many chores and couldn't be taking all day just to get the water.

Each time, when they arrived at the river, Annah watched her mother and sister and then imitated their actions: stepping into the brown water until it came up to their knees, planting their feet firmly, and then swinging the pot down in a graceful arc and holding it under the surface to fill with water. Annah carefully followed the same routine, holding her pot before her and pouring out a little water before carrying it out of the river. Once they were standing on the bank, each of them placed her jug carefully on her head. Toto and Magdalene simply placed the pot there and began walking; village girls who weren't as adept at this would hold the pot with upraised arms for most of the journey. Annah dripped water as she raised her little pot up over her head, but eventually she mastered getting it up there and balancing it as she began the return trek. The water rarely made it all the way home, though.

By the end of her fourth year, Annah had decided that she was too big for the metal pot.

"Toto, I am careful now, and see how steady I can hold my head?" she would demand as she walked. Finally, her mother agreed she would look for a very small clay pot. The next day, when Magdalene was arranging her clay pot on her head, Toto came to Annah with the pot that Papa liked to drink his beer from.

"This is the smallest clay pot I have, Annah. If you are sure you are ready, I will let you carry water in it, but you must be very careful."

Annah walked ever so properly to the river and back that day, and she proudly took the pot, nearly full of water, off her head when they reached home. Even Papa would be proud of her when he heard how she had done today. That night, her papa laughed when she told him she carried the pot all the way without dropping it.

"I knew you were strong from the moment I saw you in your mother's arms, my Frances," he said. Annah went to bed with a triumphant grin on her face that night.

The little pot only spent one day in its new status as water vessel, though. The very next day, although Annah was being as careful as she knew how, she tipped her head just once and the pot crashed to the ground and broke. Annah cried all afternoon, worrying that Papa would yell at her when he learned of her failure. He only shook his head and looked hard at her as Toto told him the story.

Annah was better at collecting firewood, although she often set her bundle down to chase the beautiful butterflies through the low brush that grew in clumps around the compound. She loved the colors of these little creatures, and the way their wings trembled when they alit on a leaf; she never got tired of following them on their journeys from bush to ground to fence. Annah liked going to get wood; she felt grown up and important as she ventured out alone and then toted her bundle back to add to the pile beside the cooking hut. Toto said Annah collected the best tinder, which was important because she couldn't start the fire without it.

Sometimes, while fetching water or gathering sticks, Annah would see neighbor boys herding their animals down to the river to graze. How she wished she could have that job. She knew she would be good at it—women in the village liked to point out how long her arms and legs were for a girl of her age, and how swiftly she could run. She surely could keep up with the goats and cows. As she watched the boys chasing down a stray, she plotted ways to get them to race her—she knew she would win. Occasionally, just within the compound, Annah chased some of their goats, shouting to them and giving them swats to move them in the direction she wanted. She was certain she could control them all the way to the river.

She had observed that, once at the river, the boys were free to rest and play as long as they kept a good eye on the animals. They liked to make noise however they could, and it was a rite of passage for a boy to master the art of playing whistled tunes by cupping his hands over his mouth and blowing into them. For all her fevered practice, Annah could never acquire this coveted skill. Some of the boys sat cross-legged and whittled flute-like instruments, while those who had finished theirs sat nearby and played halting tunes. The older boys could play full melodies that haunted Annah through the rest of her day. When the boys were in a rambunctious mood, they played a kind of soccer with handmade balls. To create a ball, a boy would gather grass and the spongy bark and leaves of banana trees. Then he would wad up the grass and wrap it tightly in the bark and leaves to create a rough sphere that could withstand a good, hard kick. Annah could hear their shrieks as one boy tossed the ball high into the air and the others scrambled to catch it.

The men who had no sons also took their animals to the river, once in the morning and again in late afternoon, after they had rested through the heat of midday. Papa and the other men always took their animals further upriver, away from where the boys played and shouted. There they sat, alone or in small groups, talking while the animals grazed. On most afternoons, Papa came back from his second trip to the river looking sad. Once, she asked why he didn't like to go to the river with the animals, and he said, "If your mother had given me sons I would not have to do this job. It is work for boys, not men."

After bringing the animals back a second time, Papa always went into the village, not to return until suppertime. In the meantime, Toto called the girls to the cooking hut for the hardest job of all: grinding the various grains and dried tubers into flour. Like most northern Ugandans, Annah's family grew a variety of grains, tubers, and vegetables in their fields. Annah especially liked the sweet potatoes, groundnuts (peanuts), squashes, and tomatoes. Cassava was their major crop, but it was tasteless to Annah. Right after harvest, there were fresh vegetables to eat, but as the year wore on, the family had to rely on the things they could preserve: millet and sorghum that they had stored in thatch-covered huts that were built off the ground to keep the contents fairly dry, or sweet potatoes and cassava that they had split and dried in the sun. All of these had to be ground into a fine meal for use either in porridge or in a pasty concoction called atap (uh-TAP). The atap was made by boiling water and then stirring in the millet or tuber flour until it reached the consistency of wet clay. At supper, Annah learned how to dip the atap into meat stew when there was meat available. It was

good for filling the stomach on the days when there were no vegetables, fruit, or meat.

The women used a very large mortar and pestle to grind the
grain and tubers into flour. Some women liked to sit with the mortar braced between their knees, but Annah's mother usually stood
to do the pounding. Their mortar, made of carved wood, was so
large that Annah thought she could probably put Rebecca in it, but
she knew better than to test Toto's patience by trying that. The pestle was a long wooden club, worn round and shiny on the end, that
Toto held in front of her with both hands to drive it into the mortar with as much force as possible. Magdalene was able to do some
good with the smaller pestle that Christopher had made for the girls,
but Annah was mainly the helper for this chore, carrying water and
bowls of grain when asked. The sounds of the pestle repeatedly beating against the mortar reminded Annah of the drumming she heard
each evening, but the rhythm was heavy and repetitive, and no song
came to her mind as Toto raised and lowered the pestle to smash the
grains. Once the grain was broken out of its covering or the tubers
were beaten into small pieces, Toto and the girls all sat down on the
cool dirt to beat and grind the pieces against a large, flat rock. They
brushed the flour that was produced into a clay pot for use in making supper. Toto used a large stone to grind the grains, and the girls
had smaller stones, about the size of one of their hands. This work
made Annah's arms ache, and her hands got blisters from working
the stone. She knew that one day, when she had become good at
this work, the blisters would turn into hard calluses—the mark of a
competent rural Ugandan woman's hands. Magdalene already had
small ones forming on her palms.

Although Annah groaned when it was time to make the flour for
supper, she had already learned that as time went on past the year's
harvest, the food they had to grind became scarcer and scarcer. She
watched nervously as Toto poured out the day's ration of grain or
tubers to be beaten, silently calculating whether this would even
make a whole bowl of atap for each of them. As much as she didn't
want to do the work, she had already learned the tough lesson of the
Ugandan growing cycle: with months between the two rainy seasons, food didn't always stretch well to the next harvest. A woman's
work was never ending, but a wise woman was thankful there was
work to be done—and food to be prepared.

Annah had also learned that women's work had to be done very
carefully. Toto instructed her and Magdalene to take turns on dif-

ferent days, one making the atap and the other making the sauce, so that they both got practice making the meals. Sometimes, the girls would let a small stone fall into the atap or put too much salt in the sauce. At those meals, Papa would look up suddenly with a frown on his face.

"So, which girl made the sauce today?" he would ask, and the girls would know immediately that something was wrong. If the sauce was too salty, he would just say "Frances made the sauce today, hmmm?" because she was always sprinkling in too much salt.

"That's Esther and her girls," he would mutter, and Annah would feel bad that Toto was being criticized for her mistake.

Annah was always glad when evening came. After supper, as the darkness began to fall, the whole family would gather near her grandparents' hut and Toto would build a small fire to keep the mosquitoes away. No matter how meager their store of food had gotten, her grandmother, Tata, her papa's mother, would have saved a few potatoes, cassava, or groundnuts to roast and give to the girls so that they wouldn't go to bed hungry. Once they had settled by the fire to eat their treats, Tata began telling them stories, especially about their ancestors. Annah liked to hear about her great-grand-father, who had twelve wives, all living in huts in a circle around his main hut. Annah was amazed by this image; she had been told that Lucy was the second wife and that the girl Lucy carried on her back, who was just a little older than Rebecca, was Papa's daughter, too, but she never saw her father going to spend time with Lucy in her hut, so how could a man want to have *twelve* families all living around him?

Her favorite evenings were those when Tata told about the ancestor, Acam (ah-CHAHM), for whom Annah had been named. Acam had lived a long time ago, even before Papa was born, and all the family spoke reverently about her. She was a strong, wealthy woman who had many animals and large fields. She bore many powerful, handsome sons, and she loved all children. When Acam went out into the village, all the people called out to her and she greeted each person and spent time checking on all of the elders. Annah imagined herself walking through the village one day, wav-ing to the adults and giving treats to the children.

As Tata finished the stories, the sound of drumbeats began to roll toward them from different directions as men all over the neigh-borhood sat drumming by their fires. Annah loved how she could feel the deep, rumbling sounds in her chest as well as in her ears. Slowly, the sounds intensified until drumming seemed to fill the sky over their heads. Then, after the drums had had their conversation and the echoed sounds faded, a man's voice sang out, relaying the news of the day. Soon other voices joined in, and the air became filled with chants of who was in love with whom, whose child was born or died, whose wife was pregnant. Once the local news had been shared, the men joined together in songs of joy for the harvest, or lament over the drought. These songs differed from night to night, and Annah wondered how all the men knew them. Always, the longest and loudest songs praised the man named Milton Obote—the one they called "president." Sometimes, after the last song, her father called Annah to him. Still humming, he would pick her up and sit her on his knee, singing softly, "Frances my angel, Frances my angel, I love my angel." She never saw Papa do this with any of her sisters. She would nestle against his strong chest, look up past his dark face to the starry sky, and think about how perfect her world was.

But there was a shadow that began to haunt her that year when she was four. Sometimes, as she lay next to her sleeping sisters, she could hear her parents still sitting and talking by the fire. Many nights the quiet hum of their conversation lulled her to sleep, but sometimes their voices rose in anger and she knew her father was displeased with someone. By that time, Annah had heard the story of why she had a middle name that could be either a boy's or a girl's name. She knew that her father had wanted her to be a boy, and that was why he called her "Frances" while Toto called her "Annah." She also knew that her father was disappointed that Toto had already given birth to four girls. Rosemary, who was four years older than Magdalene, had been sent to live in a larger village with an aunt who had no children. Earlier that year, her toto's stomach had gotten large and Magdalene had told Annah there would be a new baby in the family.

One day, Toto said she was going to the hospital to get the baby out of her stomach. She hugged each girl and told them to be good while she was away and then started walking down the road. When she returned a few days later, she showed Annah the tiny girl wrapped in her shawl and said Annah had a new sister. The baby cried softly sometimes, but she would quiet quickly when Toto nursed her. Annah thought this new baby should be good news, but there was a heavy sadness all through the compound and Toto cried a lot. After two weeks, Toto said the baby was sick and she had to take her back to the hospital for medicine.

Toto finally came home, but the bundle she carried in her arms didn't look like the baby—it was stiff and completely wrapped up in the shawl. Annah went to the doorway of their hut and watched as Toto took off the shawl and unwrapped her little sister. She lay the baby down on the bed, and the child didn't move or whimper. "Toto," Annah called, and her mother came to the door and held Annah in her arms. Her mother was crying hard, with tears running down her face and loud sobs coming from her chest. That was when Annah knew her little sister was gone.

"The baby had a hole in her heart," Toto said sadly. "She couldn't live, so she had to go away from us." It was hard to see the baby lying there so still and pale, while Toto cried and cried. Annah felt sad and scared. Did the baby's heart get hurt because she wasn't the son Papa wanted? Did Papa wish Annah would go away, too, because she wasn't a boy?

On many nights after the baby died, Annah could hear Papa yelling at Toto out by the fire. Lying there in the dark hut, Annah knew that if she could just change herself into a boy, the yelling would stop. But how could she change herself? The shouting grew louder and louder until Toto came into the hut and lay crying in her bed. Annah heard her father come in quietly a long time later. The next morning Toto and Papa were very quiet at breakfast. Annah would look at her father and he would gaze back at her, with a hard look on his face. On those days Toto worked in the field with the girls and soon sent them to play while she finished the work alone.

Annah and Magdalene's favorite game was "house," where they would gather with neighbor children and pretend that the shade of a small shrub was their hut. The girls often argued about who would be the toto, but Annah always wanted to be the papa. "I am Francis," she would say, "and I'm going out to tend the animals." While Magdalene and the other girls cut sticks to be the "babies," Annah was striding around outside herding her pretend goats. No matter which of the girls ended up being her "wife," Annah would never yell at her, and when they pretended to be gathered at the fire at night, Annah would sing songs of love to all the stick babies, whether they were girls or boys.

Chapter 2

ONE ORDINARY FRIDAY in January, Toto announced that the girls needed to go to bed early that night because she was getting up very early the next morning to go to Ngora Township. Toto almost never left their village unless someone was sick, so the girls worried all day that there was something wrong. That evening, they asked her what the trouble was.

"No trouble," she said, with a long look toward Annah. "I am going to buy a dress for Annah." Annah was confused by this: play clothes for the girls consisted of cloth rectangles that they wrapped around themselves and tied, and she already had one dress, a faded and much-mended one that had belonged to Magdalene. She had never thought that a dress could be bought at the market.

Toto was already gone when the girls awoke on Saturday, and they played close to the hut all day, eager to see what Toto would bring home. Trips to town always resulted in rare treats, like yellow bananas, oven-baked bread, or sweets—things the children never saw in their village, Agu. Annah looked forward to her treat, but mostly she wondered what a dress from so far away would be like.

Finally, late in the afternoon, Toto came home with a parcel on her head. She opened it and there was the most beautiful blue cloth that Annah had ever seen. Toto shook out the dress, took off Annah's play cloth, and slid the dress gently down over her head. Annah was engulfed in a wonderfully clean new smell, and then she was looking down at her slender body covered in the dress. It hung from her shoulders without even being tied, and it came down below her knees. Annah grabbed the small mirror from the little wooden table that stood against the wall and tried to angle it so she could see her full body, but she could just glimpse a girl's face over what seemed like a piece of the sky. She didn't even recognize herself. She was ready to run out of the hut to show the world her new dress, but Toto took hold of her arm.

"This dress is only for school, just like Magdalene's blue dress," she said sternly. "You must take it off now and we will keep it in a safe place for Monday, when the new school year starts for Magdalene and for you. This dress has to last from now until the end of the school year, in December."

School on Monday! Annah couldn't believe what she was hearing. All weekend, she kept finding a minute to slip into the hut to peek at her dress. She had to pinch herself to make sure all this was real: she was going to school. Her mother had told her many times that school would be her way to what her mother called "the world."

"I don't want my girls to be just 'village women.' You are too smart for that. One day, you'll be educated and you'll go out into the world," Toto had said so many times. Often, as they worked in the fields or sat by the fire in the evening, Toto told the girls about this world. "We live in Teso District because we are from the Iteso tribe, but the world holds many other districts, and even countries other than Uganda. There are big towns and even cities," she said, "where the people don't work in the fields. They use pen and paper to make wonderful lives for themselves, and they wear new clothes all the time. They wear watches and shoes, and they are always clean and beautiful." The girls giggled when she said these things: how could these people eat if they didn't grow things? Annah's whole world was her mother, so it frightened her a little to think there was another place and that she was expected to go there. But when Toto spoke of this world, her beautiful face softened and her eyes glistened so brightly that Annah knew this was her destiny. Whenever they walked to the river to get water, Annah peered off into the distance to see this world, but always there was nothing but trees and a blue sky. Maybe she could only see it after she had gone to school.

On Monday, Toto got out the dress and carefully washed Annah, made sure she brushed her teeth, and then pulled the soft cloth down over her head. Once again, Annah was engulfed by its marvelous smell. She stood up straighter and walked a few steps to practice being a schoolgirl. The dress swished softly about her legs. Rebecca was crying because she wanted to go to school, too, but Toto just shushed her and told her she would be old enough soon. Annah petted Rebecca and tried to soothe her, as a big girl should do for a little one.

"My Frances, we will go to school now," Papa announced. He looked proud, and taller than usual, as he took her hand and began the walk to the Agu Village school. Magdalene, who had started school the previous year, walked proudly just ahead of them, assuring Annah that she would enjoy the school very much. They walked down familiar paths through the village, but soon they had gone beyond where Annah had ever been. All along the way Annah saw people looking out of their huts at her. She wondered if they were admiring her blue dress, or if they knew she was about to enter a new world. Annah felt nervous about what lay ahead, but mostly she was excited. If she hadn't been trying so hard not to muss the dress, she would have skipped for joy over being a schoolgirl now. Eventually they reached a long, low building made of mud and grass, like the family huts. It was so big that it had to be the school. Annah wondered if this was the world her mother talked about. Surely nothing could be larger than this.

"Come Frances, we will register you," her father said as he led her into the building. They walked into a small office where a man sat. Her father called him "headmaster" and was very polite in front of him. Annah sat where she was told to and tried to listen as her father spoke to the headmaster.

"You're sure she is five?" he asked. Papa answered yes, but the headmaster came around the desk to her, took hold of her hand, and pulled her arm up and over the top of her head.

"OK," he said. "She is old enough to be enrolled." Annah looked to her father in astonishment.

"You see, Annah Frances Acam," the headmaster said with a chuckle, "you must be five years old to enter my school. Many children in Teso don't know their exact age, so I do this little test. If you are not five years old yet, you cannot reach your ear when you stretch your arm over your head. But your fingers did touch your ear, so you may come to my school." Annah was frightened to think that if she had not passed this test, she would have been sent home. She wanted to reach over her head and reassure herself that her fingers could indeed reach to her ear, but she was afraid of angering the headmaster. Papa paid the fees for her to attend, and then he bought her a book and a pencil.

"Take very good care of these, Frances," he said, leaning down close to her. "I will leave you now and you must walk home with your sister Magdalene after school. Do everything the teacher tells you."

"I am Mr. Ekilu (AKE-ee-loo)," the headmaster said, looking down at Annah with a smile. "Shall I call you Frances?" Annah paused for a moment, and then she thought how happy Toto would be if only she were Papa's son, instead of just another daughter.

"Yes," she said. "I am Frances."

Mr. Ekilu turned out to also be the teacher of the first grade, Primary I. He walked Annah to a large room with many children. They were all about her age, although Annah noticed that she was taller than most of them. The girls all had on blue dresses like hers, and, like her, they were quietly looking around as if making sure this alien place held no threats.

Mr. Ekilu stood at the front of the class and began to teach them the English phrases that they would say every morning.

"Good morning, sir."

"Good morning, class."

"How are you, sir?"

"How are you, class?"

"We are very well, sir."

"Sit down, class."

"Thank you, sir."

The children sat on the dirt floor, and Mr. Ekilu began to teach them the alphabet in their native language, Ateso. He told the children that the vowels are the most important letters, because they are in every word. He wrote the vowels in chalk on the blackboard and drilled the children until they were all able to recognize them. Then he told them to line up at the door and led them all outside to the enormous tree on the northern edge of the school compound. He had the children sit on the dirt, in a line, and he moved them so that they were about three feet away from each other.

"Now we will practice writing the vowels," he told them. "Take your hand and brush it across the dirt, like this, so that you have a nice, clean space in front of you." He stooped to demonstrate for them, and then he wrote a large A with his finger. "Now each of you write an A in your space. Make it nice and straight," he admonished. While Mr. Ekilu walked behind the children, leaning over to guide their hands when they struggled, they practiced writing each of the vowels over and over.

Suddenly, he clapped his hands and said it was time for PE. The children all marched across the compound to a field, where the teacher led them in running and jumping. Mr. Ekilu was a very distinguished-looking man—tall with nice trousers and a clean white shirt. But outside he ran and played with the children, smiling at them with affection.

Once they were all tired out, Mr. Ekilu called for them to line up. They walked a short way down the road to a public well that had been built to serve the school and the neighboring villagers. Two boys took turns pumping while all the children washed their hands and had drinks of water. Back in the classroom, the students went to sit at the few wooden desks. There were only about ten desks, so they had to sit two and three to a desk. When the benches were full, the rest sat on logs. Mr. Ekilu told Annah to sit in the back, since she was so tall, and that became her place in school. Sometimes she wondered if it was bad to be tall, but the kindly teacher called on her often and praised her work. Annah worked hard to sit up very straight and remember everything she was told.

When it was time to walk home, Annah found Magdalene with a large group of students. They all walked together down the road, children occasionally breaking off from the group when they reached their homes. Annah was amazed by all the boys and girls and by how happy they were, as they laughingly teased and chased each other. When she and Magdalene arrived home, Toto was in the field, but there were roasted potatoes set out for the schoolgirls to eat. Toto came to the hut and instructed Annah to change out of her dress and put it away for tomorrow.

"So, how was your day at school, my Annah?" she asked.

"It was so good, Toto," Annah said, but then she began to cry.

"Oh, you are just tense, my girl. Finish your potatoes and go out and play. Tomorrow you can help in the field after school, but today you just play. You are a big, strong girl now, and you are getting ready to see the big world," her mother said gently. So school was not the world her mother spoke of, either, Annah thought. "I surely must work very hard to be ready for such a big place."

Soon school days became a comfortable routine for Annah. She would awaken and dress herself and get ready for school just as Magdalene did, and she would wait eagerly for the other kids to pass by on their way to school. Annah ran on her long legs to join the throng and raced along with ease as they all made their laughing way to school. She looked forward to their break time, when they played outside and ate the snacks they had brought from home. Toto usually roasted a potato, or sometimes a cassava, depending on the season. The children liked to share their snacks with each other, so no child went without food, and there was usually a variety of treats, including mangos and nuts.

She worked hard at math and reading, but it was the crafts that she loved best. Mr. Ekilu showed the children where to find dirt for making clay in a special place near the swamp, and he taught them how to collect reeds and sisal leaves for crafts as well. Then, at the end of some days, he would instruct them to gather one of these things and bring them to school the next day. Annah always brought as much as she could find and carry, because making crafts was her favorite activity. They learned to make important, useful things like pots, baskets, and ropes. Annah discovered that she was good with her hands, even though Magdalene still accomplished the household tasks much faster than she did. Each day she looked forward to eating her snack at home and then joining her mother in the field to help with the work while telling Toto all about the new skills she had learned.

One day in the middle of the term, Annah and Magdalene came home to find that four strange children were sitting in their compound, eating some of the groundnuts that Toto had put out for the girls' after-school snack.

"These are your new neighbors, girls," Toto said. Two boys and two girls, all around Annah's and Magdalene's ages, stared at them with reddened eyes. "This is Ojulu [oh-JOO-loo]," she said, indicating the oldest boy, "and these are Oumo [OO-moh], Aluka [ah-LOO-kah], and Akutoi [ah-KOOT-wee]. Their mother and father have died, so they will be living with their grandmother, who lives in that hut." Annah was surprised that her mother was pointing at the tiny, broken-down hut of an old, bent woman who sometimes yelled at them when they played too near her home. She couldn't imagine that four more people—even ones as thin as these children—could fit into that hut. "Their grandmother is weak and can't take care of them very well, so we will help her. You must be good to them."

It was odd to have these new children living so near their compound, but Annah and her sisters invited them to play whenever they were out. Often, Annah could hear them crying in their hut.

"Why do these children cry so much?" Annah asked her mother one day.

"They are orphans. They have lost their parents and they are sad, and also there is not enough food for them, since their parents aren't here to work the fields. I give them as much food as we can spare, but still they are hungry."

From that day on, Annah began sharing her after-school meal with the children, but still they cried and grew thinner. One day, Annah gave them not just her portion of the meal, but some things that were in the cooking hut for that evening's dinner. When Toto discovered this, she gently took Annah's arm and sat down to talk with her.

"You must not do this again, Annah. I give them all I can, but I need for you to eat and remain strong enough to do your schoolwork and help with the chores. You must trust that I am giving them as much as they need."

Sometimes Annah would see the orphans helping their grandmother with the chores. Of course the boys didn't do this work, but the girls tried to be of use. The girls went about their chores with long, sad faces—so unlike the busy times Annah and her sisters shared in the cooking hut with their mother: laughing and working together. "Orphan" seemed to Annah to be the worst thing in the world to be.

One morning, when Annah and Magdalene left for school, Ojulu and Aluka joined the crowd of children walking to the village. The two children went into school with them and stayed all day, working hard to follow the teachers' instructions. They looked odd in their dirty play clothes, and they struggled to imitate the work the other students knew how to do, but Annah was so glad that they would now get a chance to see the big world, too. The orphans attended school all week, but on Friday the headmaster asked the boy if he had brought their fees. Looking down, Ojulu went and got his sister and left the school, never to return.

A few weeks after that, Mr. Ekilu had the class sit down after their lessons, and he took out a big black book. He told them it was the Bible and he began to read to them from it. Annah learned that there is a God who lives in heaven but is everywhere all at once. Heaven seemed to be high in the sky.

"He can see everything you do," Mr. Ekilu explained, "and he hears your thoughts. God loves you very much, and if you pray to him he will listen, because he always answers the prayers of children."

That day, Annah tagged along behind the group of children making their way home. She kept her head down so she could think hard about what she had learned. She wasn't comforted by the news that God was watching her every move, but her mind kept returning to Mr. Ekilu saying that God will listen when a child prays. When she arrived home, she went quickly to the hut to change into play clothes. Making sure her sisters and the orphans were not around, she went outside the hut where she could be under the sky. She crouched next to a small bush beside the hut, so that no one would see her praying.

Looking up to the sky, to this new place called heaven, she prayed to God. "Please, God, I am scared and I don't want my Toto and Papa to die. I don't want to be like the orphan children. I want to have food and go to school so that I can grow up and see the world." Annah knew that God was listening to her, but it seemed like she needed to promise something in return, so she went on: "God, if you will let Toto and Papa live, I promise when I grow up I will take care of all the orphan children."

After that conversation, Annah felt she had made her deal and that her parents were safe. She had learned that her soul was the center of her being, and she felt peace there, knowing God would answer her prayers and keep his side of the bargain. In the following weeks, her family began going to the Catholic Mass that was held in the school building on Sundays. Annah always glanced up on her way in, just to confirm that God was up there and that their deal still stood.

On Sunday afternoons, when her sisters wanted to play house with the stick babies, Annah always ran and got the orphan girls so they could play, too. She still played the father, Francis, and she would always assure the stick babies that they would have good educations, even if they became orphans. And then she told them about the big world that was waiting for them beyond the compound, beyond the school, and even beyond the village.

Chapter 3

THE HOT, DEMANDING LANDSCAPE of rural Uganda creates an environment where children quickly gain an inherent wisdom beyond their years. When the sun set over Annah's little compound each evening, and her family sat around the fire listening to the village's songs and drumbeats broadcasting the lives of her fellow Ugandans, she was filled with contentment. Even at the age of six, she had a sense that she and her family were among the more fortunate dwellers in this quiet farm community, even though they sometimes had to skip meals.

Like her sisters, Annah was keenly aware of the effect their illnesses and aches had on their mother. Toto's face would crease with concern at the slightest complaint, and whenever one of them was truly sick, the others were aware that they had only a portion of their mother's attention. Even out in the fields, it was obvious that Toto was attuned to whichever child lay ailing in the hut and that she would somehow know immediately if she needed to rush home to tend to the child. Annah had been aware of the deaths of many children in the village: most younger than she. Instead of making her timid or worried, these events caused her to feel strong and lucky. She felt fortunate that she had survived to school age, and she felt secure that her long, slim body and smooth, black skin would protect her from any real harm. She had bouts of various diseases as a child—colds, dysentery, malaria—but she always knew she would bounce back and return to all her normal activities.

Early in Annah's second term in Primary I, when life had settled into an easy routine of school, chores, and play, she noticed what seemed to be a tiny cut on her foot. After a few days of ignoring it while she made her usual treks to school and the fields, she realized that the sore was getting larger and more painful. It became red and swollen, and she soon found that she couldn't put her full weight on that foot. When it was clear that Annah couldn't make the walk to school, Toto announced that they would go to the hospital for medicine.

The following morning, Toto got Annah up early and cleaned her up, carefully bathing the infected foot. She wrapped some roasted potatoes in a cloth and placed it on her head, and then picked Annah up so that she could ride on Toto's back. It was a hot morning, and Annah could hear her mother's breath become labored under the burden of her weight. She rested her head on Toto's back and heard and felt the muscles grinding under their load. But Toto strode on determinedly, stopping to rest only when Annah began to shift uncomfortably on her back. She would set Annah under a tree for shade and then go to a well or stream she had noticed and get them a jug of water to share. When Annah said she was hungry, Toto fed her portions of the potatoes, carefully rationing so that they would have enough for the trip. Annah dozed on her mother's back through the day, but even in her dreams her mother was there, towering and strong, saving her from all threats.

At last they arrived at Fredika Hospital near Ngora, where Annah had been born. As Toto approached the strange building, Annah thought that this was surely the world her mother wanted her to enter. The hospital was a long, tan building with a roof that extended out to provide a shady porch on the concrete step. When they entered the building, Annah was startled to find that they were in a room with white, smooth walls and a hard floor. Toto walked to where there were benches along the wall and sat down with Annah on her lap. From the safety of this position, Annah looked out at the bright, clean room. The benches were filled with women in dusty dresses, holding their sick children. Some children whimpered, and some just slept in their mothers' arms. The women all looked as weary as her toto did. But Annah noticed that there were some women who walked proudly past the benches wearing beautiful white clothes; even their shoes and caps were white. When one of them came over to speak to her mother, the woman looked into Toto's face and paid attention to her firm, strong voice. The woman leaned down to look at Annah's foot and Annah smelled a sweet, clean smell that she had never encountered before. It was as beautiful as the woman's clear, smooth face.

"Stay here with her and I will bring him to look at it," she told Toto and walked briskly away.

"Annah, you must look at the women here," Toto whispered. "They are nurses, and they work here. This is the world I want for you, my girl, and you will get it if you stay in school. Your big sister

Rosemary plans to study nursing. You both will be nurses and wear white and give comfort to people every day."

Just then the nurse returned with a terrifying creature. Annah was pretty sure he was human, because he had eyes and a mouth in his head and he reached out two hands with fingers on them. But his skin was a strange, pale, whitish-pink color, and his head had wispy strands of straight brown hair on it. Annah shrank back when he leaned toward her, but Toto held her tightly and she knew she mustn't cry out or say anything. When he spoke she couldn't understand his words, but she realized he was a man like her papa, but so different.

The man lifted her foot and peered at it; then he motioned to the nurse and she told Toto and Annah to come with her. The four of them entered another room, and as they walked in, the nurse touched something on the wall and a round object in the ceiling suddenly shot out a bright light. Toto carried Annah to a tall table under the light and placed her there, still holding onto her with both hands. The man began speaking again and the nurse told Toto what he was saying.

"Annah, this is the doctor, who will give us medicine to make your foot better," Toto murmured into her ear, and then she turned Annah's foot up the way the nurse had instructed. Annah only flinched a little when the man's cool, dry hands touched her foot. He peered down at the wound while asking questions that the nurse translated to her mother. After her mother had explained how long the foot had hurt and what they had been doing for it, the nurse translated instructions for Toto to take care of it. The doctor walked over to a white bowl on the wall and turned a handle. Suddenly, water was running out of a pipe into the bowl. Annah watched while the doctor washed his hands right there in the room.

After he left, the nurse cleaned her foot with a wet cloth and put something white and creamy on the sore. She gave Toto the container of cream and wrapped the foot in a white cloth while talking to her mother in rapid sentences. Annah watched her mother and felt very proud. She had no idea that her mother could speak to these people whose lives were so important, and that they would listen respectfully when Toto spoke.

On the way home, Annah could tell her mother had gotten some extra energy from their encounter with that strange, new world. Her mother hummed a little to herself while she walked, and when they stopped, Toto reminded Annah that she could one day enter that world just by working hard at school. During one rest under a tall tree, Annah asked about the strange man, and her mother explained that there are many "white" people all over the world and that they are basically the same as black people except for the color of their skin. Toto said these people have to be very careful outdoors because the sun will burn their skin. Once again Annah marveled at the endlessness of her mother's knowledge.

Annah spent another long week out of school, waiting for her foot to heal. She developed several sores just like the first, and her mother put the cream on each of them and scolded Annah when she got them dirty. At last, the sores healed and Annah could walk again, although she had white marks on her foot where the sores had been. She would study the pale marks and think about the doctor's strange skin.

Magdalene wasn't as lucky as Annah when it came to her health. That fall, she became ill and spent several days lying in the hut while Toto washed her to keep her body cool. She developed red spots all over her skin that she scratched at constantly. Toto called the spots "measles." Magdalene moaned and thrashed in her bed, and it seemed that nothing would make her more comfortable. Annah helped her mother with the chores and caring for Magdalene when she was home, but still she would see Toto up very late in the night, leaning over Magdalene's bed. At last, Magdalene began to lie quietly, and then she was able to sit and sip the soup that Toto fed her. Although Magdalene gradually grew stronger, her ears never did: after her illness, she was unable to hear people outside the hut speaking to her. She eventually returned to school that term, but she soon stopped going because she couldn't hear the teacher speaking to the class. Magdalene became frustrated and embarrassed, and so their mother told her she would not need to continue in school.

The walks to school weren't as much fun without Magdalene, but Annah continued to do well in her studies through the second Primary II term. Home life continued without serious difficulties: crops were good and no one else became seriously ill. At the fire after supper, the sky still filled with the thunder of the drums being beaten all over the village, and the men's voices still rang out with songs of happiness and hope. After the songs, even though she was growing bigger, Papa often sat Annah on his lap and sang his little phrase, "Frances my little angel, Frances my little angel, I love my angel."

It was still the nights that produced Annah's only unhappiness.

Lying in bed, she continued to hear her father's voice raised in anger at her mother. In that year, Annah learned more about the pain that always seemed to lurk behind her father's eyes. The woman Lucy, who lived in a hut on the other side of the compound, occasionally joined the family for dinner. Her daughter and Rebecca were both four that year, and they sometimes played together and sat beside each other on the ground while eating. Papa ate sitting at the table, but the women and girls sat on the ground nearby to eat their meals. Toto and Lucy didn't seem to like each other very much—they were always quiet and stiff as they served the meal and ate. There was a lot of extra tension at those meals, and any small problem would make Papa speak angrily and get up and leave the table.

Once, during the morning walk to fetch water, Annah's mother told her that Papa had expected Lucy, as the second wife, to give him a son. Annah knew that her father often became angry with Toto for not giving him a son, but she was afraid to ask her mother why all her babies had been girls. Toto told Annah how important it is for a man to have a son, to tend the animals and help with his work, and to take over the family land. A son would be their heir and pass the land on to more generations, just as it had come to Papa from his father. Annah said she would do this for her father, but Toto just smiled and said that was not how life was in Teso.

"When you grow up you will probably marry a man, but never settle for being the second wife, Annah," her mother told her. "Remember that if you work hard in school you will be able to go into the world that I have told you about. You can be a nurse and work indoors for your living and not have to bend over all day tending the fields in the hot sun. But even if you do all this, your life will be miserable if you are not the first wife. Don't ever forget this, Annah. It is very important."

So Annah now had two goals: to grow smart enough to go to the big world, and to be someone's first wife. She thought about these things every day as she walked to school, worked on her lessons, and did her chores. She still lagged behind Magdalene in her ability to do the home chores, but her schoolwork improved every day. Annah was proud of the knowledge she was gaining, and she worked hard each day to learn more and more.

At the end of the term, Annah graduated from the Agu primary school. The village school, which was less than a mile from her home, provided only the two grades, so the following year she would attend Okoboi (oh-KOH-bwee) Girls' Primary School in the township of Ngora, which meant she would be walking fourteen miles each day to get to and from school. It was a Catholic school, so she would have nuns for teachers there. Sometimes she felt nervous about going so far away to a strange new place, even though she knew she would be walking there with several other girls from the village. But then a village elder would see her and call her a "schoolgirl" and she would feel proud and determined to succeed at this school, too.

Chapter 4

AS THE TIME DREW NEAR for Annah to set off for her new school, Toto had to buy her a new uniform. It was blue with yellow trim, and Toto assured her that this was what all the girls in the third, fourth, and fifth grades would be wearing. Just thinking about looking like a fifth-grader made Annah feel proud and scared at the same time.

On the appointed day, Annah got up very early to get ready for school. Their hut had no clock, but her mother watched the sun and woke Annah in time. After putting her lunch of roasted potato in a cloth and checking her uniform one last time, Toto sent her out to join a group of children from the village on their seven-mile walk to school. The boys would be going to St. Aloysius Demonstration School, while Annah and the other girls would be in Okoboi Girls' Primary School.

It took the children about two hours to walk the seven miles, so they played and talked as they made their way along the path. More children would join them when they passed more huts, so there was a large group of them by the time they got to Ngora. Once they reached the township, the boys ran shouting and laughing off to their school while the girls headed toward the long, low mud-building compound that was their school. This school was much bigger than the village school, but it looked very similar. Through the open windows she could see dark, dusty classrooms with assorted tables and desks. A few had chalkboards on the walls, but all of them had various makeshift chairs, stools, and stumps for the girls to sit on. The floors were concrete, which looked quite fancy to Annah, but she soon learned that her feet preferred the soft, beaten-down dirt floors of the old school.

Although Annah slept at home and walked back and forth each day, many girls lived at this school. Okoboi school was operated by nuns, and Annah was fascinated by their dark blue habits that covered all of their bodies except for their faces. She quickly came to love the gentle Sister Nicodem, the headmistress, who also taught all the children about the Bible and the world. Although Annah spent parts of each day trying to figure out if Sister Nicodem had any hair under her wimple, she worked hard to pay attention and learn everything she could from her wonderful teachers. Annah particularly loved geography class, where she was shocked to learn that most of the countries in the world are larger than her country of Uganda. She learned about the neighboring countries of Sudan, Tanzania, Kenya, and Zaire, and she was amazed to think that there are all these different places with the same black people speaking different languages.

It was in those years that Annah came to prize her body—its long, strong legs that carried her to and from school each day and its eager brain that never seemed to fill up in spite of how much it absorbed. While in school she sat erect, never moving her eyes from the blue-clad figures who were the source of so much wonderful knowledge. Annah received prizes each year for excelling in science, although her favorite time during the school day was when the girls all sat quietly to hear their teacher tell them stories in English. Annah, like all of the other kids from her village school, wasn't as fluent in English as her Okoboi classmates, so she had to work hard to understand the narrations. But she knew now that this was the key to that incredible world that her mother so wanted her to enter, so she didn't mind the work. In this school, all lessons except writing in their native language of Ateso were conducted in English, and students were sent to stand in the corner or given a sharp spanking when they made mistakes. Annah rarely had to endure either punishment.

While Annah was working hard in school, her mother was always working at home, in the fields or in the kitchen. One weekend morning, Toto told Magdalene to stay home and watch Rebecca while she and Annah went to catch some fish in the river. Annah was delighted and ran happily to get the fishing equipment. The long, narrow woven basket was what Toto would sweep through the water to trap the fish. Annah was to stand nearby holding the gourd with its narrow mouth up so Toto could drop fish in it. Then they would carry the gourd, sloshing with water and fish, back to the kitchen to prepare supper. Annah was proud that Toto trusted her with this important job: she didn't dare let any fish escape from the gourd. The family needed to eat all the fish they could catch.

On that day, Toto waded into the river with her basket and Annah worked to keep up with her, dragging the large gourd through the water. When the water reached Toto's knees, she instructed Annah to wait there with the gourd while she went deeper into the water to fish. The water was up to Annah's thighs, so she had to plant her feet carefully to stay standing. She plunged the gourd under the water to fill it about halfway with water and then waited for Toto. Toto caught one fish, then another, much larger one. She whooped when she caught the big one and carried it in the basket to Annah.

"Look at this one, Annah! It will be enough to feed Papa all by itself! This is called a lungfish. See how it has two sharp fangs on the top and bottom in its mouth? It's ugly, but it tastes really good." Toto pushed the fish into the gourd and Annah could feel its weight thrusting against the sides of the vessel.

While Toto went out to catch more fish, Annah tried to peer into the gourd to watch the lungfish swimming around, but it was too dark in there for her to see. Finally she stuck her hand in to feel the big fish as it swam. Suddenly, she felt a sharp pain in her finger. Screaming from the pain, she pulled her hand up and the big fish was hanging by its fangs from her index finger.

Toto was beside her instantly to see what had caused the scream.

"Hold still, Annah," Toto shouted, grabbing the fish around its middle. Toto made a fist and hit the fish hard on its head, and it let go of Annah's hand. Toto quickly dropped it back into the gourd with a splash. Toto held tight to the gourd containing their meal while she inspected Annah's finger.

"Alright, alright, Annah. It didn't cut you, but you have a dent in your finger—it will be a bruise for sure, but nothing more. Come on, let's take these fish home. We've had enough fishing for one day." Annah was crying softly now, partly from the pain and partly in frustration that she had let that fish bite her.

"Stop crying, girl; you're fine now. Annah, have I told you that you are to be a big sister again? We're having another baby." Annah was so excited by this news that she forgot all about her bitten finger.

That day, and on all their subsequent morning walks, Toto sang songs asking God to place a boy in her womb. Over those months, Toto got bigger and bigger, and her movements became slower and more difficult. Finally, the day came for her to go to hospital. She left to make the day-long trek while Annah was at school, so Annah tucked herself in that night and prayed that the baby would be a boy, and that Toto—and he—would be fine.

The next day, as Annah and her friends walked home after

school, they could hear drumbeats and joyful songs coming from somewhere near her compound. She ran ahead to see, and there was Papa, who grabbed her in his arms and said, "Frances, you have not one but *two* little brothers!" Annah was very happy to see her father's joy, and she quietly celebrated that now there surely would be no more fights for her to overhear from her bed in the hut. That night, drums beat all over the village, and Annah went to sleep to the sounds of songs of congratulation and celebration. She felt a deep pride, in her mother for producing two boys, and in herself for helping her mother pray for these gifts from God.

A few days later, Toto arrived home with two tiny bundles containing George and Charles. Annah couldn't believe that they both had fit in Toto's tummy, and yet she also couldn't believe human beings could be so tiny. Her grandmother, Alamo (ah-LAHM-oh), who was Toto's mother, stayed with the family for many weeks, and Magdalene and Annah had to do extra chores. It seemed like one of the babies was always crying, and Toto looked so tired when she awoke Annah for school that it was clear she had had very little sleep. And yet, Papa's joyous voice could be heard at all hours of the day, calling out, "How is my precious wife today—the mother of my two strong sons?" And so, once the boys were there, the entire family completed their work with broad smiles on their faces. It wasn't until the twins were several months old that Annah was allowed to hold them, and when she did, she was extra cautious to care for these two miracles.

As Annah's family grew, so did her love of learning. She proudly passed the third grade, feeling content that she had caught up with the students who had spent all their years at Okoboi school, and then she completed the fourth grade with the same ease. It was in fifth grade that Annah began learning that there are actually other continents beyond Africa. One weekend Toto took Annah to the market area of Ngora Township, where there were many stands set up on busy streets. Annah had never seen Ngora like this, since Saturday was market day. The people looked like the pictures in her textbooks—some were light-skinned with long blond hair, and there were Asians and Indians. It seemed that all of them were either selling or buying something, and many of them were loudly disputing the price of a sparkling trinket or a ripe, juicy mango. So that was it, Annah thought: life is all about the selling of merchandise. Annah began to wonder how much Toto knew of this expanded world, and she was surprised when Toto walked so comfortably among the vendors, counting out money to buy their wares. Still, by the fifth grade Annah often found that Toto couldn't help her with home-work; she had to go to Papa with her complicated math problems and social studies questions.

It was during that year that Annah learned in school about a black man named Nelson Mandela who had been imprisoned in South Africa simply for trying to help black people live like the white people there. She asked her father how this could be, and he told her that whites rule South Africa and blacks are not allowed to go and live there.

"But Papa," Annah argued, "Africa is the place for black people."

"Yes, my Frances, but South Africa is home to whites, too, and they have the rule of the country now," he answered her sadly. Annah remembered her teacher's having said that God answers the prayers of children, so she began praying often for the release of Nelson Mandela from the jail in South Africa.

As Annah learned more about Africa, she developed a strong sense of her place in the world. She learned that Uganda is the source of the great Nile River that flows all the way to the Medi-terranean Sea and laps at the shores of the great nations of Europe. She was certain that this meant that she, like the humble Ugandan waters that set out daily on their journey down the Nile, was des-tined to make her way out into this enormous and beckoning world. Along with her dreams, her body was growing and strengthening. She was always the tallest girl in class, and she liked to look down past her slim torso to her long, powerful legs. She excelled in every-thing physical: basketball, baseball, track, just racing her friends as they made their way to school. But it was basketball that Annah truly loved to play. Her teachers all saw the passion in Annah and quickly put her on whatever team they were assembling. They chuckled at her pure love of sport and competition.

It was at a basketball game that Annah first saw the boy. Although theirs was an all-girls school, boys from St. Aloysius were brought over after school to watch the girls' ballgames and to par-ticipate in singing and dancing lessons. Annah noticed that one boy watched her closely throughout the game, and then in the next few weeks she often saw him looking her way during singing and danc-ing. She also noticed that she wasn't the only girl looking at him. His dark eyes sparkled as if he were planning some mischief, and he always had a playful grin. The girls began to whisper among themselves that his name was Anthony, and he was in the seventh grade; and they all pronounced themselves totally in love with him. Annah noticed that some of the more outgoing girls would smile at him, and they often fought to sit beside him during lessons, but she also realized that those deep brown eyes sparkled most when he looked at her.

Annah had no idea what all this meant. The nuns strictly forbade any sort of physical contact between boys and girls, so Annah obediently stayed away from him. But no matter what she did, she noticed that all the cells in her body seemed to light up whenever he was near. She watched him out of the corner of her eye, and she was pretty sure his cells were lighting up, too. Could it be that they were in love with each other? Annah couldn't think what to do about Anthony, so for the rest of that year they just exchanged small, awkward smiles when their eyes met. Since Anthony seemed to live in another direction from school, she usually only saw him under the watchful eyes of the nuns. Sometimes, she would think about him as she jogged home, wondering if he could beat her in a footrace, and then wondering if she would let him beat her. There were just two occasions when Anthony left school and waited a little ways down the path that Annah walked. In person, she didn't have the courage to challenge him to a footrace, but they acknowledged the instant bond between them and had short, shy conversations.

Although the distance to and from school was hard on the children from Agu, Annah came to love these treks. She used the trip to practice running, and she became the fastest girl in her class. She loved the feel of the wind rushing through her short hair and swirling her uniform skirt around her legs. No one in the family except Toto and Papa had ever had shoes, but the soles of Annah's feet never even felt the sticks and stones that she pushed into the earth under them as she ran down the paths. One boy, a cousin who lived next to their compound, liked to run, too. He could run the whole distance without stopping, while Annah had to rest a few times. Every day she resolved to at least keep pace with him, but she never quite did—she had to settle for keeping the sight of his muscular back in front of her as she ran. But she rarely fell back far enough that she couldn't at least see him.

Annah's runs through the early mornings were pure joy for her, with birds twittering around her and the grass and trees glowing in the rising sun. Her feet kicked up small clouds of the orange-brown earth, and she could hear the rhythmic slap of her soles on the soft dirt. On those days Annah felt as if she could just keep running forever—maybe even to Kenya, but of course her only goal was to reach school and continue her learning. Many of her school days didn't allow her these glorious runs, though, as the first and longer rainy season in Teso lasted from March to July. On rainy days, the children would dash quickly from one hut to another. Even when the residents didn't know any of the children, they would bring the wet kids inside to stay dry and wait for a lull in the downpour.

Annah didn't like running and stopping as much as just racing all out to school, but it was fun to have all the kids to run with. When it rained, the path became muddy and then rutted with rivulets of water that they had to splash through. Snakes thrived in these conditions, so they had to watch where they put each foot as they ran. Sometimes a child would spot something slithering across the path and yell "Snake!" Annah never worried that she would be unable to run fast enough to get away from the snake, so she would be dashing through the rain laughing, until her side hurt from the combination.

Once into the school building, the children had to sit all day in their wet, scratchy uniforms. Since the family's food from the previous rainy season had become scarce by that time, Annah rarely had enough food at home to provide a lunch, so she sat cold and itchy all day with only the prospect of a wet run back to her house on an empty stomach to look forward to. To further add to her unhappiness, on those rainy days the children weren't permitted to take any schoolbooks home with them, since they would be ruined in the rain. Thus her time at school and at home became sharply divided, and her evenings were spent dreaming of all the knowledge that awaited her in the textbooks.

One rainy day in April of her fifth-grade year, Toto gave Annah the money for school fees and lectured her on the importance of taking the money directly to the headmistress and bringing back a receipt. Annah knew how hard Toto worked to sell produce, milk, and even the beer she brewed just to keep Annah in school. Sometimes when she was very hungry at school, she reminded herself that her mother gave up meals and many other things to be sure that her daughter would get an education. So that day she ran all the way with her head down and the cloth that held the money firmly clasped against her chest. When she arrived, she went to Sister Nicodem and paid her fees proudly, waiting patiently while her teacher wrote out the receipt. When school let out it was still pouring rain, and Annah carefully wrapped the receipt in the cloth that had carried the money and held it against her as she ran home. However, the cloth was soaked and the receipt that she had wrapped up so carefully was unreadable. "We won't worry," Toto said. "Sister Nicodem is a careful person and I'm sure she recorded our payment correctly." Annah noticed the wrinkles across Toto's forehead and knew, though, that there would be no way to make up this money if the school should mistakenly ask for it again.

Annah slowly lost her worry over the ruined receipt, but one day in May, Sister Nicodem took Annah into her office to tell her she could not continue at school until the fees were paid.

"I paid them in April," Annah stammered, knowing what was coming.

"I don't have a record of that, but if you're sure then just bring me the receipt tomorrow." The tears began to pour down Annah's cheeks at this. The money had been paid, and Toto had no more.

"Oh, Sister, I did pay you. Remember, I stood right here in the office and you gave me the receipt. But it was raining that day, and the paper got all wet and I gave it to Toto, but there was no writing on it." Annah was crying so hard that Sister Nicodem took her to a chair and patted her while she calmed down.

"I will let you stay today then, Annah, but I have no record that you paid. Tomorrow you must bring me those fees."

She walked slowly home that day, sobbing softly to herself as she went. When she told her mother of the problem, Toto became angry and said she would go and speak with Sister Nicodem tomorrow. Annah worried all night. What if Toto makes Sister angry and I can never go to school again, she thought. It seemed as if she could feel the world crowding in around her, taking away all the freedom and promise that her schooling had given her.

The next morning, Magdalene awoke with a cough, and Toto needed to stay home with her. Toto said she would go to the school with Annah the next day, if Magdalene felt better. Annah decided she would go to school by herself that day, because she had paid the fees and she belonged at school. All the way to school she practiced telling Sister that she knew she had paid, but the moment she entered the compound she became scared and wished she had stayed home.

"Frances!" Sister Nicodem was calling to her from the doorway, waving a piece of paper. Annah knew immediately what it was. "I found the record! You did pay your fees in April. Everything is fine." Then Annah and the headmistress both entered the building with huge smiles on their faces.

Annah was still smiling that evening when she arrived home, and Toto knew immediately that the problem must have been solved. As she told her mother the story of the found record, her elation was replaced by a new realization. She was just one small girl on this enormous planet, and nothing in that world would change if she suddenly could not attend school. Only Annah and Toto would suffer; Annah's life would be hard and sad instead of the exciting, important one her mother had described to her. And Toto would have worked all those years to educate Annah only to see her dreams for her daughter ruined, like so many of the crops she had toiled in the blistering sun to tend when God sent no water to sustain them. Never again would Annah stride into the sunlight expecting the world to give her what she sought. Like her mother, and all of her women ancestors, Annah would face each day with one shoulder lifted slightly, to ward off the blows that life could deliver, suddenly and cruelly.

Chapter 5

IN SPITE OF THE WARINESS that maturity had bestowed on Annah, she reveled in her growing body and mind. By the sixth grade, she noticed that she had developed high, full breasts, although her body remained thin and long. Her legs had strong muscles in the calves and thighs, and she took pleasure in stretching them beyond comfort to increase their power. She engaged her classmates in races, and basketball was her first love. Since foot-power was her only means of transportation, she walked or ran everywhere and never thought that any place might be too far for her to reach on her strong legs. She knew that villagers told each other stories about the swift, graceful girl who sped past their doorways every day at sunup. Okoboi school was due east of Agu Village, so in the morning Annah always ran into glowing skies, streaked with rose and gold by the sun's play at the edge of the world just before rising. She welcomed these vivid displays, knowing that they were just hints of the glories that each day held for her.

Her run to school ended slightly differently when she reached the sixth grade, for she had been selected as one of a handful of girls to attend St. Aloysius school. She was told that her serious approach to her studies was the reason she would be studying with the boys, instead of with the other girls at Okoboi. It was strange and a little scary for her to be taught by men again instead of the nuns of Okoboi school, but she soon felt comfortable in the boys' school. The schools were on opposite sides of a large church, so the priest came to teach religion at St. Aloysius, since the male teachers were all laymen. Anthony had graduated from St. Aloysius the previous year, but he and Annah had met after school on his last day and agreed to continue their budding relationship. "I'll write you letters," Anthony had said, smiling timidly at her. Annah had surprised herself when she replied, "I'll write you back."

It was new for the school to have a girls' basketball team, but the principal was excited about Annah's abilities and immediately had a girls' court prepared. The first poles were just wood with reed baskets—a step down from the metal poles she had been used to at Okoboi, but Annah was happy playing anywhere. Like the one at Okoboi, the court was just dirt, and also like Okoboi, the girls' games attracted many fans once the news of Annah's skills spread. Annah poured herself into the games, speeding down the court and dodging opponents with a shriek and a grin. She discovered that she felt most free and alive when she was lobbing the basketball into the air to reach the basket. It was as if her whole body soared after the ball, stretching for the goal. Annah joined the baseball and track teams when basketball season ended, but only basketball gave her that sense of flight.

Her days had become a beloved routine: running to school, learning wonderful and important new facts with all her brain-power, playing sports with all her physical strength, running home, and then settling in for the night with her family. Although she came home late many days because of basketball practice, she helped whenever she could with the cooking chores, and she rejoiced that she was always a part of the family gathering as night arrived. She and her sisters prepared the fire in the middle of the family com-pound, and then Tata told stories as the children roasted potatoes or groundnuts. Sometimes, Annah sat near the fire's light and did her homework, but she always listened carefully to her grandmother's stories as well. Overhead, the moon seemed to be watching over them as Tata told them many ancient tales about the moon. Some-times she recounted the story about the moon being the husband and all the stars his wives, and the children argued about which star was the nearest—the favorite wife. Annah would look over to where her parents sat and note happily that her father smiled at Esther and reached out to pat one of his twin sons when the subject of the favorite wife came up.

The family had further reason for celebration that February, because Annah's older sister Rosemary returned to their compound to be married to a young man from Soroti, which was twenty-five miles from Agu. Annah was kept busy all week helping Toto pre-pare food and beer for the event, but when the time came for the ceremony, she watched in awe as this lovely young woman who was her sister accepted the handsome man called Cooper as her husband. Rosemary had become a nurse, meeting Toto's dreams for her girls, and Annah was fascinated by how different her sister was from the village women that age. Rosemary was confident and sophisticated, and the wedding was a joyous, colorful event with singing and dancing that went on for two days. Watching Rosemary and Cooper as they left to begin their exciting new life together, Annah's determination to succeed became even stronger.

Nothing was lost on this curious girl, and she studied everything that happened to make sure she understood its meaning in her life and that of her family. Annah observed her own growth with both concern and excitement. Her mother was the most beautiful woman in the village, so Annah was pleased to see that her own body was growing more like Toto's every day. Many of the village women wore cloths wrapped around their hips and left their breasts uncovered, but Toto always wore dresses that covered her full breasts and made her look even more feminine. As Annah matured physically, she also made sure that she wore dresses when she wasn't in her school uniform.

That year, she noted also that the worry lines in her mother's face had deepened. She often heard her parents and grandparents speaking of *magendo,* which means "times of need." They quietly muttered about the shortages of food, and even of ordinary things like soap, that they were facing more and more each day. The elders no longer sang about President Obote; in fact, they seldom beat the drums and sang anymore when the family gathered around their small fire at night. Annah knew that there was less food to prepare for their growing family each night, and she rarely had food to take with her to school. When she helped her mother and sisters wash the clothes in the river on Saturdays, they had no soap bars, so they used a paste that Tata made by burning wood and collecting the acidic ashes. This paste smelled bad and since it was hard to rinse out of the clothes, everything they wore made their skin itch and burn.

As the river dried up during the weeks of drought, the women had to go farther and farther to reach water. Where Toto and the girls had usually gotten water, the river was more a soupy clay mud than water. The men and boys drove their animals into the mud to drink what water they could find, but the women had to walk farther up the river where there was still some water. Sometimes an animal got its legs stuck in the mud and then the men had to pull it out. Some couldn't be rescued, so the river also smelled of rotting animal carcasses. Many weeks passed when they simply could not wash clothes or bathe because the water was so scarce and so dirty. By the time the rainy season finally came, it brought new problems.

Everything had become so dried that the strong winds of the season blew a stinging, powdery orange dust into every crevice—Annah had to wrap a scarf around her head to keep the dust out of her nose and mouth and ears. With the huts being dried and blown so, many of the thatched roofs leaked when it rained and the family would find themselves sleeping in muddy puddles in the morning. On those days, Toto would be preoccupied with trying to stem the leaks while Annah prepared herself for school. She grew even thinner and was too tired to run all the way home some afternoons, but when she arrived home and saw how thin and worried Toto was, she said nothing.

One rainy day, Annah came home and couldn't find her mother. Magdalene told her Toto was sick and lying on her bed in the hut. Annah had never seen her mother in bed during the day, so she was terrified. Annah, Magdalene, and Rebecca made dinner that evening and took broth to Toto, but she only sipped at it and looked sadly around at the walls of the hut. The rest of the family gathered at the fire that night, but no one sang or told stories.

Over the next weeks, Annah often came home to find Toto in bed. The family settled into a subdued routine, doing the necessary chores but without the joy and laughter that had usually accompanied them. Then a day came when Annah arrived home to find Magdalene working with a tear-stained face.

"What's happened?" she demanded, though deep inside she didn't want to hear the answer.

"Toto has gone away," Magdalene said softly. "We don't know where."

Annah ran to the river, following her mother's usual path, but she was not there. On the way back, she checked the fields, and then walked toward the corral and found her father. One look at his face told her that he had no answers, either. Suddenly, she could see that her father was no longer a young man. His shoulders drooped, and his face was etched with deep lines around his mouth and across his forehead. She had been running at her top speed, but she slowed to approach him quietly.

"Where can she be, Papa?" she asked gently, but he just shook his head.

None of the family spoke through dinner that night, and they did not light the family fire. Annah finished her homework and went to bed early, but no sleep came to her. She lay on her back staring up into the darkness and prayed to God, telling him all the ways that she and her family needed her mother. She reminded him of her pledge to help orphans if only he would keep her parents safe, and she felt heartened as she remembered Mr. Ekilu telling her that God always answers the prayers of children. She prayed her rosary over and over, until at last she fell asleep. Annah arose before dawn, just as she would have if Toto had been there to awaken her. She got Rebecca up and told her to get ready for school. As Rebecca rubbed her face, she looked up at Annah and her eyes widened in alarm.

"Annah, what's happened to your hair?" she asked.

Annah took out the small mirror and peered into it. Behind her right temple, along the hairline, she saw a line of white where the roots of her hair were growing out.

"I don't know, Rebecca. I just don't know anything anymore!" she cried. Then, seeing the terror in Rebecca's eyes, she gathered her little sister to her. "We'll be alright, Rebecca. Toto will be home soon and everything will be the way it was." After her long talk with God the night before, Annah truly believed this would be so, although she trembled as she wondered how long they would have to wait.

Annah and Magdalene decided that they would have to continue to go through their daily routines so that Rebecca and the twins wouldn't be too frightened. Before she became ill, Esther had given her husband another son, Joseph, but he was only one year old. He was irritable and clung to Magdalene all day. No one seemed to feel right. Papa was the worst—he ate and worked as if in a dream, and he seemed surprised to see them when the children spoke to him. Sometimes at dinner Papa roused himself a little, looked distractedly at the girls, and said, "This is good, girls. It tastes just like when Toto makes it." The girls looked down, embarrassed. They didn't think he meant it, and they weren't sure they would be happy if he did. The family felt utterly empty, without purpose or direction.

After several days, a man—a stranger—came to their compound.

"Your wife is with me, in Bukedia [boo-KEH-dee-ah] District to the south," he said to Annah's father.

Suddenly, the old energy came into her father's eyes, but it burned with a depth of anger that Annah had never seen. "What on earth is my wife doing in your home?" he demanded.

The man took Papa's arm and drew him gently away from the children. Annah heard a few words of what he said: "possessed," "demons," "medicine," but she didn't know what to make of them.

Soon, the man walked quickly away and Papa came back to where the children all sat, waiting.

"Your mother is very sick," he said. "She has to stay with that man until she is well."

"But Papa," Annah said, "he says she has demons. How can this be?" For all the years of Annah's life, she had seen her mother praying the rosary as she worked and rested. Had all Toto's prayers, always directed to Mary, Mother of Jesus, been wasted? How could such a good woman fall prey to the devil?

"My Frances, you always see and hear more than is good for you," her father said kindly. "He says the demons entered her when she was near the river getting water—they probably came from someone she spoke with. Only he has the strong medicine that she needs, so we must wait and hope it works."

Annah was frightened by these words, but she was comforted to know that someone was helping her mother. She renewed her efforts to pray frequently to God to return her mother first to health and then to her family. Many times a week she crept to the little bush near the hut and knelt there, reminding God that she would take care of all the children without parents as long as he kept her parents safe.

Annah and her sisters fell into a routine of running the family in the way their mother would have, and the younger children soon became comfortable with the new procedures. When they became cranky or sad, Annah reminded them that their toto was working hard to get better and that she wanted them to work hard and be cheerful, too. In the evenings, they resumed sitting by the fire, and Tata told the same stories. Often on those nights Tata told them the tale about how the moon was a wise and revered woman who had had many children and grandchildren, and who was loved by all her descendants—the stars. She watched over her descendants and protected them when they were in troubled times.

After the stories, they sang a song their grandmother had taught them: "Oh, how I wish humans could be like the moon. The moon dies, but the moon will rise again, mighty and beautiful throughout all the ages." In the darkness no one noticed the tears running down Annah's face as she sang. She poured all her longing for her toto into that song.

Annah continued to run to school, play hard at sports, and work hard at her lessons, but her classmates and teachers noticed a new gravity about her after her mother became ill. The boys teased all the girls who had shown up in their midst, but they were bolder, and a little meaner, to Annah. There was one particular boy who always cheered for Annah when she played basketball, but when she looked at him, she saw that he was grinning at her with a strange glint in his eye. One day, as she walked across the compound to PE class, the boy was suddenly standing right in front of her. He was very dark-skinned, with deep black eyes that were looking her up and down. He reached out and grabbed her breast and pinched hard, while grinning into her face. Startled, Annah immediately punched him in the stomach, knocking him to the ground. A teacher grabbed the boy's arm and led him to the principal's office. Some kids told Annah later that he had gotten a whipping, and she was glad.

A few days after that incident, on a rainy afternoon, Principal Olupot came to Annah's classroom and told her to come with him to his office. He held an umbrella over them both as they walked across the compound. Annah's mind raced with the frightening images of what might be wrong: Had her work suffered? Did that boy say she had invited his actions? Were her school fees not paid? They entered the office and the principal closed the door and walked around behind his desk. Mr. Olupot was a short man, who until then had always seemed to have a kindly smile beneath his serious expression. Today he looked very grave.

Annah stood before his desk as he picked up a piece of paper and turned it over so that some written words were facing Annah. She gasped when she looked at it and saw "I love you" written in bold, black letters. Her classmates in the girls' school had said this to each other often, but Annah had never heard the word *love* from a male. She grabbed the paper and scrunched it up as if she could force the words back into the whiteness of the paper, and said, "But I am just a child" to the principal's now-smiling face. The year before in health class the nuns had taught her about what a man and woman do when they are in love, but surely he didn't expect this from her?

The principal's deep laugh rang out. "No, you are not, Annah Frances," he said reprovingly. "Look at your big breasts and your long legs. You are a woman now." He came around the desk as he said this, and suddenly he was pressing Annah against the wall, running his hands over her breasts and breathing into her face. He leaned even closer and stretched his lips toward hers. Annah fought to keep her mouth closed and tried to turn her head away from him, but he was overpowering her.

Just then, there was a knock on the door. She dashed into the corner of the room as soon as he let go of her, and he adjusted his tie and opened the door. The seventh-grade teacher was standing there, asking the principal to unlock the supply room for him. The principal reached into his pocket.

"OK, Frances, everything's fine now," Mr. Olupot said without looking back at her. "You can go back to class." His voice had lost the smooth, wheedling tone he'd been using and sounded business-like now. Annah walked out into the compound, shaking, just a few yards behind the principal and the teacher as they chatted casually.

That afternoon, Annah walked home slowly, feeling she had nowhere to go. She felt deeply ashamed of herself for what had happened, for surely it all had been her fault. Although she vowed she would never tell anyone about this—not even her mother, whenever she came home again—Annah ached to be returning to the warm glow of Toto at the fire making the family supper. School, which had been her refuge from the barren home life she led, was now a place of ugliness and danger for her.

It was only a few weeks after that day when Mr. Olupot once again came to Annah's classroom. He handed a stack of books to her and told her to take them to his home, which was located at the far end of the school property. She was terrified, but defying him was impossible. All of her upbringing and school training had taught her that obedience was her only choice. Sadly, she took the books and began walking across the school grounds. After a few yards, she became aware that the principal was following her at a distance. She reached his house and walked in to set the books on the table.

Mr. Olupot strode into the room behind her, shutting the door firmly. "I didn't get to finish what I wanted to do, Frances," he said grimly. "Come here and fix my tie."

Annah began to tremble and she stepped forward slowly, thinking that she didn't know anything about tying ties. As she stepped forward, Mr. Olupot leaned his face in close to hers. She could smell his breath and his aftershave, and her stomach wrenched. Just then, a wailing sound came from somewhere behind Annah.

"Bah," Mr. Olupot said, pushing Annah roughly to the side and walking to a closed door on the opposite wall. He began murmuring gently and entered a small room where a young child was crying in his bed. Annah ran out of the house and didn't stop until she reached her compound.

Although the principal ignored Annah after that day, it wasn't long before her English teacher handed her some books and told her to take them to his house. Annah accepted them wearily, knowing now that this was simply how school would be for her from now on. Once again she was in a strange house with a man whose authority and knowledge she had respected, and she was being fondled in an intimate and frightening way. This time, the saving interruption came in the person of the teacher's younger brother returning to the house from his day at school. Once again, Annah had escaped the teacher's purpose, but her image of herself continued to diminish, and she continued to yearn for the comfort and safety of the family life she had lost.

It seemed that the teachers had known something about Annah that she didn't know herself, because it was just a few days after the last incident that Annah made a shocking discovery as she walked across the school compound to basketball practice. She felt something sticky on her thigh and discovered blood trickling down her leg. She walked quickly out of the school compound and sat down beneath a tree along the path that would take her home. After she calmed down from the shock, she realized what was happening. Her mother had never talked to her about this, but she knew from health class that women bleed monthly unless they are pregnant. But she couldn't imagine how she would handle school, and the home chores, and the teachers who had suddenly turned into predators, and now this insult from her own body as well.

Annah walked home slowly that afternoon, looking only at the orange earth beneath her feet. She didn't think she would ever again run with carefree grace over this path, and she no longer cared to notice the sun's glowing display over her head. This day would end, but tomorrow would be just like today.

Chapter 6

THE HOT SEASON CAME EARLY and forcefully that year. First the rains became scattered and the showers left sticky, humid heat rising from the dirt; and then the countryside simply baked in the scorching sun. It seemed that the harder the sun beat down, the further behind Annah fell in her work, both at school and at home. She and Magdalene strove to keep the family together, to give the younger kids the same routines and support that Toto had, but it was impossible. On top of these worries, they watched Papa grow more and more distant. He was able to travel to Bukedia a few times to see Toto, and he would always leave in good spirits, but when he returned he would have to report that Toto was still weak and thin, and he would barely be able to get through the next few days.

As Annah entered the final term of sixth grade, her worries increased. At the end of each year in Ugandan school, the students must pass an exam to move up to the next level. She knew that these exams were particularly hard for sixth-graders because they would have just the seventh grade before entering secondary school. It was in these two grades that many children found they simply couldn't keep up, and they began to plan their lives without a secondary education. For girls, this meant marriage to a man who probably already had several wives, and it meant a lifetime of toiling in the fields and kitchen from sunup to sundown while bearing and raising children. Toto had made it clear that this was not an alternative for Annah, so she felt great pressure to succeed in the sixth grade and earn the right to prepare for secondary school.

Annah's efforts to keep up with her studies were further compounded by the new cycle that governed her life. She determined that all she could do when it happened was to stay home from school while her body righted itself and the bleeding slowed. Eventually, Annah noticed that other girls would be absent from school for a few days every few weeks, and she began to see a pattern in her body's changes as well. She realized, one night when the family sat around the fire, that she was thinking the bleeding would begin soon, and she noticed that the moon was a mere crescent in the sky, as it had been the last time she bled. It soon became clear that her body was answering to the same rhythms as the moon, and each time the moon had diminished to a tiny sliver of pale, pearly light, her body began its flow.

One evening, while the moon was at its fullest, she felt that something portentous was about to happen. Annah had learned that she sometimes had premonitions that others didn't, so she kept the feeling to herself. It wasn't a bad feeling, like the onset of her period; she felt almost elated as she tossed in her bed that night. She awoke early, but the day began like all the others—the heat hadn't broken and there were no clouds to suggest any relief. She spent the day fidgeting and wishing for it to end quickly, to the point that one of the teachers spoke sharply to her once. When the day finally ended, she burst from the school and raced over the familiar path even faster than normal, never stopping to rest.

When she arrived at home, she found Magdalene and Papa together in the compound. They grinned at her as she approached them.

"What is it?" she demanded eagerly.

"It's your toto, Frances," Papa answered. "She'll be home in three weeks, on Friday. A messenger from the medicine man in Bukedia just left us."

"Oh, Papa! Why so long?" She had known this day would come, but why now did she—did they—have to wait another three weeks for it?

"She must prepare for the journey," he replied, "and we must prepare for her homecoming. The medicine man and his helpers will bring her, so we must get the compound ready so they can rest for a few days before traveling back. And we must prepare the feast!" He nearly shouted the last sentence. Picking up on his joyful mood, Annah grabbed Magdalene's hands and they began dancing around in circles.

"Alright, alright, my girls," Papa laughed. "Let's get some dinner and plan our celebration."

The next three weeks were a flurry of activity, but for Annah they were agonizingly slow. She and Magdalene began that very night brewing the beer that would be the celebratory drink. Toto's beer was known in the whole district for its fine taste, so they knew theirs wouldn't be as good, but they didn't think anyone would mind. In the following days, aunties arrived almost daily, bringing food that would be needed or helping set up the space where the guests would stay.

At last the preparations were finished and the day had arrived. Once again, Annah barely made it through the school day, but at last she was heading home. She and some other students from Agu were jogging down the road from Ngora when the bus passed them, also heading west.

"My mother's on that bus," she shouted as she took off running after it. She was about a half mile away when the bus stopped at the lane to Agu and several people got out. Annah immediately spied the tall, stately woman who stepped slowly to the ground while two women reached up to assist her. Annah ran even faster, and caught up to the group while they were still collecting their bags and getting organized. Feeling suddenly shy around these efficient women and the one man whom she recognized as the medicine man, she stood quietly at the edge of the group, observing. But there was just one person who had Annah's full attention. This was not the thin, weak woman who had disappeared all those months ago. With hungry eyes, Annah took in her mother's return to grace and beauty. Toto seemed to be the center of the activity, and she remained still while the others were fretting and hurrying to ease her way. Annah realized that her mother must still be weak, but she could also see that this was the Toto she had always known. Mother and daughter exchanged fond, joyful looks, and then the entourage surrounded Toto and she obeyed their commands.

Annah slipped away from the scene and ran up the lane to the family compound. She shouted to her father and sisters as she came running, and they all gathered under the big tree to greet Toto. It was here that Annah got her hug from her mother at last. How complete she felt as soon as those familiar arms were around her. She realized then just how empty she had been during all those months.

The family celebrated all weekend. They ate fresh goat meat, vegetables, and rice with groundnut sauce, and they drank the beer (not as good as Toto's, but good enough) and danced and sang. Toto seemed to enjoy the feasting, but mostly she sat and looked at Papa and her children as if drinking in their features. For her part, Annah stayed as close to Toto as she could while still helping serve the guests, and the gentle smile that glowed from Toto's face was all she wanted or needed that weekend. After all the guests left, calling back good wishes as they walked down the dusty lane, Annah felt a sense of elation over the realization that the family that remained in their compound was whole again.

It was hard for Annah to focus on anything except her mother in the next few weeks. Thankfully, the school term ended and Annah had passed her exam, although her grade had been considerably lower than she usually earned. Toto still needed a great deal of help from the girls, who were glad to give it to her. Sometimes she acted strangely, but Papa and the children all worked hard not to notice—to pretend that all was back to normal. One morning Annah got up early and collected all of the fishing equipment. When it was assembled, she went to the compound, where Toto was sitting under the big tree.

"Toto," she called, "can we go fishing today? I think the children would like fish for dinner."

"No—no fish!" Toto cried. Then she took a deep breath. "I'm sorry, Annah. I didn't mean to startle you, but it's just that I must never eat anything from the river again—the medicine man said it was something from the river that made me sick. I must never eat fish. In fact, even when I am strong enough to walk that far, I won't be going with you to get water. I won't go near that river."

As the school break ended, Annah was becoming more and more concerned about how Toto would cope with her and Rebecca away all day. Papa had admonished the girls to keep their mother quiet and not let her get tired, but Annah had seen Toto try to go and cook or do some chores when Papa was away. At those times, the old, weary look would return to Toto's eyes and she would suddenly sit down in the dirt to rest. It frightened Annah to think of her mother becoming so sick again that she would have to leave them. After much thought, Annah went to Papa and told him she would stay home from school that year, to help Toto.

"Oh, my Frances," he replied, looking fondly at her. "You always know what we need." Annah was a little shocked that he didn't try to argue, but she felt glad to have been so grown-up about this, and to be a solution to her parents' problem. Of course, she knew her mother's reaction would be totally different.

"Oh, no, Annah—you must go to school. This is what I want for you—what I planned for you. You're not staying at home to become a village girl." Toto's voice was strong in spite of her illness.

"Toto, I will never stop going to school until I am a nurse, but I can stay out for just one year and then return. It will be good for me, too, to learn how to take care of you. I must do this, Toto!" Annah surprised herself with the forcefulness of her reply. She had never stood up to Toto before. She could see that Toto was shocked, too.

"Alright, my girl," her mother said quietly after a long pause. "But this is only for one year, and then you will go back to school and never stop again until you are educated. You must promise me this."

"I promise, Toto," Annah replied immediately, already wondering how she would hold up through a whole year without school.

At times, it was very difficult. Annah would catch sight of other children skipping along together on their way to or from Ngora and she would feel a sharp pain in her stomach. How could she bear not being at school for a whole year? The work she needed to do to take care of Toto and the family was always there, though, and she knew that Magdalene couldn't have done it alone. On most days she was too weary to spend much time thinking about school, and after a while she didn't think about it at all. After a few months, Annah watched the children walking to school and she felt so distant from them and the life they were leading that she wondered how she would ever go back.

It was during that time that Annah began to realize just how far Toto had gone from them—not just physically, but spiritually as well. One day, Toto told her to go and gather the leaves and roots of certain plants. Annah knew just where to find these, for most of them were plants the family used for medicines when someone wasn't feeling well or had a cut or scrape, so she enjoyed her walk out into the bush to get them. When she brought them back, Toto took her into the main hut and began arranging them against the wall. She put some of the vines and leaves in an arch over a space that she had brushed clean in the dirt. Under the arch, she carefully placed the medicinal roots and leaves.

"Now go get a small gourd and bring it to me, filled with water." Annah was mystified, but she did what her mother told her to do. Toto placed the gourd next to the roots.

"Toto, this looks like a shrine," Annah said, thinking of the little alcoves in St. Aloysius Church.

"That's just what it is, Annah." Toto was rearranging the vines, making them look neat and symmetrical. "You see, one of the things I learned from the medicine man was that I have not honored my ancestors' spirits properly. So you must help me keep up this little shrine. It will be your job to keep the water supplied and to give them bits of our food, too, in case they are hungry."

Annah was speechless. Her family was Catholic—she and Rebecca attended Catholic schools. Like the other girls there, Annah wore her rosary around her neck every day, as did her mother. She had seen her father fingering the beads of his rosary and praying as he walked with the animals or sat in the shade in the afternoon, and she had heard Toto praying continually to Mary, Mother of Jesus, as she worked. The nuns and priests never openly criticized the local beliefs about healing and ancestral spirits, but they taught that Western medicine was the correct way to handle illness. Annah knew her family revered their ancestors. After all, she was named for Acam, the woman who had been so admired and had brought great respect to their family. But they had never done anything like this. Besides, the family's Catholicism—the rosaries, the religious songs they sang weekly, the belief that God would protect them—was a main source of comfort to Annah. How could her mother be worshipping spirits?

In time, Annah developed an uneasy acceptance of the shrine, as well as of her ancestors' spirits, she supposed. Her mind was taken off the strange little shrine by the increasing difficulties the family was having getting enough of the basic necessities, like soap and rice. It was becoming harder and harder to buy these supplies at the market, and everyone in the village seemed to be getting along with less and less.

Uganda that year was suffering politically, also. Although Annah only heard small scraps of the men's conversations in the afternoons, she realized that the new president, Idi Amin, was letting his soldiers attack villages to steal and pillage. Women had to be especially wary, and all the villagers kept a constant lookout for soldiers. While the men grumbled quietly, no one dared say the name of Idi Amin, because soldiers would kill a person for saying bad things about the president. It seemed that all of Uganda was just waiting. Annah heard the adults grumble that they were just waiting for something worse to happen.

In spite of this, Toto had gained strength, and she announced to Annah one day that it was almost time for her to get ready for the school term. Annah was excited but terrified by the prospect of returning to the rigors of school, but she had promised Toto and she would keep her promise. The previous year, just after Toto got home, the principal had called Annah into his office and told her that her schoolwork had slipped so much that he felt she should repeat the sixth grade. Annah had told him that her mother had been ill and was just home and clearly still very weak.

"I may not come back to school right away. I may stay for a while to take care of my mother." The words had surprised her as she said them, but she had known in her heart this was what she wanted to do.

"Very well, Frances," he had said slowly. "But you are a gifted student, and I expect you back here to finish your schooling."

When she marched back into school the following year, with her school fees in her hand, Mr. Olupot smiled broadly at her. He gave her a receipt and said, "Get back to work, Frances. Your teachers have missed you."

Annah buried herself in her studies, and in her beloved basketball and track, and before long she was the same bright, athletic student she had been before. The one aspect of school that she had hoped to avoid also plagued her as before, though: she continued to catch the attention of male teachers and had to fend off advances from them. By this time she was more comfortable with herself as a young woman, which made her all the more fierce about protecting herself. She also had settled into a true relationship with Anthony. He was now at secondary school in Mbale, far away from St. Aloysius, but they had continued to exchange letters, which had become more frequent in recent months.

Anthony actually visited Annah at home during one school break, and Papa announced immediately that he didn't like this boy who was taking up his daughter's time and attention. Toto had been more accepting of him, once she had ascertained that he intended to become educated and one day to work in an office job, not farming.

"Just make sure you're his first wife, Annah," she said, "and you'll have my blessing. But only after you've finished your schooling, too, my girl." Annah didn't really want to think about any of this—it was all too far off in the future.

But it was pleasant to get Anthony's letters, and to imagine holding hands with him. Annah had another important male figure in her life that year: her math teacher, Mr. Oluka (oh-LOO-kah). He was a gentle, humble man, and the only teacher who never looked at her with a leer or said or did anything suggestive to her. He had a beautiful wife and lovely children, and Annah wished fervently that Anthony would prove to be a similar husband one day.

Once again, school was Annah's joy, and she excelled in her final exams and went happily into her final year at St. Aloysius. Seventh grade in Uganda is a watershed: at the end of the year, all seventh graders take the comprehensive test known as the Primary Leaving Exam. Those who pass move on to secondary school and begin preparing for their futures, while those who fail begin making their lives in the village. Annah knew her mother had become a village girl, and she saw how hard Toto's life had been. Magdalene seemed content with the village life she would continue to live, but Annah was determined to get out into that great world that Toto had been telling her about since she was very little.

For most of that year, Annah and her classmates were all so focused on the impending exam that they talked of little else. The students and even the teachers were nervous about how many of them would pass this important test. This was when Annah heard about a legendary seventh-grade teacher: Mr. Emuge (EH-moo-gay). Her teachers praised him, telling the children that each year every one of his students passed the exam and went on to secondary schools all over the country. Some children claimed to know kids who attended Olio (oh-LEE-oh) Primary School, where he taught, and they assured their classmates that he was handsome and kind in addition to being an excellent teacher. Even the principal spoke of Mr. Emuge's accomplishments, and he urged his teachers to prepare their students well so that St. Aloysius would look good compared to Olio. Annah wished that she had been able to attend this marvelous school, although she knew it was far to the west, near Serere (suh-RAY-ray) Township.

Finally the day of the exam arrived. The seventh-grade students stayed in one classroom all day, and the test was divided into subjects like math, English, history, and biology. About an hour was allotted to each portion. They had a short lunch break, and some of the children discussed the harder questions and compared answers. Others just listened wearily and worried about the afternoon's subjects. Annah left school that day drained but optimistic that she had passed.

The tests would be sent to England for scoring, so the results wouldn't come for about a month. It was early December, and the children in the other grades would be in school longer—until the break at the end of December. Annah felt odd thinking she would never see St. Aloysius again, or many of her classmates. But mostly on that walk home she thought about what she would become. She pictured herself, tall, slender, and beautiful, in a stark white nurse's uniform. She would give medicine to children and mothers and make them well and happy. Her tiredness vanished and she raced the rest of the way home to tell all her family and neighbors that she had finished primary school.

That December was hotter and drier than anyone could remember, so Annah's days were quickly taken up with the search for water and food. Their stores of vegetables from the rainy season were nearly gone, and the cassava and potatoes that could normally be dug at this time of year were drying more rapidly than the girls could harvest them. The daily journeys for water became all-consuming.As the sources of water began drying up, the girls had to go farther and farther to fill their jugs each day. Annah, Magdalene, Rebecca, and their mother began getting up at four in the morning, long before light, to walk to the nearest source—a distant village's well. When they arrived, there would already be a long line of women and girls waiting. One day they didn't get back home with water until midafternoon, weary and hungry and frustrated by the wasted day.

The lesson was clear: never go late to fetch water, so Toto began getting the girls up at midnight to walk long distances and be the first in line. Once they were home again, they barely had time for chores before they had to prepare supper with the meager rations that were left.

The entire country was in the same situation. On Saturdays, when Toto and the girls went to the market in Ngora, the shelves were nearly empty. There was no paraffin for candles, and no salt to make the food they did have taste better. On the rare days when the store had gotten some food items in, the customers fought over them. Toto would get what she could and then urge the girls to think positively as they walked home. She would talk about the better world that was there for Annah and Rebecca if they stayed in school, and Annah was optimistic about her own life. But she saw how her parents were getting thinner and more careworn, and she saw that they were powerless to do anything about their situation. They lived in want and in fear—fear of the ever-present soldiers, who stole or just demanded whatever they wanted from the villagers. The family's only hope came at prayer time, when they prayed for food and water, and for peace in Uganda and in their village.

It was during that sad time that Annah's waiting ended—she got her exam results. She had not finished in the top level, but she was in the second level, which also qualified her for secondary school. Annah had indeed passed out of primary school! She told her family, and saw tears in both Toto's and Papa's eyes.

"You will go to secondary school in Soroti, and you'll live with your sister Rosemary," Toto said. "We'll slaughter one of the goats and sell the meat to pay your school fees." Annah looked to her father, worried that he would resist killing one of their precious animals, but he just nodded, smiling.

Her new adventure was still a few weeks away, and it didn't seem real that she would actually leave the family compound and the village for a life she couldn't even imagine. Some days Annah could barely work in her excitement and eagerness to get this life started. But then she began to think about how her life now followed such a strict pattern: wake up early every day to the same struggle that was women's work, toil long into the afternoon, prepare a scant supper and sadly place it before the ever-hungry family, clean up after the meal, put the children to bed, and then fall into a deep sleep knowing it would all begin again tomorrow.

She thought about how this had been her mother's life since long before she was born, and how it would continue to be after Annah left for Soroti. Her mother was the strongest woman in the world, and Annah believed she would never be that strong. Still, she could see the strain of the days taking their toll on her mother's body. How could she leave her mother to do all this with one less helper? Annah knew that she was a big help in the household, and that she would be sorely missed. But when she voiced her concerns to her mother, Toto just sat down, wiped the sweat from her brow, and smiled at Annah with visible joy.

"This is what I've always planned for you, my girl," her mother said gently. "When you graduate and get a good job, you will send me money so that I can hire help. That is what I want from you. If you want to truly help me, that is the way I want you to do it."

It felt unfair that her mother would not get to experience this life of the outside world, but Annah knew that she would enter it with her mother's blessing. Her best tribute to her mother would be to succeed at everything that she would get a chance to try.

1974 to 1983

BY THE MID-1970s, the world had denounced "Big Daddy" Idi Amin as a buffoon and a despot, while in Uganda the citizens lived in constant fear of the murderous whims that drove him and his soldiers to terrorize them. He fostered the tribal divisions within the country, especially the animosity between the northern regions and the tribes of the south who had gained much of their power during colonial times. Amin, a convert to Islam, had his soldiers carry out raids in which members of other religions, especially Christians, were targeted. Although he was denounced by Muslim leaders in general, he received aid and support from Libya's president, Muammar Gaddafi.

In 1977, Amin declared himself President of Uganda for Life and began amassing an invasion army to obtain territory from neighboring countries. Amin's forces were defeated in 1979 by Tanzanian troops, who, with the help of thousands of deserters from Amin's army, attacked Kampala and drove Amin into exile. After finally escaping his country, Amin found refuge and a life of comfort in Libya.

There were two interim presidents after Amin's ouster, and then former president Milton Obote, who had been in hiding in Tanzania, returned and was elected president again in 1980. He struggled to bring the country back from the ruin left by Amin's reign, and although he was accused of many human rights violations in his handling of his political enemies, Obote managed to establish several programs to improve the plight of the citizens. Using foreign aid, he accomplished some rebuilding of the infrastructure, and he emphasized education as a key to economic growth.

However, Obote continually faced opposition from rebel forces who maintained that he had rigged his election. The most powerful, the National Resistance Movement, was headed by Yoweri Museveni. This group was primarily composed of members of southern tribes, while Obote's loyalists were from the northern tribes.

Chapter 7

ANNAH'S SISTER ROSEMARY arrived one day in February 1974 to take her to her home in Soroti, where she would live while she attended secondary school. The family gathered for a final dinner, and although her parents and Rosemary talked cheerfully about the adventures that awaited Annah, she and the other children were subdued. No one could quite imagine family life without Annah in the middle of it. The next morning, Annah bade a tearful goodbye to her brothers and sisters, and then hugged her papa and toto one last time. She and Rosemary climbed onto the bus that would deliver them, two hours later, to Soroti.

Only a girl whose mother's sole purpose in life had been to prepare her daughter for a larger life could have handled all the changes that Annah experienced. Certain that she was headed for her own special destiny, Annah entered the bus that day not realizing that she would never be a village girl again.

Rosemary and her husband, Cooper, and three children, George, Joseph, and Steven, lived just a half mile from Annah's secondary school, Erimu's (AIR-eh-moo) College. Their house was made of concrete blocks with a smooth, beige plaster finish on the outside and a brown metal roof that made raindrops sing. Inside, the smooth walls and ceilings were all white. Annah was certain that no palace could look any more elegant than this home. There was electricity to power lamps in the house, and water ran from a tap in the kitchen. Although Annah had visited Rosemary, and had even stayed a few days to help out when her youngest nephew was born, she couldn't believe she was to wake up every day in this house and venture out into the town. Rosemary worked as a nurse, and her husband was an administrator for Teso District. They lived among professionals—a doctor on one side and a high school teacher on the other. Although Annah would be helping out with household chores, most of the hard work was done by Akutoi, one of the orphaned children who had come to Agu Village when Annah was younger.

On Annah's first day at her new school, Rosemary walked her to school and introduced her to the principal. He was sitting at his desk, and as he looked up to see his new student, he broke into a huge smile.

"You must be a basketball player," he exclaimed, looking hopeful.

"Oh yes, I am!" This was the one topic that took away all of Annah's shyness. The principal stood and took measure of her full height and then came around his desk to shake her hand and welcome her to the school. Although it was unheard of for a student in Senior 1, Annah was made captain of the basketball team during her first semester.

As always, learning was a pleasure for Annah. Secondary school offered her such a wide range of courses, and she had music, drama, and basketball to look forward to at the end of the day. She studied from nine to five, with an hour lunch break which she was able to take at home. She generally got home in time to help with dinner preparations, and then she ate with the family, did her homework, and went to bed to dream of more days just like the last.

Every day was pure joy for Annah, and she found that she put even more enthusiasm into her work at Erimu's College. Although she missed her runs to and from school each day, she poured that extra energy into her new school and town activities. Her happiness showed in her basketball playing, where she nearly flew down the court with the ball. When she was playing, she felt that only she and the ball existed, using teammates and opponents alike just to accomplish her goal. She became known for her prowess not just at school but also in town, where shopkeepers and strangers would see her and ask how she had gotten so good at basketball. She had no easy answer for that question, because for her the game was simply a part of her, like the orange soil of her village, the easy chatter of her mother and sisters as they worked, and the earthenware water jug she had once carried daily on her head.

The founder of Annah's school, Erimu, was a famous Pentecostal minister who now preached in churches all over Uganda. Annah found that the school's religious teachings were not very different from those of her Catholic schools, but she had to get used to not having nuns in her life. The Erimu's College teachers were enthusiastic and kind, and her principal was especially friendly to her. He was a true basketball fan, and he never missed a game or an opportunity to compliment her playing when he met Annah in the school compound. He encouraged her in so many ways, telling her she would be a very successful woman if she stayed in school and studied hard. As her secondary years progressed, Annah was able to put her past incidents with male teachers behind her and begin to trust and respect her educators again.

While Catholicism wasn't a part of school life here, Christianity was, and Annah began finding new solace from the Bible and from her friends' and teachers' religious opinions. She still wore her rosary around her neck, but she was thirsty for the differing ideas that she learned from people of other faiths. She often went to the school library to do homework, and while there she would sometimes take a break and read the Bible. It was unusual for her to be reading it on her own: in Catholic school, reading from the Bible was something the nuns and priests did aloud to the children. Annah found great comfort in sitting quietly, reading random passages and pondering their meaning all by herself.

It was from friends that Annah first heard the term *born again*. Many of the girls she knew insisted that it was only through this experience of being reborn that one could be cleansed of her previous sins and become worthy of a place in heaven. Annah secretly worried that she would never merit such forgiveness, since she had helped her mother in what surely was idolatry, so she just listened to her friends and read the Bible, seeking each time the one passage that could lead her out of her dilemma.

Mostly, though, Annah and her friends just took each day's adventures as they came. Like Annah, many of the girls had come from rural schools and were experiencing life with running water, electricity, and cars for the first time. They giggled together about these things but pretended to the town girls to be comfortable with all the new experiences. All the girls talked about their grade school years, and Annah was surprised to hear again the name of the famous seventh-grade teacher, Mr. Emuge. Finally, Annah met Angela, who had attended Olio school.

"He was the most handsome and fun teacher in the world," she told Annah once. "He was really a hard teacher, but we loved him so much we didn't mind." Annah couldn't imagine a teacher being so perfect. Some of the girls from Olio school acted like they were better than the others, but Angela became a good friend of Annah's and they both began to measure teachers as well as boys against the lofty standard of Mr. Emuge.

Annah and her girlfriends found as many opportunities as they

could to leave thoughts of school behind and get to the really important topics of discussion: hair, clothes, and boys. Annah let her hair
grow during her time at school, so for the first time she had to comb
and style it. She figured out a way to comb it so that the white patch
was covered up and enjoyed the fact that no one asked about it or
teased her. Although they wore uniforms to school, the girls talked
constantly about their church clothes and what styles suited them
best. With Annah's height and slender build, the girls enviously told
her she would look beautiful in any style. Her friends also assured
her that she could have any boy she wanted, but throughout secondary school Annah had only one boy in her heart: Anthony.

Anthony and Annah continued to exchange letters, and when
other girls talked about going for romantic walks with their boy-
friends, Annah felt content that she just sat at home and read his letters over and over. She had one small photograph of Anthony that
she kept in a bookcase so that only her eyes would see it. On many
nights, Annah would go out to her sister's porch and look up at the
sky. It seemed so different here, but the moon always shone just as
it had over her family's gatherings around the fire. Annah took comfort in knowing that her family was sitting under this moon, telling
the same stories and singing the same songs. It seemed, though, that
the moon was farther away from here. Although she had always
checked the moon at home to see where she was in her monthly
cycle, in Soroti she was more likely to be surprised by her period
and then realize that the moon was just a sliver overhead.

By the first school break and visit home, in May of her first year,
Annah had changed so much in three months that her little brothers were shy with her, and even the villagers remarked that she had
gone away and become a grown-up. She settled back easily into the
routines of the household, and she felt proud that she worked as an
adult now. She easily carried a full-sized jug on the morning water
trips, and she fished, cooked, and toiled in the fields with a new ease
and authority. Most pleasing of all to her was that sometimes Toto
would just sit and rest while her girls worked. Annah loved the contented little smile her mother wore at those times.

Annah reveled in her mother's joy in her three sons. The twins
were seven, and little Joe was a cheerful four-year-old. Papa was
teaching them how to tend the animals and take them to the river
to graze and drink, and Annah could see that the other villagers
were impressed by these little men. Her mother's status in the community had risen because she was now the mother of not just one

but three strong boys. Rebecca was happy with her schoolwork at Ngora Township school, and Magdalene, whose wedding to a village boy would be in a few weeks, was content with her quiet, homebound life. Magdalene giggled when she assured Annah that she was to be the first wife. Annah wanted to be a part of her sister's celebration, but the family could not afford to bring her home for it, and she shouldn't miss school.

On her two trips home that year, Annah noticed that the divide between the teens attending secondary school and those who remained in the village widened with each passing month. The girls who stayed kept their village ways and stared openly at Annah's different clothes and hair. Although Annah tried to strike up old friendships, the girls would grow silent and look away as she talked, as if they didn't believe what she was telling them. The boys from Annah's grade school were either working their family farms or off becoming soldiers in Idi Amin's army. Although it was jarring to think of her former playmates behaving like the soldiers she encountered in Soroti, Annah could hardly blame them. It seemed that the soldiers were the only people who had everything they needed, partly because they simply took it from citizens if they wished to.

It was clear that, as much as Annah's life was expanding and improving, Uganda was suffering a terrible fate. Annah could tell from the careworn looks of her parents and the other villagers that times continued to be hard. Although her family generally had enough to eat, the shortages continued, and they had no salt for their food, or soap, or paraffin for candles, or much of anything that had to be purchased instead of grown or made at home. Even in Soroti, people were losing jobs and becoming beggars. Rosemary was lucky that there was always a need for nurses, and her husband was lucky to own a car that he could hire out as a taxi for additional money. By her second term in Soroti, Annah was hearing about raids by soldiers who would just walk into homes or schools and begin shooting. There, as in larger towns throughout Uganda, educated and powerful people would simply disappear one day. Apparently their prestige threatened the power-mad president, so he ordered his soldiers to make them vanish.

Annah began hearing many stories of soldiers coming to schools and taking girls out and raping them. Although they never came to Erimu's College, all the students and teachers became wary, and looking over her shoulder became a way of life for Annah.

At just sixteen years old, Annah was a thoughtful and analytical person, and she saw the irony of her life at that point. In most ways, her life was truly beautiful: she was experiencing things most village girls couldn't even imagine, and she was preparing for an important job in a large and exciting world even as that world seemed to be shrinking faster than her dreams were expanding. Even more ironic, she knew, was the fact that Idi Amin continued to be afraid of people with education. He had people killed just for being able to speak English. And yet, she worked hard every day to perfect her English and to become as educated as she possibly could. There were days when a small doubt about her future would creep into her head, but it would quickly be replaced by a vision of her mother repeating that a vast and wonderful world awaited her, if she just continued to excel at school. Rosemary had met their mother's expectations, and she hadn't been bothered by Amin's soldiers. Annah's faith remained strong and she was certain there was nothing for her to do except to go forward to meet that world, with the same focus and determination that sent her flying down the basketball court.

Chapter 8

ANNAH BROUGHT IMPORTANT NEWS to her parents when she returned home after her second semester at Soroti: she had passed the qualifying exams for acceptance into Kangole Secondary School, a Catholic boarding school for girls that was about 125 miles northeast of Soroti. Kangole was a more prestigious school, and Rosemary had told Annah that she and Cooper would help with expenses, so that the burden of school fees wouldn't be too great for Toto and Papa. Although Toto was clearly saddened by how far away her daughter would be, Annah could see that her mother was pleased and proud that such a school wanted Annah.

When Annah had arrived home that December, she discovered that Toto was quite pregnant: the baby was due at the end of the month. Toto was in her forties, so the nurse at the hospital near Ngora told her she must be very careful and that she should make sure she was in the hospital when labor started. On December 18, Toto told the girls she felt she needed to go to Fredika Hospital to wait. She asked Annah to come and be her helper—family members were expected to bring in food for the patients and help them with their baths, since just a few nurses had many people to care for. Annah was thrilled to be of such help to Toto, so she happily walked Toto there and stayed in the small building that housed family members. Each day she arose wondering if she would have a new sibling that day.

On the day before Christmas, Toto asked Annah if she would go to the market to get some beef for her lunch, so Annah set off on her errand. When she returned two hours later, Toto lay in her bed with a tiny child lying at her side.

"Annah, your sister came," Toto said with a tired smile. Annah couldn't believe how small and new the baby looked. With a shock she realized that she was actually old enough that this child could have been hers.

"Toto! Tomorrow is Christmas; we must name her Christine."

And so the baby became Florence Christine. Annah would always feel a special bond to this little sister, and her experience at Fredika Hospital made her more determined than ever to become a nurse.

A few weeks later it was time for Annah to begin her journey north to her new school. The family had a quiet final supper, and then Annah packed her meager belongings for the eight-hour bus ride to Kangole. Toto wrapped up a small meal of potatoes and groundnuts for the trip, and some extra nuts and dried fruit for Annah to have once she reached the school. As with all the sacrifices Annah knew her family made to support her education, she smiled happily to cover the ache she felt inside and took the gifts gratefully.

What joy to be back in a Catholic school! As she entered the compound she saw the familiar figures of serene, black-clad nuns walking between the buildings. Her dormitory was a large, open hall with bunk beds about four feet apart in long rows. Annah found an empty lower bunk and carefully placed her suitcase on the floor against the wall, to serve as her closet. Then she crawled onto the bed to revel in the amount of space that was solely hers. She stretched out on her back and looked at the slats of the bed above her and said a quiet prayer of thanksgiving and hope to God. She would be everything he, and her mother, expected of her in return for this opportunity.

As the semester went on, Annah came to feel she had arrived in heaven. Everything she needed or wanted was right there. Pipes with spigots were placed near the dormitories, and the girls just had to fill their basins and take the water to the building where they bathed and used the latrines. When they walked to the dining halls, they stopped to fill their mugs with water to drink with their meals. There was no carrying water on her head for miles, or building fires to make meals, or taking care of little siblings or cousins. For the first time in her life, Annah was leading the life of a child. Her classmates were all chatty, happy teenagers, just like her, whose worries were limited to getting their homework done and finding the most flattering hairstyle. For weeks, Annah would find herself thinking she was ignoring a chore that needed to be done. She had never lived without work to do and siblings to take care of. It was a wonderful feeling of freedom, but she felt guilty sometimes that Toto and her sisters were home working while she was playing ball with friends or just sitting under a tree, talking. They all rose each morning except Saturday to attend Mass, and then they filed into the dining hall for breakfast. After their classes and extra sports and activities, they ate dinner, attended prayers at church, and then settled in to do homework, write letters home, and go to bed.

Friday night was movie night, held in the dining hall after prayers. Annah had seen a movie only once, a small, grainy production shown in her grade school classroom. She relished sitting close to her friends in the dark and being transported to other worlds. Some Saturday nights the school held dances, with the girls all dancing with each other to the latest songs blaring from a record player.

Since the students at the Kangole Secondary School were teenagers, their relationships with the nuns were more relaxed than Annah had experienced at Okoboi school. The teaching nuns were all white-skinned and from faraway places like the United States and Great Britain. Uganda had black sisters in those days, but they were elementary teachers, or they cooked and cleaned in the upper-level schools. Annah's favorite nun was Sister Ruth, who was from Maryland in America. Sister Ruth was the youngest in the convent, and she taught English and sewing. She was like an older sister to Annah—even teaching her important female things like how to sew pieces of cloth to make sanitary pads. Once, Sister Ruth took Annah to her room in the convent and gave her some of her old "civilian" clothes. Annah couldn't believe she was wearing dresses from the other side of the world. Annah still pondered her old childhood mystery about nuns: what exactly was under those wimples? She begged Sister Ruth constantly to take the wimple off, if only for a minute.

"Oh, silly Frances! Stop it," was the only reply Annah ever got, but they both would break into fits of giggles—Sister Ruth because of the repeated question and Annah because she was imagining that the nun had no hair under there.

Sister Ruth and Sister Theresa were in charge of the theater program at school. Sister Theresa was a jolly, sweet nun who was beloved by all and returned the affection boisterously. She had a passion for groundnuts, and all the girls from the villages brought her a few precious handfuls of them when they returned from vacations. She would squeal with delight as she unwrapped the little cloth-bound treasure from each girl, and then, with a wink, she would promise to share them with the other nuns. Kangole was in a desert region, so no groundnuts grew anywhere near the school.

Annah got involved in theater because she wanted to work with these two nuns, but she soon discovered that she loved acting as well. Because of her height she was usually given the male roles in this all-girls school's productions. Annah had costumes with trousers and all the nuns laughed when she dressed for her parts. Secretly, Annah liked it because she had always wished she had been a son to her father, and this was her chance to pretend that she really was his boy Francis. With her statuesque figure, Annah looked striking even in male outfits, and in no time at all she was attracting the attention of the boys from the nearby boys' school who came to watch the girls' plays and basketball games. She noticed that the boys especially liked to look at her legs beneath her basketball shorts, and after a drama production they often became bold and patted her back or took her arm when she emerged from backstage in trousers.

Annah enjoyed the attention of the boys—both at plays and at basketball games, when her royal blue uniform shorts showed off her long legs. But still the only boy for her was Anthony. Although they kept up their correspondence even now, while Annah was in Kangole and Anthony was away at school in Kuchonga Secondary School in the Bukedia District, Annah gave little thought to marriage—that was still far off in her future. She had so much to do first, and school was the key to accomplishing all that.

One aspect of life at the Kangole school that made Annah especially happy was that, for the first time in her life, she wasn't the tallest girl in school. As soon as Annah had arrived, she had been told about a girl in her grade who was much taller than she. She could hardly believe it, but then she met Joy, who was nearly a foot taller than Annah. Even stranger was the fact that Joy didn't play basketball. How could she have gone through school without learning to play? The two girls soon became good friends, and Annah never stopped feeling a little thrill when the girls lined up by height and she was not the very last person in line.

The phenomenon of Joy's lack of interest in sports made Annah understand why the principal and so many teachers had been slightly tentative when they asked if she played basketball. But even on that most familiar ground for Annah—the basketball court— things were different at Kangole. There was already an established team captain, who was in Senior 4, so Annah was made her assistant rather than captain. Annah was disappointed at first, but she soon found great pleasure in being free of the leadership role and able to concentrate only on herself and the ball during games. Her speed and agility improved, and she found that her time on the court became an even greater release for her.

Everything about the Kangole school gave Annah a feeling of

peace and well-being that she had never experienced before. Still, her favorite time of day continued to be at night, when all the noise in the dorm had ceased and she heard only the rhythmic breathing of her classmates. That was when Annah basked in the little space that was hers alone, and she lay quietly, staring at the dim light of the moon through the dorm's open windows. She counted off the familiar, worn slats of the bed frame above her while repeating the prayers that she had been saying all her life. She still prayed directly to God, but the nuns had also taught her to pray to Mary, Mother of God, since she could influence her son in ways only a mother could. Annah always drifted off to sleep content that God was hearing her, and that Mary was making sure he paid attention.

Annah's trip home for the midyear break was a sobering experience for her. The bus she boarded for the eight-hour trip was jammed with people, including some other girls from her school. At first, the girls chattered and laughed about things that had happened at school, but they soon realized that the other people on the bus were unusually quiet and sober. After a few hours, the bus abruptly came to a halt in the middle of nowhere. The girls heard murmurs about a road block while some of the passengers began stuffing personal belongings into their clothes to conceal them. The girls were mystified until a soldier with a machine gun climbed into the bus and ordered everyone to get off.

"Take nothing with you," he shouted. "Just get off now—hurry up!" He was pointing the gun up and down the rows of passengers, who ducked when the barrel was turned toward them.

The passengers walked quickly down the aisle and stepped onto the dirt road. Their heads were lowered and they avoided the eyes of this soldier and his compatriots who stood near the bus gesturing with their guns for the people to line up several yards away. Soon all the luggage from inside the bus and on top of it was heaped on the ground and several soldiers were pawing through it while two of them kept their guns trained on the silent passengers. Occasionally a soldier would hold up some food or usable clothing with a whoop, and one of the passengers would flinch. After the bags had been ransacked and tossed aside, the soldiers walked up and down, stopping in front of individuals and demanding to have anything they had hidden. With the gun barrels aimed at their faces, the passengers quickly complied. The soldiers ignored Annah and her friends—what could a schoolgirl have of value?

At last, the soldiers ordered the passengers to get back onto the bus and fired some bullets into the air as the driver ground the gears of the bus and sped away. For a while the bus was silent and then the girls heard some women weeping while male voices rose in anger. Others shushed both the women and the men, looking around fearfully to be sure no soldiers had remained on the bus.

"We are fortunate to have our lives," one man said. "Stop complaining."

The remainder of the ride passed in silence, although no one slept or even relaxed. All eyes were peering across the landscape, watching for more soldiers. Annah and her friends sat quietly, subdued more by the behavior of the adults around them than by the incident with the soldiers.

Home was waiting, unchanged, at the end of Annah's journey. The smiles on her parents' and siblings' faces were just as broad, their eyes shone with just as much love as ever. After a few days, though, Annah realized that villagers were coming to stand quietly at the edge of the family compound while her mother or father wrapped up small parcels of cassava or potatoes or filled small jugs with milk. Although Annah knew that her parents were always willing to help their neighbors, she had already noted that her own family was eating just two meals per day.

In spite of continued hardships, Annah's siblings were growing and seemed content. Her father now had twelve children from his two wives, Esther and Lucy. As usual, Annah saw little of Lucy and her children, but her three brothers and the two sisters who lived at home sat talking with her late into the night. Although they all worried about the food shortages and their parents' need to work so hard, they fell quickly into their old ways of laughing and teasing each other. As the children had grown bigger, it had become necessary to build more huts, so now all of the girls slept in one hut while all of the boys slept in another. Papa and Toto slept in the hut that Annah and her sisters had once shared with them, and Lucy had a similar arrangement across the compound, with her girls in one hut and her boys in another.

The May school break occurred during planting season, so Annah spent her days with the family hoeing, planting, and weeding. As usual for this time of year, the work was overwhelming, so there was no question but that Annah would help them. She put aside her school clothes and her shoes, and went barefoot with them to the fields every day. Toto was clearly relieved to have the extra pair of hands. Once Annah adjusted to doing physical labor all day, she enjoyed working with her mother and siblings, and the four weeks of the break passed quickly.

The bus trip back to Kangole was long, hot, and scary. The bus was stopped twice by soldiers, and each time the passengers endured the same routine that Annah had experienced with her friends on her trip home. The second time the bus was stopped, the soldier who was shaking down each passenger stopped in front of Annah and waved the barrel of his gun in her face. She stood frozen, her eyes fixed on his toes sticking through ragged, filthy boots.

"What do *you* have hidden in there?" he asked. She glanced up to see a cruel smirk on his face as he looked her up and down.

"Nothing," she stammered.

The soldier laughed and looked at her a moment longer, but then he shrugged and turned his gun to the man next to her. She barely breathed all the way back to Kangole, where she entered half-heartedly into the happy greetings that the girls were giving each other. That night, she lay in bed unable to collect her thoughts enough to pray. God granted the wishes of children, she knew, but now that she was becoming a young woman, would she lose his protection?

Annah's fears eventually quieted, although it seemed that most of the girls had returned from break with an increased awareness of the precariousness of Uganda and its people. Discussions in class about government were carefully guided by the nuns to avoid any criticism of Idi Amin or his regime, but the girls learned about the workings of other types of government, and it was not lost on them that their own situation compared badly to most other nations. Some of the girls would murmur among themselves that surely some other country would see what was happening in Uganda and send its armies to stop this.

That semester, the girls began to see large trucks passing by the school compound, driven by soldiers. In the back, where they usually saw huge mounds of cassavas behind the slatted sides, they could see the bodies of people of all ages, some nearly naked. Once, Annah saw a soldier standing atop the pile of bodies, looking out over the side, and lazily pointing his gun at the people he passed. When the girls asked the nuns about the trucks, they were told to turn away when one passed and never, never to look a soldier in the eye. It was hard for Annah not to look at the faces she could glimpse in the tangle of arms and legs. She felt somehow that she must look at their frozen features, to affirm for these people that they had existed. As she lay in bed on those nights, Annah would be haunted by the faces she had seen, and she would pray to Mary, asking her to tell her son that Idi Amin needed to die.

The girls found solace in the normalcy of school. Although food was becoming more and more scarce, the teachers and students brought whatever they could find and it was shared among everyone. Sports, drama, and Friday-night movies continued unchanged, and they had occasional dances on Saturday evenings. The school had a young priest, Father John, who came to the dances, but he only danced with Senior 4 girls. The younger girls would watch enviously and criticize the older girls when they tried to dance too close to him.

"Tonight I am going to dance with Father John," Annah told her friends one Saturday.

"He won't do it, Frances," they giggled.

"Just watch me," she said as she strode off across the floor.

Smiling mischievously, Annah went up to the dancing priest and tapped his shoulder.

"I'm cutting in," she said loudly.

Father John looked surprised and then bowed stiffly. "I would be honored to dance with the school's star basketball player," he said, his eyes twinkling. He took her hand and danced a few steps while all the girls laughed and pointed. That night, in their dorm, the other girls couldn't stop asking Annah what kind of dancer he was.

"Oh, he was dreamy," she said. "Too bad he is a priest."

"Oh, Frances—shame on you!" the girls exclaimed, while giggles arose from every bunk.

It was only a few days later that Father John was again the talk of the school, though for a very different reason. One afternoon, a truckload of soldiers drove straight into the school compound and six armed men jumped from the truck. The nuns quickly told the girls to get down behind the classroom walls and be silent. They could hear that Father John had gone out to meet the men, and he was speaking with them in a calm, friendly voice.

"Get those nuns out here," the girls heard a man yell. "We want some white women." There was a rumble of male laughter. The girls couldn't quite hear what Father John was saying, but his tone was still calm and placating. Annah inched closer to Sister Ruth, who was on the floor beside her. She could feel the nun trembling and squeezed her hand hard, wishing she could make the entire school disappear. In a few minutes it sounded as though the voices got quieter, and then there was silence from the compound. No one moved, and soon they could hear the soldiers again, laughing and talking loudly. The truck engine roared, and they heard it drive off.

One of the other nuns came into the classroom and told the girls that they were all to go to the church for prayers. Once the girls and the nuns had all assembled, Father John came out to the altar. His face was white and his hands shook as he made the sign of the cross and began to pray. After some prayers of thanksgiving, he looked around the church, meeting the eyes of each of the nuns.

"We were in great danger today, but the Lord blessed us. The soldiers decided they would take our food and go, without hurting anyone here. We have nothing for dinner tonight, but we have each other and the peace of the Lord, so we are truly blessed. Please go quietly to your dorms, do your homework and go to bed. You should offer your hunger up to God, and ask him to continue to bless us."

The girls filed silently to their dorms and settled down with their schoolbooks. Soon, most were lying in their beds, ready to try to sleep. No one mentioned being hungry, and eventually the whispered "Good nights" ended and Annah could hear soft breathing.

That night, as she drifted off to sleep herself, Annah was praying hard to Mary to keep them all safe and to ask God to bless her and give her a good life. "I want to keep learning, and then use my knowledge to help others," she prayed. "Please keep me alive to do this."

Suddenly, Annah could see a white-clad figure hovering over her. She was confused, because it was not Mary, to whom she had been praying, but a young male figure, huge and both fierce and gentle at the same time. Could this be Jesus?

"Annah," the deep voice said to her, "you will live a long time. You will be married, and you and your husband and two children will leave Uganda and travel far away from here."

Annah sat up in her bed, her heart pounding. "How can this be?" she wondered. "I am getting educated so that I can build a life of my own, working in a profession and helping my mother and father in their older years. Why would I be married and going with my husband away from my parents? Oh, this must have been just a horrible dream." She began praying to Mary, and as she did so her heart calmed and she was able to lie down again. Eventually she drifted off to sleep, without dreaming the rest of the night.

From that night on, although Annah continued to work hard to get her education, she carried in her heart an image of herself as a wife and mother in a strange place, protecting her children from the strange world around her. In church, she would gaze at the statue of Jesus and feel a sense not just of peace but also of companionship. She felt she had been lifted above her childish bargains with God and given the gift of knowledge of her own place in Creation.

Chapter 9

FOR THE FIRST TIME IN HER LIFE, Annah felt a mix of sadness and joy as she packed to go home for the year-end break that
December. She longed to be with her family—especially Toto and
Papa—but she would miss the carefree days she had enjoyed in
school. She also felt a strange sense of foreboding. Through all of
her life she had only looked forward with purpose and faith, and
yet this semester her sister Rosemary had told her to pack all of her
belongings because she might not be returning to Kangole, and it
had caused a turmoil of doubts in her mind. Rosemary had learned
of an internship offered by the hospital in Olio where she had once
worked as a nurse, and Annah had carefully written a letter of
application, which her elder sister had corrected and then submit-
ted. This step felt right to Annah, but still she worried about leaving school for a semester, even for more learning. Was this truly
the path she should be taking? Musing on the long bus ride home,
Annah decided to leave this decision to God; if she was accepted for
the internship, then God must know this to be her true calling.

She decided to let God guide her through another situation, too.
She knew that she would see Anthony during break, since he would
be home from his school in Mbale. Lately, his letters, while still
full of tenderness toward her, had become more insistent. He was
pointing out that they were both nearly grown up, and she knew he
wanted to discuss marriage with her. How wonderful it would be
to wake each morning next to Anthony, but then Annah thought of
her mother's advice: "Tell the boys they can just ask you again after
you've finished all your schooling." She didn't want to outright
refuse him, for fear that he would simply move on to other girls,
but she knew that she—and most certainly Toto—was not ready for
serious talk of her marriage.

When she stepped off the bus in Agu, Annah felt her usual settling, as if she had once again placed her body and her surroundings
in perfect harmony. She set off down the dusty path to her house

alone, since her family hadn't known exactly when she would arrive. She enjoyed the few minutes of just breathing in the air and noting happily that the trees and the huts of her neighbors were still there. By the time she reached her compound, she was walking with an easy gait and felt that God was already working on her dilemmas for her.

Annah had grown accustomed to seeing lines of worry on her parents' faces, but it always upset her at first after an absence. They were eating one meal a day at this point, and all the family members were thin and their clothing was tattered and worn. Still, their joy at having her back was the same as always, and she reveled in their laughter and stories as they gathered around for hugs. That evening's supper was a big celebration; her mother killed a goat and made her wonderful groundnut sauce for the atap. They all ate hungrily, savoring the unfamiliar taste of meat.

Annah joined the girls in their chores each day, although she was surprised that her muscles ached at first. After a few days had gone by, she had settled back into the family routine. One afternoon Akello, one of her half sisters, asked her if she wanted to accompany the older girls to a dance in the village.

"Papa would never allow that," Annah replied, startled by the suggestion.

"I didn't say we would tell him we are going," Akello answered with a sly grin. "After they are asleep tonight, we will go."

All afternoon the girls were whispering among themselves and running back and forth to plan what to wear and how to escape quietly. At dinner, Annah and Rebecca avoided looking at each other for fear that they would begin to giggle. Still, there was so much suppressed excitement in the air that Annah thought surely Toto would demand to know what was up. But her parents ate and chatted like normal. At last, it was time for bed. The two girls went to their hut and lay down, fully dressed, to wait for Papa and Toto to leave the fire and go to their hut. It seemed to take forever that night, but finally they could hear their parents' voices from within their hut. The girls waited until the conversation had ended and then crept out of their hut and walked carefully away, down the road to the planned meeting site. Akello and her younger sister, Abego, silently joined them, and then they all ran to the compound in the village where the dance was being held. It was a compound where a family of boys lived, and Annah saw the boys' father standing near the edge. The father watched a few minutes and then waved and went into his hut.

What fun they had. Her sisters all seemed to have been practicing the wild African dances, but Annah didn't know them, so at first she just watched. Finally, a boy asked her to dance and she found she could follow him easily as they whirled about on the dirt of the compound. Annah giggled at the thought of how she would impress the Kangole girls with her new talent, even though she would just be dancing with other girls there. Maybe she would approach Father John again, she thought, and make him dance this way with her.

After several hours of dancing, the girls laughingly returned home, leaning on one another as they walked under the hazy moon. It was nearly morning, and the silent huts of their neighbors would rise up suddenly like hunks of debris floating down a misty river as they walked by. Once they had neared the family compound, Akello and Abego raised their hands in silent farewell and walked quietly toward their hut. Annah and Rebecca crept up to the door of their hut and stopped. The door they had carefully latched was standing open and their bedding had been moved around.

"Papa knows," Annah whispered.

"So we get a whipping," Rebecca replied. "It was worth it," she sighed. She quickly took off her dress and lay on her mat.

Soon Rebecca was sleeping soundly while Annah lay on her mat thinking about facing her parents when they awoke. She was a young woman now, and surely not subject to whippings, but how could she explain open defiance of her father's rules? More disconcerting was the thought of her mother's reaction. She went over the sacrifices her mother had made to keep her in excellent schools. She recalled how she was the only child her mother had trusted to know where she had buried the family's money near the wall of their hut, under Toto and Papa's bed. Only she had been sent alone on errands to purchase things for the family. Only she knew, and even understood, her mother's driving need to worship the spirits of their ancestors during that year of her recovery from the strange illness. By the time dawn arrived, Annah knew she had her answer about Anthony: he would wait or not, but she would be educated fully before she even considered marriage. She would honor her mother's wishes.

Rebecca woke up and began dressing, so Annah did the same. Rebecca seemed more subdued now. They both were dressed and waiting when Papa called to them to come out at once. When they emerged, they saw that he had cut two switches from the nearby mango tree. Annah stood silently, keeping her eyes on the ground as Papa commanded Rebecca to lie down for her two swats with the switch. Rebecca wept and apologized to their parents before going to the kitchen hut to begin the chores.

Then it was just Annah. There was silence and she finally dragged her eyes up to her father's face. He was regarding her quietly, his anger darkening his deep brown eyes.

"We expected more from you, Frances. You have shamed your family." Annah's eyes returned to the dirt at his feet, hoping this would end quickly. "Lie down for your whipping."

Shocked, she took in a sharp breath, but she was too stunned to do anything but obey. The switch whistled in the air and she felt the searing pain of two swats, harder than she had ever experienced from this man. How could he be doing this to her, as if she were a mere child? Contrary to all of her upbringing, and everything she knew to be the Ateso culture, Annah raised partway to a sitting position and glared at this man who seemed to be taking away her identity.

A growl seemed to emanate from deep within him. "Pack your possessions and go now, and don't come back if you want to look at me like that. If you wish to stay here, lie down for more."

"Christopher, no!" her mother shouted. "You promised only two."

"Don't you defy me too, woman. Be quiet or you can take your girls and go."

"Where could I go?" Annah thought. No relative would take her in after this. That question was a thousand times more complicated for her mother.

"Papa, please," she moaned as she lay back down, not sure what she was begging for.

Annah's physical pain over the next several days was nothing compared to her emotional pain. Her father hadn't called her his angel for several years, but he was even more formal with her now, and her mother often wore an expression of quiet discouragement. Annah worked diligently to please them, at the same time feeling impatient with their rigid adherence to the old ways of doing everything. Sometimes she longed to tell them how much easier life could be, but she bit her tongue.

After two weeks of her holiday, the letter from the hospital in

Olio came, and she had her internship. Although Annah tried to concentrate on her home chores, she kept an eye on the horizon, as if her new life might just come flying over the far hills and carry her away. She would be assisting real nurses, with real patients. She would have her own apartment at the dispensary. She would be a grown-up!

As soon as the internship became a reality to her, Annah wrote Anthony a long letter, telling him about her plans. "Anthony, you are very special to me, but I need for you to know that I will not even think about marriage until I have gotten a nursing degree and worked as a nurse for a while. This is all that's important to me now. I understand that you want a commitment from me, but my mind is made up," she wrote. Then she softened her message with sweet remarks, but she didn't go back and change the words she had written, because she knew now that they were absolutely true.

When it came time for Annah to leave for Olio, she packed up the cooking pots that Toto and Rosemary had helped collect for her, along with some food that she knew the family couldn't spare. As the bus pulled up to the dusty intersection, she hugged her family goodbye, trying to conceal the emotions that were running through her, but her mother put her hands on either side of Annah's face and spoke quietly.

"It will be everything you imagine it to be, my daughter. And you will do very well there. You are ready for a young woman's job." Annah wondered how her mother could read her innermost thoughts so easily.

But of course, Toto had been right. In her crisp white outfit, minus the cap that only nurses wore, Annah found that she worked well with the doctors and nurses, and soon she was contributing to the functioning of the small hospital. She especially loved working with the patients, and, although she was good at calming them and helping them understand all the strange things they were encountering, she quickly realized that the hospital was barely able to meet the most basic medical needs of these people. Supplies were late in coming and then lacked important items when they did arrive. There was nothing to clean the instruments with, so she and the other aides boiled them and wrapped them in clean cloth. At first, the doctors were giving patients one-fourth of the proper dose of medicines, to stretch supplies as far as possible. When new supplies did arrive, she realized that the medicine cabinets would suddenly be nearly empty again, because those with keys to the cabinets would steal the medicines to sell at the "black market," where all kinds of real and fake medicines were sold to those with money. Once the hospital supplies were gone, all the doctors could do was to tell the patients to try to buy the medicine they needed on that same market.

After Annah had been working only two weeks, one of the nurses told her there was someone there to see her. "He's waiting outside," she added with a grin. Puzzled, Annah went to the door and there was Anthony, sitting on his bicycle and looking nervous.

"I came to talk to you, Frances. I miss you and I want us to get married. I will graduate at the end of this year, and you're already working as a nurse, so it must be time." He had stepped forward, and she had to look almost straight up to see the earnest look on his face.

Annah was so shocked that she almost blurted out her opposition to that plan, but she took a breath and smiled.

"Anthony, it's good to see you, and I appreciate your coming all this way. I can't get away right now, but you could wait until after work if you want."

For the rest of the afternoon, Annah caught glimpses of Anthony, sitting under a tree, waiting. She realized finally that she hadn't been happy to see him—just sort of annoyed that he had bothered her at work. She tried to think of the endearing things he always said in letters, but each time her mind would return to the image of Anthony hovering over her, expecting that they shared the same vision of their futures. Finally, the day ended and Annah walked with Anthony to her apartment. She shared some dinner with him while he chattered on about his life at school and his plans for after graduation that year.

After the meal, Annah took Anthony's hand and said, "Anthony, I just don't think this will work. We've become different people, and I am not finished creating my own life, while you want it all settled. I am just not the person for you." Anthony studied her face for a minute, and she met his gaze calmly. He stood up and thanked her for the meal. The sight of him riding away from her on his bike left her feeling more liberated than sad.

Once Anthony's visit was behind her, Annah quickly settled into her life. She enjoyed making small talk with the hospital staff, and she found that she had a knack for putting patients—especially the mothers and children—at ease while they awaited treatment. She realized that what she missed most from school was basketball, so she walked to the nearby school and challenged some fifth-grade girls to a game. She knew she must have been a comical sight—this tall young woman in old uniform shorts grabbing the ball from surprised girls and hurtling down the court to stuff a basket. Her life became a routine of rewarding and yet heartbreaking work at the hospital followed by a gloriously free romp on the basketball court and then a quiet evening after returning to her apartment for supper and sleep.

Like those of everyone else in rural Uganda, Annah's days were never free from the underlying threat of the soldiers, and the fear of Idi Amin and his irrational actions and decrees. Although on the radio they were constantly being reminded that Idi Amin had full control of his country, people spoke in hushed tones about how he was taking desperate measures to try to keep any sort of power. One day in July 1976, even the radio reported that Uganda had been attacked by outside forces: Israeli soldiers had accomplished a raid on Entebbe Airport. The official version was that the Israelis, aided by Kenya, had wrongly violated the sovereignty of Uganda and would face retribution from the United Nations. But the story told quietly among the people of Uganda was that Amin had aided hijackers in hiding hostages, and that the Israeli action was simply a rescue. Annah heard wild estimates of the Ugandan casualties, from fifty to fifteen hundred, but everyone knew that only one Israeli soldier had died. Far from quieting the actions of Amin or his soldiers, this incident and the UN's refusal to condemn Israel for it caused the people in the towns and villages to suffer even more at the hands of the soldiers.

Once, on a particularly difficult day at the hospital, when Annah had watched a young mother give birth, only to have the infant die while the doctors and nurses tried futilely to save it, she skipped playing basketball after work and went for a walk around the village of Olio. Along the way she met a woman who was distributing pamphlets from the United States. There were essays in them by T. L. Osborne, Oral Roberts, and Billy Graham. When the woman thrust several of each of the pamphlets at her, Annah instinctively accepted them, but when she saw what they were about she handed them back.

"You should read them," the woman said. "You'll find them very comforting."

"But I'm Catholic," Annah replied.

"Well, just take them and give them to someone else," the woman answered, already walking away down the road.

Annah carried the pamphlets home and glanced at one while she made her supper. She was surprised by how different it seemed from the catechisms she had studied in school. It talked about hope and love—not all the rules and warnings and punishments that the nuns had drilled into her. Once she had eaten, she settled on her bed and began to read them all. Oral Roberts was telling her she could be assured of salvation, right where she was, if she would just pray to Jesus. Billy Graham said the same thing—that no sin is too great for Jesus to forgive. Annah hungrily read through all of the pamphlets then, and fell asleep feeling more at peace than she had in months.

The next day at the hospital she began to ask her coworkers about church services. Christian worship had been banned in the country, so she only asked those she trusted completely, and she learned that there were some young people, led by a wonderfully wise and knowledgeable young man named James, who met on Sundays and Wednesday evenings to pray. She agreed that she would join them that Sunday, feeling again the wonderful peace that had enveloped her the evening before.

That afternoon, as she was walking home from a basketball game, a young man came toward her, slowly riding a bicycle while balancing a book bag awkwardly across his knees. When he got near, he stopped and got off, adjusted his shirt and tie, and walked the bike toward her. When he stood beside her she looked into his face and felt a strange weakness in her knees. A handsome man with a gentle, shy smile and deep brown eyes was looking at her as if she were the only other person on the planet. He was slightly shorter than she, and yet she felt that he looked at her from a lofty and peaceful place.

"Hello," he said. "I work at the school and I've noticed you before, but I've never been close enough to introduce myself." Annah marveled that such a kind face could be eclipsed by the gentleness of the voice that came out of it.

"I'm . . . I'm Frances Acam. I work . . ."

"I know—at the hospital. Thank you for your work there. I hear you've been a comfort to many people," he said softly. "I am James. James Emuge."

Chapter 10

ANNAH FELT AS IF EVERYTHING in her universe had come together to make a perfect life for her. She had been offered a continuation of the internship through the second school term and hadn't hesitated to accept it. She loved this work and was pleased to see that she was good at it. Although she felt nervous about not returning to school, Annah knew that she would pick up her studies the following term, and also that, if necessary for some reason, she could study on her own and take the qualifying exams to earn a diploma without actually being in school. But most importantly, she felt that she belonged in this job, and she wasn't ready to leave the staff and patients that she had come to love.

The apartment at the hospital was lonely, so Annah moved to a small house on the grounds of Olio school. It was just a short walk to the hospital from there, and—most importantly—being within the school compound meant that she could easily organize or join a basketball game with the upper primary students. She became kind of a player-coach, teaching the kids all of her moves, but always participating in their games. She knew she probably looked a little silly, towering over her sixth-grader opponents, but she enjoyed the opportunity to laugh and run, completely emptying her mind of all of the sadness and desperation that surrounded her daily in the hospital.

Her greatest source of peace during this time was the group of Christians that she began joining for worship and fellowship. It turned out that they met most often just three houses away from hers, and she had often heard singing and joyful shouting from there. These people were Pentecostals, and they gathered each Sunday for services led by the charismatic young James. It was in his house that six or eight of them met on Wednesdays for fellowship and prayer. Although not a formal minister, James engaged the group in discussions and prayers that increased their knowledge of—and love for—the Bible and fed their thirst for uplifting news. Annah sat quietly in these meetings at first, partly because just one look from James's softly glowing eyes would leave her throat dry and her heart pounding. Also, though, she was unsure that she belonged here. She had never before experienced the peace she felt each time the Pentecostals began their joyous noise, and yet she still thought of herself as a Catholic, and a very serious sinner.

One evening, as the group was resting and chatting after their prayers, someone asked Annah when she was going to join them completely. Startled, she looked around at the group and saw James watching her with his head tilted slightly.

"Yes, Frances," he said. "You sit each time with one toe poked into our pool of devotion. When will you let the rest of yourself embrace our worship?"

"I just don't think I can . . . I . . . I'm not really worthy," Annah told them, her eyes tracing the outline of her toes against the hard earth floor.

"Frances, don't you see?" James asked softly. "This is what we have been talking about. Jesus can forgive anything, as long as you ask. We have all needed forgiveness for something. And we all received it just as soon as we accepted that. Let him into your heart. Do that, and just see how wonderful it feels. You won't believe it!"

Over the next few days, Annah thought constantly about what James had said. When she looked into the eyes of the patients she helped at the hospital, she began to wonder whether they had accepted Jesus. Every so often there would be a patient who was quiet in his suffering and only smiled sadly when he was told there was no medicine. This kind of patient always seemed more concerned about letting the nurses and doctors know that they had done their best than about getting the treatment he was seeking. Annah began to see, too, that the nurses and doctors who were Pentecostals were more assured and peaceful with the patients, even when they could offer little more than a sympathetic ear. Was this what James and the others were offering her?

One afternoon, during a basketball game, Annah deftly grabbed the ball from one of the best Olio players. The students laughed and clapped as she dribbled it swiftly down the court and leapt into the air to send it swishing through the net. When she felt her feet hit the ground, she suddenly realized that she *wanted* to fill her heart with the Jesus who could create such joy in everyday life.

That Sunday, after the service, Annah asked the Pentecostals to pray for her. She took a deep breath, looked at each of their smiling faces, and then began to tell them about having helped her mother worship the spirits of their ancestors. She described the little shrine in their hut, and how she had tended it daily even though she never lost her fear of the power it evoked.

"I was indoctrinated into this practice, and I served spirits. I know that it was idolatry. I know it was wrong," she said softly at the end of her story. She sat looking at the floor, but no one spoke. When she finally looked up, it was into James's eyes. He was smiling as if he had just received a wonderful gift. James took Annah's shoulder and gently guided her down onto her knees. The group prayed for her, each offering a prayer for her salvation and thanking the Lord for her courage to seek forgiveness. James stood directly over her, with his hand resting on her head.

"Frances," he said quietly, "let's pray the Sinner's Prayer together. Repeat the words after me: Lord, I thank you for sending Jesus to die on the cross for my sins. I'm a sinner and I repent of all my sins. Jesus, come into my heart, and Lord, help me follow Jesus for the rest of my days. Amen."

The words seemed to pour over Annah like the purest water she could imagine. For the first time in all those years, she felt a weight lift from her. The demons in her soul were gone—there was no one there but Jesus.

James took his hand away, but she remained kneeling. Filled with sudden fear that she had abandoned her mother, Annah begged him to pray for her toto, too, to set her free from the demons.

"Remember what the Bible says, Frances," James told her, pulling her to her feet. "Anything you ask in Jesus's name will be done, if you have faith. You have the power now, Frances. Use it wisely."

From that day, Annah's life became filled with new purpose and strength. Her coworkers at the hospital noticed the joy in her eyes as she went about the daily tasks of stretching meager supplies and making do with poor substitutes for real equipment, while still finding just the right tone to reassure and comfort the patients. It seemed that everything she did was a prayer, and she felt that all of these routine tasks were just preparation for her worship and study of God's ways with the Pentecostals.

Her joy was soon offset by a new wariness, however. Idi Amin had taken bold new steps to further his power in the world and at the same time keep his people in abject terror. He had invaded Tanzania, in spite of what every citizen, at least in the rural areas, knew: there were not enough strong, whole men in this starving, terrorized country to ward off retaliatory actions by Tanzania. Certainly all the men that Annah knew were thin and weak, just like the women and children, from the massive shortages of food and medicine that plagued their region. It was known all over Uganda that Amin kept many lavish palaces for his own family. He had converted to Islam in his youth, and he embraced that religion's emphasis on polygamy. He was rumored to have more than thirty-five children with his many wives, whom he would kill at the first hint of defiance or disobedience. But the children and the favored wives lived in unabashed luxury and grew fatter every day. As if this weren't enough to break the spirits of his citizens, Amin had decided that Islam was to be the only religion in Uganda. Up to that time, Muslims had been an extremely small minority in Uganda, but they were never the targets of discrimination or deprivation.

As Annah grew closer to her friends in the little Pentecostal congregation in Olio, she became aware that most of them had suffered for their religion. Some had spent time in jail, and many had been beaten by soldiers when their group was discovered. As Amin's hatred for Christians grew, there were reports that they were being killed in nearby towns and villages. These stories terrified Annah, and she knew the others were frightened, too, but they all continued to meet and gain solace from each other and from God.

It happened one hot, dry Sunday as Annah's congregation was singing a soft hymn to Jesus. They were in a small hut in the village that they used as a makeshift church. They had purposely moved their services to this location, about two miles from Olio school, in an attempt to hide from the soldiers. The door of the hut was thrust open and two soldiers stood in the entrance, their guns aimed inward.

"What are you doing?" the ringleader of the soldiers demanded.

"We're praying," someone answered.

"That's against the law. Get out here—into the road! Now!" The soldier was waving his gun and screaming.

Once out of the house, several members of the group scattered and ran, and Annah was one of them. She dashed behind a nearby hut and hid there, peering out at the scene in the road. Eight Pentecostals, led by James, walked slowly out into the street. A few of them softly hummed the hymn they had been singing.

"Shut up!" the ringleader yelled and stood in front of them, his machine gun pointing right at James's face. Annah looked closely at the gunmen and realized that they were all Iteso—her fellow countrymen, her neighbors.

James smiled into the ringleader's eyes, who quickly took a step backward. Annah knew the power of that smile; she wasn't surprised by the soldier's response.

"If you want to die for your Christianity, stay here," the soldier yelled. "Give up your Jesus and you can walk away. Go on—just walk away." No one moved and the other two soldiers looked at the first. He waved his gun in the faces of three of the Pentecostals, but they just stood there.

Annah drew back behind the hut, afraid to watch. There was silence for several minutes and then she heard the soldier's voice again, but he was speaking, not yelling. After a silence, she got the courage to peek out at the scene again, and the soldier was standing with his gun lowered, just staring at James, who had started to lead the others in prayer.

"Sit down then, and pray," he told them. The two soldiers with him looked relieved and all three walked quickly to their truck and drove away.

One kind soldier was no reason to let their guard down, though. Throughout Olio, and Annah was sure everywhere in Uganda, people were living lives of hiding and fear. Still, Annah and the Pentecostals continued to meet. She knew they all felt what she did: that life's only peace is in prayer. It had been six months since Annah had seen her family, and she worried about how her mother and father were holding up physically, but she was comforted to know that, through her fervent prayers, her mother's soul was now safe.

Work in the hospital became more difficult as the shortages grew worse. Soldiers and police officers would just walk into the hospital and demand to be given medicine or to be the first patient seen in spite of the long line of people waiting ahead of them. No one dared tell them to go to the end of the line. One afternoon, while Annah toiled among the weary, frightened adults and crying children who were awaiting care, the chief of the village police came striding into the hospital. When he saw Annah he looked her slowly up and down, making her feel like a piece of meat at the market. Finally, he walked past her to demand the doctor's attention. One of the nurses, Alupo, reported later that the chief had quizzed her about Annah, asking her name, where she came from, and where she was living.

"She's good looking," he had commented, and he spat into the corner as he walked out.

The following day the police chief returned to the hospital and cornered Annah.

"So, I know your name and where you live," he said, his eyes roaming over her body. "Are you married? Do you have a man?"

"No, I am just a girl, and I haven't finished school," Annah answered, trying to keep the tremble out of her voice.

"Well, that doesn't matter to me. I want you anyway."

"No, I must finish school," Annah said, her courage rising. "I will think about marrying after I am educated."

The man's laugh was rough and loud, almost like a barking dog. He leaned into her face, so that she could smell his breath. "I get what I want," he told her in a low voice.

After work Annah went straight to James's house and told him about the chief.

"I think he will come tonight and do something to me," she said. James showed her a back way to get from her house to his without being seen and then instructed her to go home, wait until it was just dark, and then sneak back.

"They are probably watching you," he said grimly. "Be careful!"

Annah walked slowly home, wanting it to be plain to anyone watching that she would be in her house. She waited anxiously for darkness to begin to fall and then crept out and hurried to James's house by way of the shortcut he had shown her. They sat in his house in the dark, and around ten o'clock they could hear pounding. Peering down the way, they saw two policemen knocking on her door.

"Do you think they're there to take me to the chief?"

"I do, but you're OK here if we're quiet," James whispered.

Finally, the men gave up and strolled away in the opposite direction from James's house. James put a mat on the floor in an extra room and gave Annah blankets so she could sleep there. She lay in the strange room praying that the men wouldn't return for her, and finally fell asleep. In the morning, James urged Annah to pray and fast to bring God's protection to her. She wasn't sure what he meant.

"For three days, you must eat and drink nothing, and pray constantly, Frances," he told her. "God will protect you."

Annah began her fast and prayer that very minute. Later in the morning, one of the policemen came to the hospital and asked Annah where she had been.

"I was home," she said.

"We were looking for you and you didn't come to the door when we knocked."

"Why, is there something wrong?" she asked.

"Oh, no, the chief just wanted to talk to you." He leered at her as he spoke, and she suddenly felt cold.

The next day Annah spoke to Alupo, the nurse who had warned her the first time. Alupo told her the police chief was married, but his wife was on the other side of the village.

"Be careful, Frances," she said. "This guy's after you."

That night, though, Annah began to feel peace from her fasting and praying. She decided not to let fear drive her from her own home, so she stayed there all night. She slept little, waiting for the knocking to come, but nothing happened. The chief must have tired of his little game.

While Annah and the residents of Olio worked to keep their lives from being shattered, Idi Amin's forces had been defeated by an army of Tanzanian soldiers and Ugandan rebels who turned against their own countrymen. News of Amin's outrage spread quickly—almost as quickly as his soldiers, who now openly killed and raped through the countryside.

One morning everyone in the hospital was speaking in hushed, frightened voices. When Annah asked what was happening, she was told that the previous evening a band of soldiers had invaded the home of a family in the village, demanding to eat the goat meat that the mother was roasting. They devoured all of it, with the man, his wife, and his five children watching them. Apparently the villager had become angry that no food was left for his family, so he demanded that the soldiers pay him for the meal. One soldier put his gun to the man's head and blew out his brains. Another soldier grabbed his wife and forced her to bend over. He placed the barrel of his gun between her legs and shot her, then turned and shot the children.

Chapter 11

PERHAPS IT WAS ONLY a seventeen-year-old girl who could have found peace in this Uganda. Or perhaps the drive to make her life equal to her mother's dreams for it fueled Annah's unwavering belief that she was still blessed. The same shortages that plagued the hospital affected everyone's home lives, so there was never enough food or supplies like soap and paraffin. Annah constantly kept a wary eye out for soldiers and policemen as she walked through the town, and she kept a heavy rock leaning against her door at night. But she went to the hospital six days per week, and she prayed and sang with a group of people who had become her family and her friends. Although she hadn't heard from her own family in months, Annah continued to believe that her prayers were keeping them out of harm, and she believed the same about herself. Her life, though lacking many basic comforts, was going just as she thought it should, and she awoke each day eager to see what the new dawn would bring.

Through all this, it was James Emuge who began to fill her mind, at first not as a young man, she thought, but as her connection to the God and savior she had discovered. James was always courtly to her, getting off his bicycle to ask after her well-being when he met her on the road, and making sure to greet her when she joined the other Pentecostals at worship or Bible-reading. Annah had eventually gotten less tongue-tied with him, and she found herself thinking of him more and more. Whenever she read a passage in the Bible or pondered Jesus's ways, she felt an urge to run to him to ask his opinion. Sometimes when she let a small worry into her head, usually about her family, she knew what James would say and she would listen to his answer in her mind.

"You must pray harder, and offer a fast to your God, Frances. In your suffering he will see your piety and grant what you wish," he would tell her softly.

It was shortly after the incident with the police chief, while

Annah was still praying to God to keep the chief and the soldiers away from her, that she found herself suddenly shocked and amazed by God's personal interventions on her behalf. Annah had made the decision to stay in Olio for another year, rather than return to Kangole school. Somehow she felt she was doing more to become her real self in Olio, and she determined to study on her own and pass the exam for graduation. Coming home from the hospital one February evening, she met her friend Angela and another girl from Olio who attended Kangole Secondary School with them. They greeted her fondly, and there was something almost desperate in their hugs and exclamations of joy at seeing her.

"Why aren't you at school?" she asked. "You should have left three weeks ago."

Both girls' faces tightened, and they looked at each other for a moment, as if each were begging the other to speak. Annah looked at their wide eyes and her stomach clenched.

"Tell me . . . what happened," she demanded.

"Frances, you are so blessed to have stayed here," Angela began. "It was terrible. We had just started morning classes when two trucks arrived carrying soldiers. They all got out and ran into the classrooms with their guns pointed at us. They made us all go out in the yard and line up. Then they began choosing girls." Tears ran down Angela's face and she stopped talking and sobbed into her hands.

"Did they rape you?" Annah asked gently.

"All of us," she answered. "They took some of the girls with them when they left. The rest of us were just roaming around the school, crying."

"The principal told us to go home—that he was closing the school." She looked around her as if she didn't know where she was. Annah realized that her friend didn't know *who* she was anymore. Annah wondered what she would have done if she'd been there. How truly blessed I am, she thought.

But blessings weren't flowing over the country. Soldiers were everywhere, and they went on rampages every evening, breaking down people's doors, raping and killing. Annah and her neighbors began leaving their homes just before dark to hide in the bushes outside the village. They would creep back after midnight and, if their home hadn't been burned down, sleep on the floor until morning. All of the homes had been ransacked, so no one had beds or supplies in their houses.

Soon it became impossible to return home at all, and the villagers just hid in the bushes all night. There was a particular area where the hospital staff and also the teachers from Olio school gathered, and Annah began sitting near James there. The group would talk quietly, and then hide when they heard trucks coming. They would all go to work during the day, but the bushes became their home. They would leave work early to finish their ordinary evening routines of water-fetching, cooking, and eating before nightfall. At a moment's notice, they would run for the bushes and spend the night hiding, waiting for the terror to begin again.

Although they had been aloof toward each other, Annah and James began sitting together under a particular tree in the evenings. They talked about many things. She learned that James was nine years older than she was, and that he planned to get his master's degree so that he could be promoted to an administrative job in the schools. He wanted to help teachers become better at their jobs so that students would learn even more. Annah wanted to finish school and be a nurse so that she could help people suffering from injuries and illnesses. The more they shared their dreams, the more real they became, even though they were two small figures crouched under a shrub in the open countryside, ready at any moment to run for their very lives.

One night James began speaking about his dreams for a family. He would have many children and a loving and beautiful wife.

"So, you are looking for this perfect wife, huh?" Annah teased.

"Oh, no," James replied with a smile. "God has told me that my wife will just come to my house one day. I don't have to look for her."

"Hmm, how is he handling the fact that your house is an open field now?" she laughed, gesturing around them.

"Maybe she's already come to my house," he responded gently.

It was in the late morning one day, when Olio school and the little hospital nearby were operating as usual, that this new life ended. Soldiers stormed into the compound, shooting everywhere. Outside, Annah saw utter chaos. Children running from the school instinctively turned toward their homes, but that way was through the band of soldiers. After seeing several children shot, Annah and James found themselves together trying to herd the children away into the countryside. A few followed them, and they soon caught up with others running in the same direction. They ran all afternoon and evening, stopping to hide in the woods only after it was fully dark.

James was able to run in his work shoes, but Annah's shoes—dressy pumps with low heels that Rosemary had given her—wouldn't stay on her feet, so she ran barefoot. As they tore over the uneven ground, she knew she was getting cuts and bruises, but her fear obliterated the pain completely. Their flight lasted several days, and after the first day they found that they had to run at night and hide during the day so that bands of soldiers wouldn't find them. After each night-long run, she would sit and pull out the thorns and splinters she had accumulated, and then try to ignore the burning pain in her feet as she slept.

A man in the group of refugees had a radio, and one evening he spread the word that Idi Amin had been overthrown. A murmur ran through the woods—the quietest and yet most joyful cheer Annah had ever heard. The group's elation was short-lived, however. It turned out that Idi Amin had been in hiding for several weeks, in Soroti—only thirty miles from where the refugees from Olio were now hiding. Some of the men gathered to discuss their predicament, and James returned to tell Annah that they felt it was likely that Amin and his soldiers would be running through these very woods to escape into Sudan and then to Libya. Annah and James decided to walk to his sister's house in Akoboi Village and never return to Olio.

It was more than a day's walk, and when they arrived they found Phoebe and her family safe but just as hungry and desperate as they were. She welcomed them joyfully and gave them space to sleep and inclusion in the family's sparse meals. Annah and James were immediately involved in the struggle to find food and remain on the lookout for soldiers. James joined the young men in the area who went out hunting for squirrels and other small animals each day. When someone came upon one of the enormous anthills that dotted the landscape, they would open the hill from the top and scoop out handfuls of ants, which would be their protein that day. In spite of the hardship, Annah and James were grateful to find that they were once again settled into a family routine. In the evenings, after the meal of stringy meat with a little atap, the family would gather in the yard at a small fire. Annah went to great lengths to find groundnuts when she could, so that the children would have a roasted nut to eat while listening to the stories of the elders. Annah dreamed of nights with her grandmother, and she taught these children the song about how humans should be more like the moon, always returning when needed most.

One evening Annah noticed that James was watching her intently as she sang to the children. After the family had quieted and they were all sitting and watching the smoke rise into the sky, James took Annah's hand and pulled her away to stand alone under the nearby trees.

"Frances, if this war comes to an end and peace returns, would you marry me?"

In the darkness Annah knew he couldn't see her face and she was glad. It felt unfair for him to ask her to imagine a normal life. This had hardly been a courtship, and yet she really couldn't imagine life without him. Perhaps it was the family fire they had just left, but all she could think of was that she hadn't fulfilled her goals yet.

"Frances, can't we make a life together?" he asked gently, with a touch of fear in his voice.

"Oh, I just don't know, James." Was this man destined to be the moon in her sky? She thought of her strong toto, who had never let her think that being a wife was all there was to life. "I have to finish my schooling. I have to become a nurse. I have to become who I am supposed to be."

"Then I'll wait, Frances. I just want your commitment now. Can I have that much?"

"I can't, James. I . . . I'll talk to you later." She stumbled back to the huts and went to bed, only to lie staring upward while thoughts swirled in her brain. "What would I have done without James in this horrid situation? But what of my dreams? So many people are dead, what do we who are living owe to them? To embrace life, probably, but which life? The one that feels safe with James, or the one Toto has worked so hard to give me?"

Sometime after that night, amid the awkwardness that now lay between them, James and Annah learned of the relative peace that had finally come to Uganda. Idi Amin was gone, and there was an interim government in place. Citizens were urged to return to their homes, so the two of them walked back to the Olio school compound. They were surprised to find their little houses still standing, though they were completely empty.

Annah set about returning to her life as quickly as possible. The staff found the same problem at the hospital: the door was broken down and nothing remained inside. The workers were miserable. As soon as they arrived, patients began coming with hopeful looks on their faces, but there wasn't even a pen and paper to record their names. The staff had to ask them to leave and return in a few days, hoping they could come up with supplies by then. None of the patients complained—they had been making do with less than nothing for so long that there was no surprise in their looks, just resignation.

Those days turned into weeks and then months of waiting for help, supplies, even food. On the radio they would hear that the country was rebuilding, but at Olio nothing grew or improved. Even the most patient of individuals grew weary and suspicious that this small, barren part of Uganda had been forgotten. Although soldiers weren't rampaging into the village killing people with their guns, families still lost members to starvation and disease.

Finally one day a UN truck arrived, packed with food and supplies. Everyone ran to the truck, shouting desperately and trampling each other in their frenzy to get the food. They were willing to die just to get beans, oil, and a little soap. Annah stood in a line all day and never got food—she never got any closer to the trucks because of all the people pushing in ahead of others. And they weren't just pushing. While she was there a woman with a thin baby sucking listlessly at her breast walked up next to Annah. Another child with huge, pleading eyes was tied in a cloth on the woman's back, and three more children, naked and with swollen bellies, straggled behind her. Of course Annah let the family stand in line in front of her, but this scenario repeated itself over and over. All of these people simply could not be fed.

The next day the local chief set up a different system. Food was put into lots divided by townships, and the trucks drove to workplaces to give parcels only to the employees there. Although this system worked better, it meant that the staff members just walked away from their patients when the truck arrived. No one could afford to miss the arrival of the rations. Those people who didn't get food at a workplace were left to stand in lines at the end of the day, hoping there would be some food left over. Many people died waiting for food. For those lucky enough to get food, each individual was given a week's worth of rations: one cup each of cornmeal, beans, powdered milk, and sugar; and one tablespoon of salt. When she received this package, Annah felt as if she had been showered with manna.

During this time, James and Annah had returned to their routines of work and church, and to a relationship of friendship and shared worship. She still felt drawn to him, especially when she pondered religious questions, and after worship services she could feel his gentle eyes following her movements as she prayed and talked with the other Pentecostals.

One day at the hospital, a disheveled man rode up on a bicycle. While this wasn't terribly unusual, Annah felt herself studying the man, feeling something was important about his arrival. As she watched him get off the bike and roll it carefully to rest against a tree, Annah realized she had watched this man do this all her life. Her father turned and looked appraisingly at the hospital, and then Annah was running into his arms.

"Papa, is Toto alright?" she demanded as soon as she reached him.

"Everyone is fine, Frances. It is you I needed to check on," he replied, holding her close to him. "How have you survived, my girl?"

How could she begin to explain all that had happened, when all she wanted to do was hold tight to her father and never let go?

"Papa, come to my house for lunch and I will tell you," she answered. They walked the bike together, telling each other as fast as they could all that they had been doing to survive.

"Frances, I must meet this young man who helped my daughter through these times." So they got James on the way, and the three had a lunch with little food but lots of talk. Annah left the two men talking when she returned to the hospital that afternoon. She asked her father to come to the hospital before he left to ride home. When he arrived he was full of praise for James, but she saw no sign that he had heard of James's marriage proposal. She felt a little disappointed at this.

"Make time to come to the village and see your mother, Frances— she's been so worried about you."

"I will, Papa, I promise." It was several weeks before Annah could make good on this vow, since the soldiers had destroyed all the buses.

After her father's visit, James seemed more emboldened with her. He stopped by each Sunday to walk her to church, and he visited several times during the week to ask about her family. She became comfortable with this routine, so that she felt lost when he didn't come to see her. He arrived one day just as she was making dinner, so she offered to share her food with him.

"Oh, Frances, I would say no, but do I see groundnut soup there? I could never turn down a pretty girl offering me my favorite delicacy," he said with an enormous grin as he sat down at her table. Annah laughed at his love for a food that was like salt to her family, but James came from farther north, where groundnuts are rare. It seemed as if he couldn't get enough of the sweet, pungent soup—or of her company.

Soon James and Annah were eating together frequently. He would buy ingredients and bring them to her, waiting contentedly while she made his favorite groundnut soup. After a few weeks of this, one of the nurses at the hospital told her that everyone was talking about them and asked what was going on.

"We're just friends," Annah answered and was shocked when her friend burst out laughing.

"Only you believe that, Frances. Wake up!"

Chapter 12

THOSE MONTHS WERE IDYLLIC for Annah. James was sweet and attentive, and his company gave her a glow that everyone noticed. James's dreams became hers—sometimes she could picture the life he envisioned. She knew he would succeed when he said he would one day be a school inspector, after he had completed further studies. And he made her dreams feel real and important, too. By that time she was eighteen years old, and she had been away from school for so long that it would have been impossible for her to return to a conventional school setting, so James told her he would help her study so that she could take the required exams to be issued a diploma. She began to notice that in conversations he would pause sometimes and explain something in detail, giving her the history and theory behind it. She could tell that he enjoyed her quick mind and respected her thirst for knowledge. He was her teacher then, as well as her friend, brother, and spiritual guide.

Only one cloud seemed to mar their relationship, and that was the issue of marriage. James was gentle about it, but he never let her think that the topic was closed. Once during this time one of James's younger brothers, Jesse, came to visit. Annah loved having Jesse around—his broad smile and brotherly jokes were entertaining, and he and James clearly loved each other. After Jesse left, James told Annah that there had been a serious purpose to Jesse's visit this time. In the Iteso culture, a younger brother must wait to marry until his older brother is wed, and Jesse wanted to know how soon James would be doing that. Jesse had also told his brother that their mother had picked out a girl in their village and was planning to pressure James to marry her.

This incident sparked the first disagreement between James and Annah. He began to pester her about marrying him. Annah tried to explain that she owed it to her mother to finish her studies first, but James was determined to convince her that this was not an obstacle: he would continue to support her quest for education once they were married. All Annah could imagine was the arrival of babies and a lack of time to do anything but care for them and tend to household chores. She had seen enough of her childhood friends' married lives to find it hard to believe James's promises to the contrary.

Finally, Annah decided James would simply have to hear her case from someone else. Her sister Rosemary came immediately to mind. Rosemary had done just what their mother envisioned for both of them: she had finished her education and had her nursing career established before she married Cooper, so there had never been a question that she might give it up to stay home and raise the children. James surely would pay attention to Annah's assertive and successful older sister. She was surprised by how quickly James agreed to go to Rosemary to plead his case.

"If she's as smart as you say, she will surely realize how much I love you," he explained. It was typical of James to be so certain about his way being best. Annah smiled to think this, knowing that she mostly loved this trait of James's—when it wasn't focused on her.

That very weekend, James hired a taxi to take him to Soroti to meet Rosemary. Annah spent that Sunday wondering what was happening with these two important people in her life. She hoped James wouldn't be too disappointed by Rosemary's answer. But she found that she was spending more time hoping that her sister would like this earnest young man.

Finally, the taxi pulled into the compound outside her house. Annah stood in the doorway while James paid the driver. She was encouraged when he straightened up from the cab and began walking toward her with a small smile playing on his lips. Good: Rosemary didn't discourage him completely.

"So, you got your answer," she said, a little triumphantly, as he approached.

"Not exactly," he said.

"What do you mean? What happened?"

"Well, I found her house easily, and she was there alone." That pleased Annah—no Cooper to offer opposing opinions about the role of women.

"We had a very pleasant chat over the lunch she made me. So you aren't the only woman who knows how to make groundnuts into ambrosia," he teased, but Annah had no patience for this.

"So you told her you want to marry me?" She was starting to wonder if he'd lost his nerve.

"Of course I did—that's what I went there for."

"And . . . ?"

"She started to giggle," James said, his eyes twinkling. "So I asked her if it was really so funny to think of you marrying me."

"'No, no,' she said. 'But who am I to say no or yes to you? Frances is a strong, sensible girl, so she can say yes or no for herself. If she wants this, she has my blessing.'" James drew out the last four words and looked deep into her eyes as he said them. Annah was flabbergasted. How could Rosemary have done that? How could she have thought that? Rosemary of all people knew how important education was to their mother—to Annah. What could have prompted her to say that? Annah mused over this message from her sister for several days. Perhaps times were so different in this devastated country today that Rosemary knew they shouldn't wait to marry. Or perhaps Rosemary saw a steadiness of purpose in James that reassured her that her little sister would be fine in a marriage to him?

Of course, Rosemary's message was clear to James, so he immediately resumed his campaign to get a commitment from Annah. Finally she realized she must send him to her parents for a final answer. James immediately sent a letter to her parents, stating his desire to marry their daughter. In those days of uncertain communication on any level, he was remarkably efficient in finding someone who was traveling to Agu Village and who assured James he would personally place the letter in Christopher's hands. After a week, James arranged his second trip to secure Annah's hand in marriage and set out on a Sunday with high spirits and determination.

This time, James was just plain grinning when he alighted from the taxi, so Annah knew her parents' answer before he spoke. He walked to her and looked earnestly into her eyes.

"Yes," was all he said.

"Yes what?" she asked, suddenly feeling playful.

"Yes, I received blessings from Father Christopher and Mother Esther."

"Oh, really?" She was surprised at his reference to them as "Mother" and "Father," but it somehow felt right, too. "So, it looks like I'm to be your wife."

"Frances, if I've learned anything over these months it's that you are your own person, so I won't have my answer until you say it." Annah was startled by the sudden seriousness in his eyes. And then, right there in the dusty road in front of her house, James knelt down and kissed her hand. She expected a question, but instead he began to pray: "Thank you, God, for bringing my wife to me just as you promised. This day I have been given permission to marry Frances. Let your will be done. Frances?" When he looked up at her she could see such vulnerability and pleading in his eyes that she hastened to answer.

"Let his will be done," she replied solemnly, and from that very moment Annah felt married. She savored the sweet sensation of becoming a part of this wonderful man, and she felt enormous tenderness and responsibility toward him. Oh, let me be a good wife to him, she prayed silently as he stood and held her in his arms. When he drew back at last and held her at arm's length, he looked different— a little like he'd grown up and taken on a responsibility, but mostly just more peaceful, as if he'd ended a long journey. She realized that she would always and only feel truly at home with James at her side.

"Well, tell me, tell me. Are my parents fine? Did you meet my little brothers? What did Toto say to you?"

"OK, OK, let me tell you. I'll start from the beginning. Your father and brothers greeted me, and we sat under the mango tree and had a nice talk. George and Charles were such polite teenagers, and they sounded so grown-up when they spoke. They were clearly reserved in front of your father, but I got them laughing and talking. Pretty soon your mother came out with cups of tea, and your father introduced us. She was so interesting, Frances—she seemed kind of shy, but there was such intelligence in her eyes. She saw everything that was going on and all the children knew she was aware of them. I felt pretty sure your father approved of me, but I knew that wasn't going to be enough. If your mother hadn't liked me I'd have been sent away for good."

"So what did you do?"

"Well, after dinner when we were sitting around the fire, I sat next to her and we spoke. The very first thing she asked me was, 'Have you already been married?' I was so shocked. Did she think I was so old that I must have been married?"

Annah chuckled, knowing her toto was just making sure Annah would be the first wife. "She was just protecting me, James," she said with a smile.

"Well, I must have given her the right answer, because she didn't seem so tense after that. She asked me so many questions— had I finished college, what were my career plans, what was my job now, could I make a good living? All the while she was looking me up and down as if she were measuring me."

"Oh, James," Annah laughed. "I knew she would do that, but I also knew you would charm her."

"Hmm, I don't know about that, but I do know that when she said I have her blessing I felt that I had been given a great gift." Annah knew just how it felt to have Toto's approval, and she was so glad to hear it had been bestowed on James.

Their friends and colleagues received the news of their betrothal with a mixture of amusement and joy—amusement that these two were the only people in the village who hadn't already accepted their eventual union as a given, and joy that life actually seemed to be about new beginnings and a bright future again. Times were still hard in Uganda, and especially in their region. Although Obote's presidency had broken the power of the soldiers to terrorize citizens, eastern Uganda suffered from a devastating dearth of all the necessities of life. No one had possessions, or even enough to eat on most days, but all of the teachers in James's school and all of the staff in Annah's hospital found themselves smiling more than they had in months.

The plans for the wedding were put into place quickly. Although they both knew that they would adopt the modern concept of a wife's taking her husband's last name, they agreed that their wedding would follow the traditions of their elders. In Iteso culture, a couple has two weddings: one at the bride's home and then one at the groom's. They set a date six weeks in the future for the first wedding, and James immediately wrote to Jesse and their mother, Lucy, that he had chosen his bride. Jesse must have done a good job convincing their mother that Annah was the woman for James, because she accepted his decision without protest. James then wrote to Christopher and Esther, formally requesting them to meet his mother.

One day, Annah got out a pencil and pad to begin a list of all the preparations she needed to make. As she began to write, it occurred to her that this type of pad was what she had always used in school. With a start, she realized she could never return to Kangole school. She thought of the big, noisy dorm where she had lain in her cot and giggled with the other girls and felt the loss of her childhood. When she realized that she would never again be sitting in the classroom, eagerly soaking up new facts and theories, she felt a sharp pain in her chest. How could she be walking away from all her dreams and goals?

Later that evening, when James arrived for dinner, she was still feeling shock that she had made the decision to leave so much behind.

"What is it, Frances? Why are you so quiet tonight?" James asked as they sat together.

"I'm thinking about school, James. I will never go back, will I?"

"Not as a girl sitting at a desk, Frances, but haven't I always promised you that as long as we're together you will continue your education?" He reached over and took her hand firmly in his. "Frances, I am not a man who needs to follow all of the tribal customs we both grew up with. I will never deny your right to be an educated, liberated woman."

Annah shuddered at his mention of tribal customs. By those laws, Annah would be taken to live in her mother-in-law's home, to take care of her while James went out to work. Since James worked in a distant village, this would mean that he would live in Olio and return to his wife only on weekends. Annah knew in her heart that if James had expected her to do this, she would have called off the engagement.

The very next day, James brought Annah books from his school and began overseeing her studies for the O Level exams, which would allow her to begin formal training for her vocation as a nurse. She worked diligently, learning shorthand and even typing when he was able to borrow a typewriter. Over dinner they would discuss her subjects. Annah marveled at her fiancé's vast knowledge of history, mathematics, science, and all the other subjects she tackled.

Annah realized that she was doubly blessed—to have James overseeing her studies and to have her mother making the necessary preparations for the wedding. The one item Annah needed to handle herself was her wedding attire. According to Iteso tradition, Annah needed two special dresses, one for each day of the wedding. Iteso brides don't wear white, preferring to be married in beautiful colors. Since she had no extra money, James took her shopping and even helped choose the dresses. Both were long and extremely modest. The one James chose had flowers of red and yellow on a black background. Annah chose one that was sky blue with thin golden threads that caught the light when she moved.

When the time had come to travel home for the wedding, Annah cooked James a last meal in Olio—groundnut soup, of course. They were both quiet over dinner, but it was not an awkward silence. Annah's head swam with images of the future she saw before them.

She recalled her vision that she and her husband and children would travel far away. It had frightened her that night as she lay in her cot, to think of going away from her village, but now all she saw was that she and James and their children—yes, children!—would be together, and that was all that mattered.

The next day they said their last goodbye as betrothed, and Annah left for Agu while James traveled to Amuria to join his mother and Jesse on the trip to Agu. James's three other brothers and his five sisters would be coming later with cousins and friends who were eager to celebrate James's marriage. When Annah arrived, she found Toto busy preparing food and sending the younger children scurrying on various errands. Annah joined her mother in the kitchen hut, feeling the heavy significance of her last duty as simply a daughter.

"So, Annah, this Emuge seems a good man," her mother began tentatively.

"He is, Toto. He is a greatly respected teacher, and he is already teaching me what I need to know to pass the O Level exams, and then I'll begin nursing training."

"Hmmm," her mother said. "Ambition for himself and for you is good. I think he'll be a kind husband and father, too. But, so short—he will be the shortest in the family, I guess."

Annah burst out laughing. She knew that her mother loved tall men—she had always been especially attentive to men she had to raise her head to address. James was a little shorter than Esther.

"Oh, Toto," Annah said, "you taught me to measure a man by what's inside, and I did."

"You did well, my daughter," her mother answered, still looking a bit bemused. Annah could see that time would have to prove to Toto that a short man could be just as loving as a tall one.

The wedding would begin the next morning. James and his family had arrived and were staying within the compound, but away from Annah and her family. Annah's brothers had set a table in the center of the compound, and they were carrying in stools and chairs borrowed from all the villagers. An Iteso wedding is a negotiation between the two parties. First Annah would have to demonstrate her acceptance of James as a suitor, and then James and his family would have to offer a price for the bride. If Christopher and Esther accepted this price, then the two would be married and the celebration would begin.

The following morning, Annah arose early to prepare for her

wedding. Her mother came to the girls' hut, where Annah had slept, and told her daughter that it was time to dress. At the sight of Toto, leaning slightly on the door frame as if she were tired already just thinking about the day's events, Annah began to weep silently.

"No time for sorrow, my daughter," Toto said gently. "This day will go well and at the end of it you'll have a wonderful husband." She began to dress Annah in the blue dress. The floral print would be her celebration gown after the negotiations had concluded. Toto paused every so often while helping Annah dress to wipe away the tears that continued to fall.

"You are just overexcited, my girl. You will be fine. Come now; you are ready." They stood for a moment in the doorway of the hut. That was where Toto would remain until Annah had indicated her acceptance of James. Magdalene stepped forward and took Annah's hand to escort her to her place in the center of the compound. All of the villagers were gathered, with the elders seated near the table.

It wasn't until Annah had sat down in the chair that she noticed James, sitting across the compound, looking nervous and determined. At a signal from the elders, James stood up and walked to the table that separated the two families. He placed an envelope on it and returned to his seat. Annah knew that the envelope contained cash—the amount was intended to symbolize his love for her. It was now up to her to accept this offering or demand more.

Her knees trembled as she rose and walked to the table. She picked up the envelope, surprised by its weight. Holding it tightly she returned to her chair and then opened it, her fingers shaking. Annah looked at the money inside. It was a large number of shillings, and she knew she was supposed to count it, but she couldn't imagine embarrassing James by rejecting this token of his love. Thinking about how she knew the depth of his love not from this pile of money but from all that they had endured together, Annah merely rifled through the shillings a bit and then looked up and nodded to the elders.

A happy murmur ran through the gathered villagers. They had all been speculating about the amount James would offer. They had known Annah as a bold young girl who ran swiftly past them to school each day, and they had been curious about how readily she would accept his overture. It must be a very large sum, they whispered—just look at how thick the envelope is.

Across the compound, James looked relieved, and then he retreated with his mother while Annah returned to the huts with her mother. The bride and groom remained in huts while the two families met to settle the price James's mother would pay to Annah's parents. In the Iteso culture, the bride-price is a subject of tremendous purport for both families. The groom's parents want to seem generous yet shrewd, and the bride's parents must uphold their daughter's honor while sending a message of just the amount of acceptance they wished to convey to the groom.

Under the hot African sun, in a small village where little in life is more important than the merging of two families to create a new generation, these negotiations proceed slowly and can be fraught with quiet demonstrations of resistance and assertion. Christopher and other elders of the village were there, and James's brother Jesse and mother, Lucy. While these negotiations are normally conducted only by the men of the family, Lucy's status as a widow meant she must participate as well.

Annah and her mother and sisters sat quietly in their hut, waiting for the time to pass and the result of the negotiations to be announced to them. Rebecca and Florence kept trying to bring up some little item to discuss, like how handsome James had seemed, but Annah remained silent, tears still flowing down her cheeks.

"Annah, why do you cry so?" Toto asked.

"I guess I'm sorry to be leaving my family," Annah answered after some thought. But the truth was that she didn't know why she cried.

At last, there were shouts of joy and the family knew the negotiations had been successful. Annah wasn't told then, but she learned later that her parents had been offered fifteen cows, ten goats, and five thousand shillings by Lucy in exchange for their daughter. Christopher accepted the offer without haggling or delaying, which made Annah proud. She was glad that the process had been peaceful and respectful, and she knew this was a generous price, especially for a widow to offer.

There had been no food or drink served until the business could be concluded, so Annah's aunties and sisters immediately set out a huge feast with jugs of homemade beer. The entire village entered into the joy of the day, eating, drinking, and dancing. In spite of their plans to continue the celebration the next day, the group was still dancing and drinking long after the sun had set. The night sky shone with its twinkling denizens. Annah noted that the moon, though not yet full, seemed fat and proud as it cast its light over the revelry. In the morning, while continuing their celebrations, the families made arrangements for the remainder of their wedding.

The tradition is that the bride and groom live together for a few weeks, so that the groom can ascertain that the bride is indeed a worthy wife, both in the marriage bed and in daily routines. Normally, the bride and groom are living with the groom's family, so the mother-in-law is also observing the bride to make sure that the girl can keep a good home and serve both the groom and herself as expected. In their case, James and Annah did not plan to live with his mother, but they would still go to Lucy's house a week before the second wedding to give his mother time to get to know Annah. It was agreed that the second ceremony, which is celebrated after the bride's family has received the dowry and approved it, would be held in Amuria in four weeks.

Just after lunch that day, Annah, James, Lucy, and Jesse all left together to go to Olio for the night. Jesse and Lucy would leave from there for Amuria the next morning.

The final ceremony in the bride's portion of the wedding is the farewell to her mother. Traditionally, the bride stands before her mother, who removes her daughter's blouse and bathes her for one last time—just as she had done all through the girl's life. Toto knew her Annah was a private, modest girl, and she was also concerned by the fact that Annah had continued to cry quietly throughout the two days of her wedding. At the appointed time, Toto merely stood before Annah and gently placed her hands on either side of her daughter's face. Looking deep into Annah's eyes, Toto prayed to God for blessings of many children, good health, and a long and happy life with her husband. Annah leaned her head on Toto's breast and then turned to leave.

Her father and mother walked Annah to the car and told her they loved her. Annah glanced at James, who was ready to help her into the backseat, and she saw that his forehead was creased with worry. He wiped a tear from her cheek and looked deep into her eyes. He probably wondered if she was ill, or perhaps he feared she was changing her mind.

As they began the journey, Lucy asked Annah why she was crying.

"Because I am leaving my family to join a new one," Annah replied, although she didn't really think this was the reason.

"Oh, Frances, all girls do this," her mother-in-law laughed. "Everything will be OK." Annah took some comfort that her husband's mother could be kind to her, but her tears increased as they drove away from Agu Village.

Away from the crowds and all the attention focused on her, Annah knew she must face this sorrow and determine its source, so that she could enter wholeheartedly into her new life with James. Just thinking of that life made her heart beat a little faster and brought a loving smile to her lips. So why, why was she so sad?

Chapter 13

WHEN THE FAMILY ARRIVED at James's house in Olio, Jesse immediately began carrying in the suitcases and the few items that Annah's family and friends had sent with the newlyweds: some pots and dishes, a few pieces of cloth for Annah to use in making curtains or mats, and some bundles of food from the celebration. Lucy strode into the house to prepare beds for herself and Jesse in the extra room, calling directions to Annah, James, and Jesse as she bustled around.

As soon as Annah climbed out of the car, it struck her how different this house looked, now that it was to be her home with James. She had been in it many times, visiting James or with the Christian fellowship group, and she had even stayed in that extra room on the night long ago when the police chief had frightened her out of her own home. But now she felt a sense of ownership and belonging that settled comfortably around her shoulders like an old shawl. The house looked sturdier than she recalled, and also plainer, but she knew she could fix that. She stood looking at it for a moment, turning the word *wife* over in her mind, and then James came up beside her.

"Aren't you coming into our house, Mrs. Emuge?" He was smiling at her, but Annah could see the glimmer of worry in his eyes. Forcing the strange, inexplicable sadness deep inside, she smiled back at him and took his hand to walk together into their home. Once inside, James gave Annah a soft but quick kiss—all either of them could manage with Lucy and Jesse looking on. The evening passed comfortably, with James and his family telling stories of his childhood that Annah hadn't heard before.

She had known that James's father, a teacher and Pentecostal minister, had died when James was just fourteen years old, but Annah had never known that James had been his father's constant traveling companion from a very young age. At the age of five, James had been with his father when he was the first East African minister

111

to welcome Canadian missionaries into the region. He recalled how his father had seemed so indomitable in his minister's robes, arguing points of Bible interpretation with the white men who had come from Canada. Lucy told Annah how James's father had become ill one day when he was out preaching and died the next day. She began to tell Annah that he had been poisoned by angry residents on whose land he had built a church, but James put his hand on her shoulder. "That's just speculation, Toto; we don't know what happened."

Lucy then told Annah how she had nearly lost James several times before he was one, to measles. As Lucy described the hurried walks to the hospital with James, and the hours spent watching his small, feverish body to make sure his breathing continued, Annah realized that both she and Jesse were thinking how different their lives would have been if James had not survived. It was hard to picture her strong, solid husband perishing from such a disease, but Annah knew that many African children did. She glanced at Jesse and he returned her gaze, a partially scared and partially grateful look in his dark eyes. Amen, she thought.

Early the next morning, Annah and James said goodbye to Jesse and Lucy and returned to their home, alone at last. They paused just outside the door and James put his arm around Annah.

"We have the rest of our lives together," he said. "I have so many plans and dreams, Frances, and now I know I can fulfill them, with you at my side."

Tears welled up in Annah's eyes, and the sadness that she had been pushing away returned like a stone hanging around her neck. She leaned on James but said nothing.

Just then, a neighbor called out to James asking for his help, so James gave her a hug and went to see what the man needed. Annah walked into the house and sat on a chair. She began crying harder, and she determined right then and there to figure out the cause of this sadness.

I have everything I have wanted, she thought: a sweet, loving husband, the means to finish my education, a career as a nurse to look forward to, and a life that I never could have imagined, growing up in Agu Village. So why am I so sad?

Suddenly, Annah could see an image of her mother from her childhood. It was late afternoon, and Toto was cooking dinner in the kettle over the hot, smoky fire. Toto had the twins swathed in a shawl that bound them to her breast, and she leaned over carefully, working around the two little heads that peeped from the shawl. Toto had carried these boys with her all day: as she walked to the river for water and returned with a full jug on her head; as she guided her daughters in their chores and made sure they left for school on time; as she worked her way down the rows of cassava in the family plot, hoeing out the weeds; as she pounded the dried cassava into meal and then cooked porridge with some beans and groundnut sauce for their dinner. This was a woman who knew that she worked to make her family comfortable, and she never shirked that duty in any way. Annah thought of all the times her mother had sat quietly by the fire in the evenings, smiling as she watched Papa rocking Annah and calling her his angel. Toto was always silent at those fires—she was probably too tired to join in the loud talk and laughter of Annah's father and grandparents. But it was always Toto whose face Annah studied to be sure they were indeed having fun.

When Annah came home from school it was Toto who made sure that she had performed well and had had a successful day, and it was Toto who oversaw her homework in the evenings. Even when Toto had been so sick and weak, she had always insisted that Annah's place was in school. Nothing had pleased Toto more than the day she had been able to send her daughter back to school, after she had regained her health. Through all of Annah's struggles—running miles to and from school in pouring rain, watching the dead bodies of Idi Amin's victims pass by the school on truck beds, cowering with the other girls as her nuns and priest tried to protect them from Amin's soldiers come to rape and kill—through all of this, Annah had survived merely by holding in her heart the image of her mother's face. As she sat pondering this, Annah realized that her mother had worked all of her life to give Annah the education and the opportunities that she now enjoyed. And yet, just yesterday Annah had left to seek a new life, while Toto would continue to live the very life she had worked so hard to spare Annah.

Annah couldn't stop her sobbing then, just thinking of Toto walking miles for water, walking miles to take sick children to the hospital, walking miles and miles and yet never escaping the harshness of her life. She wrapped her arms across her chest and rocked in her chair, trying to make sense of a world that leaves a woman so poor and helpless while her daughter can walk away from that life. After a few minutes she couldn't sit still any longer, so she rose and went outside to the kitchen area, where the dirty dishes were still piled on the ground from their breakfast. The sight of those dishes upset her and she immediately began heating water to wash them. In all her time in Olio, Annah had never allowed dirty dishes to pile up, so she worked quickly to restore the clean implements to their assigned spots in the outdoor cupboard near the fire pit. As she was putting them away, she realized that she had gotten this aversion to soiled dishes from her mother. No matter how tired she and the girls might be, Toto always insisted that dishes be cleaned up immediately. Annah felt some comfort in knowing that she honored her mother through this simple chore, and she reflected that most of what she knew had come, either spoken or demonstrated, from Toto.

A calmness came over her then, and she began to realize that this was what Toto had intended. Toto had made of her own life what she could, but she had given Annah the means to make her life even more. It was now up to Annah to use what her mother had taught her to make the best life possible for her husband, herself, and of course her own children. Annah was comforted by these thoughts, but she still thought, couldn't I have stayed to help Toto just a little longer?

By the time James returned to the house, Annah was busy in the small bedroom, folding the blankets and smoothing the sheets on their bed. James walked in, looked at her a moment, and then came over and tilted her face up to his. She met his gaze with a shy smile.

"So we're going to be OK, you and I, Mrs. Emuge?"

"Yes, we are, Mr. Emuge." Annah leaned her head on his shoulder and felt his warmth and strength filling her. "We are going to be fine."

Annah and James settled into their daily routine easily, as if they had always been together. They ate breakfast together, went their separate ways to work, and met again in their home for lunch. After work, Annah hurried home to make tea for James and then heated water for his bath. While Christopher had always had his bath before the evening tea, James wanted just the opposite. Once he had bathed, they would do some evening chores or Bible reading, and then they would go together to the bed they shared.

Although the days of their marriage were hectic and tiring, the nights were sweet. James teased Annah sometimes that he was testing her to make sure she would suffice as a wife. Annah would pretend to bristle and insist that he tell her she was an excellent wife. But under their laughter it was clear that they were falling more deeply in love every day. James was a tender and caring lover, and Annah felt safe and entirely wanted in his arms.

Annah was surprised to learn that James was eager to talk after their lovemaking. Their conversations reminded her of the days when they had talked together while hiding under the bushes to escape the marauding soldiers. But now there was nothing urgent about their discussions—they spoke lazily, like people who had many lifetimes ahead of them. Finally, as Annah lay with her head on James's shoulder, she would fall asleep to the sound of his voice. Some nights, in that half-dreaming state just before deep sleep, Annah would think that she was hearing her papa's voice from the hut next to the one she had shared with Magdalene and Rebecca.

James and Annah soon had to prepare for the second part of their marriage, when the two of them would spend a week in Lucy's home. Annah quizzed James about his mother's preferences, knowing she would be expected to cook for Lucy and demonstrate her abilities to keep house and do chores. James teased her that his mother would be too afraid of such an educated girl to criticize, but that only increased her worries.

"Frances, I will tell her you are already accepted—that I am as pleased with you as any man can be, and that is all that matters."

"But James, I know of a girl from my village who was sent back to her family by the husband's mother, even though her husband wanted her."

"Well, if you get sent back to Agu, I will just go with you. Papa Christopher and Toto Esther will keep me." Annah would laugh then, too, but inside she was more nervous about this test than she had been about her primary-leaving exams.

Although this second wedding is normally no more than two months after the first, a problem arose with the dowry. Lucy had the cows and goats that she had promised, but an epidemic broke out among cattle in the northern areas and no cows could be exported to other parts of Uganda. Even though the dowry cows remained healthy, they all had to wait until the quarantine was lifted before the marriage could proceed. Annah and James resigned themselves to having half of a wedding, but they both felt as if they'd been married a long time. Just a month after their first ceremony, Annah began to feel ill. She wondered if there was something wrong with her handling of the food, because she was throwing up every day and didn't want to eat at all.

Finally, after a week of this, James sat her down one evening.

"Frances, you know I teach biology, so I need to ask you: have you had your period this month?" Annah was shocked that he knew about such things, but she thought about it and realized she hadn't.

"No, I guess it is late," she replied slowly, only to see an enormous smile spread over his face.

"Frances, you are pregnant—we are going to have a child!" He was laughing and shouting by this time. "And it is a boy!" he added. "I know this because God told me you would give me a son, even before we were married."

Annah's bouts of sickness ended in a few weeks, and then she and James settled into planning and waiting for their son. From what they could figure out, he would arrive sometime in December, so they planned for a wonderful Christmas. In the midst of all this excitement, Annah nearly forgot that she had yet to prove herself a fit wife to James's mother. But in early July, Lucy announced that, quarantine or no, Annah needed to come and undergo her scrutiny. The couple set off to complete the required week in Amuria, with Lucy and all the villagers sitting in judgment of Annah. Since they had been through the first part of the ceremony, Annah and James were allowed to stay together in a hut in Lucy's compound, but each day Annah rose early to get her assigned chores from her mother-in-law. As she set about her chores—walking for water, gathering firewood, finding the ripest vegetables in the family fields, grinding the cassava into meal, and cooking the porridge and vegetables—she would notice the village women watching her from their doorways, hands on hips. Annah's pregnancy was still just a slight swelling of the belly, but she was already feeling awkward, and the stares only made her more nervous.

When they sat to eat the first meal, Annah knew immediately that she had put in too much salt. This was something Toto had always scolded her about, so she wasn't surprised when Lucy made a face and asked Annah how she measured the salt. She stammered that she used her hand and her mother-in-law just clucked her tongue and kept on eating. Annah's face burned throughout the rest of the meal; she was too embarrassed to look at anyone—even James.

That night, Annah cried in James's arms while he tried to comfort her.

"Why do all the women stare at me so?" she asked him.

"Frances, my mother has told them you attended Catholic

boarding schools, so they are wondering what on earth those nuns could have filled your head with that would make you a good wife."

"Well, it wasn't how to measure salt," she muttered miserably. James just laughed and held her close.

"You will be fine, mother of my son. My mother already likes you more than she wants to admit, and I just happen to love you with all my heart."

At last, the week ended and Lucy pronounced Annah acceptable as a wife to her son. It was far from heavy praise, but Annah felt even better than if she had just made the tie-breaking basket on the Kangole basketball court. She was proud of herself for persevering, and she knew Toto would be, too.

The couple returned happily to Olio to wait for the quarantine to end. With her advancing pregnancy, Annah gave little thought to the ceremony that still kept their marriage from being completely official. She and James already felt as close as any two people could, she knew. Although they both were working at their jobs, they hated to be separated and spent all of their nonworking time together. They passed most evenings sitting in front of their home while James read the Bible to his son, one hand resting on Annah's belly. Once Annah had resigned from the hospital when her pregnancy was obvious, she spent long hours during the days studying for her exams. The subject of her studies had worried her at first, but James assured her that he planned to hire a girl to help with the house and the baby so that she could still prepare for her exams.

Annah had checkups at her hospital each month, and she visited Toto several times while she could still travel, so she felt confident this baby would arrive in fine condition. She knew she had the prayers of many people supporting her—her family, their Pentecostal fellowship in Olio, and James's family. Although he was working far away in western Uganda, as an agricultural officer, Jesse had replied to their news with a letter full of joy and excitement. This little boy would be beloved.

That December was even hotter than usual, and Annah became slower and slower. Finally, she awoke just after going to bed one night with pains that made her gasp.

"James, he's coming!" She had to shake James a couple times, but then he leaped from the bed and began timing the contractions. They were still quite far apart, so James settled Annah on the bed and read the Bible to her when she was quiet. Each time a contraction curled her body, he rubbed her back and spoke softly to her.

Finally, just before dawn, James said they better start walking to the hospital so that she wouldn't have to deliver the baby in the field near his school.

"I don't want to have you squatting in the field having this baby when my students begin to pass by," he laughed. Annah certainly agreed, so they set out to walk to the hospital, James clutching the suitcase and Annah holding her belly. They only had to travel about five hundred yards from their house to the hospital, but their progress was agonizingly slow. Annah had to stop several times and lean on James while the pain ripped through her belly, but she didn't fall and she didn't deliver the baby there.

James stayed with her in the hospital for over an hour, but then he had to go to school to preside over final exams.

"Don't do anything until I get back around noon," he told her with a grin.

"I'll do what this baby wants, I think. Just get here as fast as you can," she replied. Their son was too impatient to obey his father, so Gilbert Opolot was born around eleven o'clock on the morning of December eleventh, 1979. By the time James arrived at the hospital, mother and son were both resting. Once James had sat down beside Annah, a nurse brought Gilbert to them. James took the small bundle, but he was too nervous to manage keeping the baby's neck straight while holding him, so he handed his son to Annah. She cradled him gently while basking in his father's unbridled joy.

"I can't believe this boy was inside you," James exclaimed, admiring Gilbert's size. "Frances, you've been carrying an entire human being in your belly!"

"Well, what did you think was in there—a goat?" she teased, but it certainly did seem miraculous that this child had come to them in such a way. Gilbert was large and plump, with dark hair and skin, just like his father's.

"Gilbert," Annah mused. "I know that name just came to you, but it seems to fit him." Naming children is always the prerogative of the Iteso father, and James had announced as soon as she was pregnant that he would call his son Gilbert. Lucy had been given the honor of selecting his ancestral name: Opolot. This was Jesse's ancestral name, too, so it pleased James and Annah to have borne a namesake to Jesse as well as Lucy's ancestor.

Since Annah and James lived close to the hospital, Annah's friend and midwife told her to go home after just two days there. The walk back to their house was easier than the walk to the hospital had been, but James was just as nervous. Annah had Gilbert strapped to her chest in a shawl, and she leaned on James as she picked her way carefully through the grass. At last, mother and son were resting in their bedroom.

Those days were idyllic for the new parents; Gilbert nursed well and slept in large chunks of time so that the two could rest. He was a contented little boy who rarely cried or fussed. School had ended for the term, so James was able to stay with them all day, running errands and putting together their meals while Annah rested, with little Gilbert always in her arms. Just when it seemed to Annah and James that their world was perfect, a man came to the house saying he must speak with James. James didn't know him, but his business was clearly serious. James took him outside to talk while Annah stayed with Gilbert. Annah could see them through the window, standing together under a mango tree. The man spoke earnestly to James, who suddenly put his hands over his face and shook his head. The man seemed eager to finish what he had to say, and then he left quickly. James just stood still for several moments, and when he walked back into the house he looked years older.

"James, what is it?" He crossed to the bed and sat beside Annah, one hand cupping Gilbert's little head protectively.

"It's Jesse," he said, sounding bewildered. "Someone murdered him. Frances, he's dead." They leaned on each other, then, with Gilbert pressed between them. Tears ran down both their faces as James repeated what the man had told him, about how Jesse had been found, dead from a stab wound, in his house out west where he was working. Jesse had died on December eighth. The body would be arriving in Amuria any day now. Annah immediately thought about how they had celebrated Gilbert's arrival when Jesse was already gone and they hadn't known. She knew that James was thinking about this, too, but she didn't bring it up. How could they not have sensed this somehow? At last, James sat up and spoke.

"Gilbert Opolot, you have a man's job now," he said gently to his son. "You must live your life well enough for two people."

James and Annah left the next day for Amuria in a taxi. James carefully wrapped Annah and Gilbert in a blanket in the backseat so that they could travel safely. On the long, quiet ride, he looked back at them often, his face a mask of pain and grief as he stared at his small son. Annah sensed that he would be a changed man from that day forward, but she didn't realize how completely all their lives would be altered by this terrible event.

Chapter 14

ANNAH STOOD SILENTLY as her husband led his mother to the head of the fresh hole that lay open next to his father's grave on the edge of the family compound. He motioned for his brothers, his sisters, and Annah to stand beside the grave, and then for their friends and neighbors to gather just outside the family circle. James appeared to be in control, but Annah knew that inside he was wishing he could just sit down next to the wooden box holding Jesse's body and weep. The Pentecostal minister stepped forward and began intoning prayers.

"How have we come to this?" Annah thought as she stood holding Gilbert, willing him to stay asleep through the ceremony. "We just shared the ultimate joy—holding our first-born son in our arms—and now James must face the rest of his life without his brother. And I must somehow comfort him, and find ways to fill that void."

The minister finished his prayers, and some men from the village took hold of the box and lowered it carefully into the ground. Lucy began weeping loudly, so James led her away and the others began to follow. Annah watched for a moment, thinking of the finality of the concrete covering that would be poured over the grave to keep it safe from animals. All week she had been able to call up an image of Jesse's impish grin whenever she wanted, but no image came now. He just felt gone. Gilbert began to fuss then, and Annah returned to the house to nurse him, glad for the excuse to sit alone.

In Iteso tradition, the family isn't left alone for the first week after a death, so Lucy's small house was crowded throughout the days that followed. At night, the village men slept outside near the grave. Tradition held that they must remain vigilant for seven days, to protect the grave from the evil that lurked everywhere. They kept a fire burning through the night, but all week the nights were cloudy and starless, and the fire's light did little to dispel the heavy darkness. One day, a man whom Annah knew to be James's boss arrived, offering words of sympathy and understanding. Annah felt a little thrill to realize how important James was—that a district official would travel such a distance to offer condolences that would normally be conveyed in a letter. After James had introduced the man to Annah and his mother, the two of them walked across the compound and stood under the mango tree. She watched with pride as the man spoke earnestly to James, who seemed to consider his words carefully and then respond with quiet assurance. After several minutes of discussion, the two shook hands and James walked the man to his car. The car moved out of the compound and James turned and walked slowly back to Annah.

"Come for a walk with me, Frances? We must talk." Annah was surprised that he wanted to leave the compound, but she quickly placed Gilbert in a shawl and secured him against her chest. James led her out of the compound and down a narrow, barely worn path toward a small stand of trees. James had shown her this place once: there was a little glen that she had to duck low to get into. In it sat a long, low rock that was shaded by the tall trees above it and tucked into a stand of short bushes with soft, willowy branches. It had been James's favorite place to go as a child when he needed to sit and contemplate life. He settled quickly into what must have been his usual seat on the rock's surface, and then he brushed twigs off a similarly flat area for Annah. She sat down beside him, cradling Gilbert in her arms.

"What is it, James?" He reached over and put his hand on Gilbert's little head, and sat staring at his son's face, lost in thought for a few minutes. Finally, he turned so that he could look into Annah's eyes.

"I was glad Mr. Okello came to see me today," he said at last.

"I was, too, James. I know they think highly of you at the Education Department. You should be proud." James shook his head a little, seeming to flick this praise away from himself. Annah knew that he was too self-effacing to say it of himself.

"I needed to speak with him about my—our—situation," he said gently. "My mother is devastated over Jesse and she's asked me to move here to help her. I'm not sure she can bear all this without help, Frances."

Annah drew in a sharp breath. She thought of all the times when they were courting that James had assured her that she would not be taken to his village to serve his mother. She realized she had never told him that this would have been cause for her to end their engagement—he had said it would never happen. And yet, in the short time she had known James's brother, Jesse had become a vital part of her life, too. She had relied on his messages of good cheer when he was away, and she had savored every minute of his visits as he filled their home with laughter and joy. So she knew how empty Lucy must feel; but still: how could she become a typical daughter-in-law, serving her husband's criticism-prone mother and craving his undivided attention?

"We won't live in her house, Frances. I promise." James seemed to have heard her thoughts. "Mr. Okello says there is a teaching position in Amuria Primary School, so we can live in the compound there. It's only a short walk from here, so we can check on my mother without living with her. I'll still help you with your studies and we'll do all the things we planned. I just need to stay close for a while."

"Of course, James, we must stay near her," Annah replied, hugging Gilbert tightly to soothe the sudden ache in her stomach. The words surprised her as she said them, but then she knew they had come from her heart. I can get through this, she thought, and it *is* temporary.

"I knew you would understand, my Frances." James beamed at her and took her hand to help her up. The two of them stooped under the branches and walked together to the path. She leaned against his side as he walked her back, one arm encircling her shoulder and the other cradling the tiny bundle that was their son.

James and Annah returned to Olio for just a few days, to pack up their belongings and move them to their house at Amuria school. It was hard for Annah to leave this community—so many important things had happened here: finding her career in nursing, meeting James, joining the Pentecostal church, falling in love, becoming a wife, and giving birth to Gilbert. How could such a small community have given her so much? On the morning they were to leave, Annah walked to the hospital for one last farewell, thinking of all the times she had followed that path. She chuckled to think of the morning she and James had walked it while Gilbert was insisting it was time to be born. How long the way had seemed on that day, when it had been so short on all the others. After a tearful goodbye to the hospital staff, she returned home to accompany her husband to their new village.

Life in Amuria began peacefully. James liked his new school, and Lucy was content to see them each weekend, when either she came to their house or they went to hers. Annah sent letters home often, and Toto and Papa responded joyfully to every snippet of news about their grandson. Annah and James continued to grow in their love, and Gilbert flourished. James had always liked children, but Annah was amazed by the relationship he developed with little Gilbert. She loved to watch as James held his son on his lap and lectured him about the Bible. James would position Gilbert so that they were facing each other, and Gilbert would stare intently into his father's eyes as he spoke.

While Annah and James were content with their life, Lucy remained inconsolable about Jesse. She seemed to work at finding things to complain about. She had been critical of Annah's fitness as a wife to James, but now she appeared overcome with unhappiness that they were not fully married.

"Toto," James would say patiently, "what does your grandson look like to you, if not the perfect evidence of a marriage that was meant to be?" Lucy always softened at the mention of her "Opolot," as she called him, but soon she would be fretting again about the second part of the wedding.

Finally, in March, the quarantine was lifted and they could finalize their marriage. Christopher and Esther arrived, overjoyed by the chance to see little Gilbert and eager to settle the marriage bargain. In keeping with tradition, Lucy had her son John pen the cows and goats together and take Christopher to inspect them. Papa walked solemnly around all the animals, and then came to the house. With a wink toward Annah, he pronounced them all fine specimens and said he would be happy for his daughter to be officially married to James. As in the first ceremony, friends and neighbors came to Lucy's compound from all over, and there were two days of dancing, singing, and feasting on goat's meat and beer. There were no rituals like the parting of Annah from her mother, so James, Annah, and Gilbert just bade goodbye to Christopher and Esther as they began their journey home. After a few days, James and his twelve-year-old brother, Benjamin, left to herd the animals to her father's land in Agu.

Annah stood with Lucy, watching them drive the animals down the lane with sticks. Benjamin looked pretty much at ease, but James was talking to the animals, coaxing and scolding as if they were reluctant pupils in his classroom. Annah glanced at Lucy and saw a trace of a smile playing on the older woman's lips.

"It's going to be a long journey for them, I think," Lucy murmured.

"Yes, for the animals as well as for James and Benjamin," Annah replied with a grin. It was good to see Lucy smile, fleeting though it was.

Both women were visibly relieved when James and Benjamin returned. They were tired and dirty, but they had clearly enjoyed working together and were in teasing moods.

"Now, ladies, Emuge men have been herding animals for generations," James pointed out. "There was no need for you to worry."

"Unfortunately, the more recent trend has been for Emuge men to work with their mouths," Lucy pointed out.

"Well, I won't say my brother talked those animals all the way to Agu, but it was *most* of the way," Benjamin put in with a sidelong glance toward James. Annah was impressed that these three could laugh and joke, in spite of the father and brother who were so clearly missing from the group. This was a good family, she thought, even though they tried her patience at times.

It wasn't until a few weeks later that Annah learned just how perilous that trek to Agu had truly been. Their district of Teso was bordered on the northeast by the Karamonjong district. It was through this area that Idi Amin and his soldiers had fled, and this was also the district where the Iteso people's bitterest enemies resided. The Karamonjong felt that all cattle in the area belonged to them ancestrally, and they had raided Iteso farms for years. While the raiding of farms had slowed during the epidemic of cow disease, the Karamonjong returned to cattle rustling with a vengeance once the sickness stopped spreading. But it soon became clear that there was a new twist to this age-old hatred: hosting Idi Amin and his followers had left the Karamonjong armed with rifles, while the Itesos still protected themselves with knives and spears.

James wouldn't tell Annah much, but she learned that while he and Benjamin had done their traveling in daylight, they had slept little at night, when they had to hide the animals from bands of Karamonjong. Once home, James had instructed her not to go far from their house and never to linger near farms with cattle. Stories of violence increased, as the Karamonjong enjoyed their new superiority over the Iteso. They were killing farmers for their animals, and soon after they were raiding and killing more for sport than just to acquire animals.

By May, there were so many raids on homes in the evening hours that Annah found herself once again hiding in bushes, but this time she also had to shield her small son from the horror. She and James would sit numb under the low trees, not daring to speak a word for fear of rousing Gilbert. A cry from him could bring the evil raiders to their hiding place, and Annah wouldn't let herself think what would happen then. Annah was relieved at least that James had not sent her and Gilbert to live with his mother, in spite of Lucy's request that he do so. James had told his mother that he would keep his family with him, to protect them the best he could, so Annah rearranged their little house and Lucy moved in with them.

One night, as Annah sat under the bushes, she began to review her life. How much death and fear had she seen in her twenty years on earth? How much more could she take? She never questioned God's willingness to care for her, but why was he content with the suffering that was once again the way of life in Uganda? Things were better: President Obote had returned to power and the government was maintaining peace in some areas, near Kampala. Even Agu was peaceful and regaining some prosperity, but here she sat, in hiding from her own countrymen, while the government did nothing. Her thoughts seemed to spiral down from there, until she was asking herself if she had made a bad choice in the family she had joined.

Just then Gilbert awoke with a whimper, and James reached over and pulled the baby onto his lap. By this time Gilbert was almost a year old and walking, so it was all they could do to keep him from toddling out of the bushes to find adventure. It was a night with a bright, almost-full moon, and she could see their profiles against the silent sky. James leaned down and whispered in Gilbert's ear, and then the two of them began drawing with their fingers in the dirt. She watched as Gilbert would carefully study the shapes that his father had created in the dust and then add his own little squiggles. Finger to his lips, James would nod approval and then elaborate the picture so that Gilbert would want to add to it again. The two of them worked at their art for over half an hour, with James deftly directing Gilbert's attention back when it began to wander. Seeing this father-son game, played in absolute silence but seeming to shout to Annah about their love for each other, she realized with a grateful sigh that this man, and now also his small son, truly were her destiny in life, no matter how terrible the world around them might become. A sense of ferocity settled over her when she thought of the forces that threatened to harm these two, and she knew she would give up her own life in an instant to protect either one of them.

Somehow through all this turmoil their lives did go on, and after almost a year the region began to suffer less violence. President Obote finally sent soldiers to maintain some order, and the residents were able to stay in their homes again. Karamonjong still roamed the area occasionally, and Annah knew they were simply a people who cared nothing for human life: if you had what they wanted, they killed you. It was that simple.

One day in August, Annah realized that she was probably pregnant again. She felt an instant of dismay, wondering how she could protect yet another helpless little person in this chaos, but then she was overwhelmed with joy and awe that she would again give birth. I will protect you from it all, my dear one, she thought. For a few days she kept silent about her discovery, making sure it really was happening, but soon she was bursting to tell James that their family was growing again. She waited until one evening when they were alone in their room, with Gilbert sound asleep in his crib. They were sitting together on their bed and James was telling her in a soft whisper how Gilbert seemed to be getting smarter every day.

"Well, James, I hope our next child is just as smart," she said, looking at him intently. His eyes widened and for a moment she could see that his first thought, too, was keeping another family member safe.

"Oh, Frances, you are the most remarkable woman. I don't know how you could be creating new life out of all this." His voice trailed off as he waved a hand out toward the world around him, and then he grabbed her and hugged her hard.

"Shhh, careful, Papa; you'll startle both our children." They spent the rest of that evening wrapped in each other's arms, praying quietly to God. They thanked him for their enormous blessings and asked him to ensure that they would always be together to help each other through whatever might come in these uncertain times.

A few months later, James received a letter from the minister of education informing him that he had been promoted to the job of district inspector of schools. The minister cited James's outstanding record of successfully preparing students to pass the Primary Leaving Exam and stated that he had made a special exception for James, so that he would not need further schooling. He was to report to Kampala to find out which section of the country would be his post.

"James," Annah said immediately, "can we get out of here? I'm so tired of the hiding and the fear and the gunfire."

"I'll do my best," he replied. He returned with the news that they were to report to Masindi in western Uganda within the month. Masindi was a large town, about the size of Soroti, and Annah knew that life in that region would be much safer for them. Six months pregnant, Annah cried tears of relief as she packed up their belongings. This would be the beginning of the life she and James had dreamed for themselves and their family. Lucy had assured them that she would never leave Amuria, but that James's brothers and sisters would be there to help her. James was so happy about his new job that he danced and sang his way through the days, and even little Gilbert seemed to know that his life was about to be better. Annah and James reminded themselves humbly that they would always do God's will no matter what, but Annah sent frequent prayers of thanksgiving to God for finally rewarding James for his hard work.

The house in Masindi seemed enormous, with a separate room for Gilbert to sleep in, and electricity and indoor plumbing. Like the electricity, the water ran sporadically, but the family felt like they were living in pure luxury nonetheless. Just as they had planned, James had arranged for his young cousin, Mary, to come with them to Masindi to help with the children and the housework. Mary had her own room, also, and she walked to the town well on days when the taps were dry.

As part of his job, James traveled to schools all over the district, so he had a car and driver available for his daily use. James received frequent praise from his boss, and all the school administrators greeted him eagerly when he visited and sought his advice often. Into this perfect world, on May 9, 1982, Ruby Anyumel was born. Annah's labor wasn't difficult, and the hospital in Masindi was luxurious compared to the Olio hospital. Gilbert was a gentle, protective big brother, and Ruby was a contented baby. Suddenly, Annah was the matron of a prosperous family; she enjoyed teaching Mary the ways of a city as well as how to care for the children and the house. Both she and Mary struggled to understand the local language, Bantu, when James wasn't there to help translate. But it was a comfort to have someone to help her, and also to speak Ateso with her when James was gone.

Annah was too wrapped up in her little family to pay much heed to the political situation, but it was clear that the resistance to President Obote was increasing, and that he was using force and instilling fear among the citizens in order to assert his power. His biggest threat was the National Resistance Movement, headed by

Yoweri Museveni, who was from a district just south of Masindi. Once again in Annah's life, she was living in the center of unrest. She had to be particularly careful in public, since she spoke very little of either the local dialect or Kiswahili, which had been declared the national language. The rebels suspected anyone from a northern tribe of being a spy for Obote, and neither group trusted anyone who spoke English. As pressure from Museveni's army increased, government soldiers became boldly aggressive: setting up roadblocks and challenging anyone who passed by. Both groups were terrorizing citizens: looting, robbing, and raping. This time it was best for the family to remain inside their home at night, although they often heard shouts and gunfire that were alarmingly close.

Throughout these times James continued to do his work, and his reputation grew with each passing week. When Ruby was eight months old, James was told that he was to be trained to become the next minister of education. To prepare him, the government offered to send him abroad for a PhD degree in education. He had his choice of going to school in either London or the United States. Annah barely breathed as he told her this news. When she finally realized that he was actually telling her that the whole family would be sent abroad while he got this degree, she was dizzy with a mixture of relief and dread; relief that they might actually escape all this misery, and dread that it might all just be a wonderful daydream.

"Frances, I want you to choose which place we move to," James told her.

"James, this is too big for me. We should pray for direction from God." James knelt down with her there in the living room and said his prayer.

"Oh God, please guide us in this decision, so that we move to the place that will be best for my wife and children. My family can face any hardship, as long as we are together. Help us choose the place where Frances and our children will grow and flourish with me." Annah bowed her head and tears of gratitude rolled down her face—gratitude to God for this opportunity, and to James for thinking of her and the children first.

After a week of prayer and fasting, Annah told James she felt certain it should be America.

"If that's where you want to go, then we'll go there," James said. He immediately began applying to universities in the United States, and in less than a month he was accepted by Ohio University in

Athens, Ohio. It sounded as foreign as the moon to Annah, but she knew there would be peace there, so she felt no qualms at all about going.

In June the family moved to an apartment about five miles outside Kampala so that James could spend the final two months before their departure preparing for his studies and training his replacement. Each step that brought them closer to America was a blessing to Annah, so she settled happily into the apartment. It felt safe there, although of course they couldn't go out at night. As with all the homes they had lived in together, James and Annah immediately began inviting other Pentecostals over for Christian fellowship as soon as they moved in.

A week after they arrived, they were hosting seven young men, all originally from Teso, in a Bible study and dinner gathering. At about eight o'clock, the men were sitting with James in the living room while Annah finished up her dinner preparations with Mary. Once the meal was ready, she went and sat with the men to hear James finish his preaching. Gilbert had been very tired that day, so he was asleep in the bedroom and Ruby was curled up on Annah's lap. Mary had left the apartment to sit outside for the few minutes before dinner.

Suddenly, the living room door swung open and Annah could see Mary walking in, very slowly and stiffly. She was about to scold the girl mildly for barging in when she saw that a man in a camouflage jacket was behind her, holding a gun to her back. Annah froze in fear—she couldn't even look at James to signal to him to turn and look at the scene unfolding in the doorway. When the gunman entered the room, all the men stared at him, just as paralyzed as Annah. More men—about five in all—burst in behind the first and began shouting for everyone to lie face down on the floor. Annah was moving slowly, trying to hold her baby while she obeyed the command, when she glanced up into the face of one of the intruders.

"Don't look at me, Iteso!" he shouted and jammed the barrel of his gun against her face, right between her eyes. "If you do that again I'll blow your face off."

Annah curled her arm around Ruby, who was crying in terror, and pressed her own face into the floor. She heard another man tell James to give them money. James led the man to the bedroom, where they kept a small cloth bag with household cash. A third gunman followed them into the bedroom and Annah could see that he was carrying out the packages they had purchased just that day—new clothes for the trip to America. The others kept their guns trained on the men and Annah and Mary, while the one kept picking up things and piling them near the front door. She saw their radio and more clothing added to the pile, and then one of them stuck his gun in her back and told her to get up. She struggled up with Ruby under her arm, being careful not to look him in the face. He pushed her into the bedroom, where she saw James standing in the corner with his face against the wall. The ringleader had his gun pressed into James's back and he was shouting.

"Give me your money now!" the second man yelled at Annah. She went to the place where the bag normally hung, but it was empty. The gun jabbed her hard in the back and the gunman yelled, "Where is the money?"

Annah was surprised by her own calm. Lying on the floor in the living room, she had prayed to God and then said, "Let your will be done here this day," and at that moment she had let go of worry about her own life.

"James, where is the money from the bag?" she asked softly.

"I already gave it to them," he answered. "Please don't hurt my wife and children," he pleaded. "Take whatever you want but don't hurt them. We don't have any more money."

"Down on the bed," the man said to Annah, shoving her with his gun. It was awkward, but Annah managed to lie partially on her side, curled around the baby, while she kept her face down against the bed. Miraculously, Gilbert seemed to still be asleep in his crib. She realized the man was crouched over her and then she felt his knee press into her side. She waited, resigned, to be raped in front of her husband and children.

"Please forgive us," James begged. "That's all the money we have, I swear." It hurt Annah to hear James so desperate, and she realized suddenly that she was just tired—tired of Idi Amin, tired of the Karamonjong, tired of the soldiers and the rebels. I am ready to go to God, she thought. There will be peace there.

Turning her head slightly, without looking at his face, she addressed the gunman. "Please, sir, if you kill me, could you make sure you also kill my children? They can't live without me." She pulled Ruby into her chest so that the baby was directly in front of her heart. Any bullet aimed at her would have to go through her child as well.

Suddenly, the weight of the man's leg was lifted from her side. She squeezed her eyes shut and then heard his footsteps. He was walking backward, slowly, out of the room. Then the one who had been holding James was walking out of the room also. Even Ruby sensed something, because she stopped crying. The only sound in the room was her ragged breathing after crying so much. Annah lay there wondering what was happening.

Finally, she heard James walk out of the room. When no sound came from there she got up and went into the living room. James was standing in the middle of the room, Mary was still lying on the floor, and all the gunmen as well as their Iteso friends were gone. James walked over and shut the door and locked it, and then turned off the lights. The two of them went into the bedroom and simply collapsed on the bed, with the baby between them. Annah lay in the dark, trying not to think about what had happened, knowing she would never sleep soundly again. And then it was daybreak.

Gilbert was awake and crying for food. Annah looked over at James and they both stood up stiffly.

"You feed the children," he said. "I'm going to headquarters to get a car and get us out of here." He returned a few hours later with a truck. The two of them loaded up as many of their belongings as they could and drove across Kampala to an apartment that James had been given when he told his story.

Just three weeks later, in August of 1983, the family climbed into a taxi to go to Entebbe Airport. Annah had been too afraid to go to Agu Village to say goodbye to Papa and Toto; she sent Mary back there to give them all the things from the apartment. They hadn't been able to buy more clothes for the trip, so James and Annah were carrying just one extra set of clothing for each of them and the children. They each wore the only pair of shoes they owned. Neither of them cared; James had prayed every day since the night of the intruders: "Just let us go there and be together in peace, Lord."

All through the taxi ride, Annah watched out the windows, certain that soldiers would appear and tell them at gunpoint that they had to return because they were staying in Uganda. Once they were inside Entebbe, they had to sit and wait for the plane for two hours. There were soldiers in the airport, and every time one passed them Annah's heart raced and she broke out in a sweat. Finally, the time came to board the plane. Gilbert was excitedly trying to run across the tarmac while James held his hand firmly. Everything in Annah's being wanted to do exactly the same thing, but she was certain she would be pulled back into Uganda if she ran. The family walked slowly up the steps of the plane and settled themselves in their seats. Finally, the plane taxied and lifted into the air. Annah watched as they flew out over Lake Victoria, away from Uganda: away from the soldiers and the guns and the hatred; away from Papa and Toto and Jesse.

"The seatbelt sign is now turned off," a strange, disembodied voice told the passengers. "You are free to move about the plane."

Annah wanted to shriek with laughter. "Free?" she wanted to shout. "How will we ever be free? We are Ugandans."

James Emuge's passport photo from 1982. *(Courtesy of Annah Emuge)*

Annah's father, Christopher, in front of her sister Rosemary's house in Soroti, in 1997. *(Courtesy of Annah Emuge)*

Annah's sister Rosemary and her mother, Esther, beside Rosemary's house in Soroti, in 1997. *(Courtesy of Annah Emuge)*

James's mother, Lucy, taken at her son's house in Kampala in the late 1990s.
(Courtesy of Annah Emuge)

The main hut in Christopher's compound in Agu Village, taken in 2004. *(Courtesy of Annah Emuge)*

Annah and James Emuge, taken at church in St. Charles, Missouri, in 1998.
(Courtesy of Annah Emuge and Lifetouch Church Directories and Portraits)

1983 to 1994

PRESIDENT OBOTE CONTINUED to struggle to maintain control of Uganda. In addition to unabated pressure from Museveni's National Resistance Movement, animosities broke out among the northern tribes that made up Obote's army. In 1985, one of Obote's own commanders overthrew him, and then Museveni quickly seized control of the government, assuming the official title of president in January 1986. That year Museveni conducted a counterinsurgency campaign against northern rebels, called Operation North, in which thousands of civilians died. Out of this environment of insurgencies and counterinsurgencies, Joseph Kony was able to create his band of rebel warriors known as the Lord's Resistance Army. This group quickly became an additional source of terror and destruction in the north, as it pillaged and burned villages and forced the residents to join the movement or die. Children were conscripted to serve as soldiers, slaves, or concubines, and any resistance meant death.

In responding to the atrocities, President Museveni created enormous refugee camps housing hundreds of thousands of northern Ugandans, but these camps became reviled throughout the world because of inhumane living conditions and mass starvation and disease. Nearly two million Ugandans ended up living in refugee camps for close to two decades, creating a generation of Ugandans who had never known community life or learned the basic skills of self-support.

Chapter 15

THE PLANE WAS ABOVE the clouds now, so all Annah could do was imagine Agu receding below them. I will be back, Toto, she said over and over to herself until she felt calm enough to look around the plane. The flight attendant was coming down the aisle, offering drinks to the passengers.

"Water for all of us, please," James said when she reached their row.

Annah's eyes widened when she saw the woman pour a clear liquid into their clear plastic cups.

"James," she whispered, "water really *is* clear. I can see my hand through this full glass. Even after I boil it, it's brown at home." James was beaming at her.

"This is the first of many marvels I will introduce you to, Frances," he told her, laughing. But she could see him looking through the water when he lifted his cup, too. Nowhere in Uganda was the water like this: Annah had thought it was an exaggeration when she read in books about clear water.

Each member of the Emuge family got through the four long flights to America differently. The children immediately accepted the inside of the plane as their universe. A kind flight attendant taught Gilbert how to use the headphones to watch the movies, and his sister spent most of her time toddling up and down the aisle, befriending as many passengers as possible. James talked gently with the children when they needed his attention, and he spent much of the time sleeping or gazing out the window with a contented smile. Annah seemed to be the only one of them who was wracked with every emotion possible during the long journey. When she tended to the children she looked at their trusting faces and felt torn between gratitude that they were on their way out of Uganda and concern about the unknown world she was making their home. Thoughts of Agu and Papa and Toto only saddened her, and yet she would begin to think about her mother's description of that great world out there and she would break out in a happy grin, wishing she could exult with Toto that she was actually on her way to that world. But under all these emotions lay unadulterated fear that somehow this would all turn out to be an unreachable dream.

The family landed in Brussels and had to find their way to the hotel that was to be their overnight layover. Annah followed James through the airport, amazed by his ability to navigate all the strange signs and directions they received. Finally, they had their suitcase and were told to walk outside and across the street to the shuttle that would take them to the hotel. Annah was thrilled by her first breath of fresh air in ten hours, but she was soon concentrating on holding Ruby and keeping a firm grip on Gilbert's hand while following James as he carried their bag. They came to an intersection filled with cars and trucks.

"Mommy, look," Gilbert shouted, trying to point in several directions at once.

"Yes, this is a big city, and there are cars and trucks all over the roads," she answered while tugging on Gilbert to follow James across the street. Suddenly, she heard a loud whistle and saw a policeman waving his arms.

"They've come for us, James, we have to go back!" Annah cried as she froze in the middle of the street. James dropped their suitcase on the curb and ran back to her. He took hold of Gilbert's hand and put an arm around Annah's shoulders.

"He's just directing the traffic, Frances," he said gently, guiding her across the lane of stopped cars. He stood with her once they had reached the sidewalk and took her face in his hands.

"Frances, listen to me. We're not going back until we decide to. You, and Ruby, and Gilbert, and I are all safe now. We're going to America!" James balanced the bag awkwardly on his shoulder and kept a hand on his wife's arm as they walked to the shuttle. Her trembling never stopped until they were on the plane to New York the next day.

By the time the family reached the Columbus, Ohio, airport, they were too drained to notice the landscape of their new home. James found the bus station, thanks to the directions the university had provided, and they set off on the two-hour ride to Athens. The children slept all the way, while Annah gazed out the window, barely seeing the countryside. When the bus pulled into the Athens station, they got their bag from the luggage compartment and walked slowly into the building.

Suddenly, there was a smiling man, holding a sign that read "Emuge," standing right in front of them.

"You must be James," he said, grabbing the suitcase and clasping James's hand. "I'm Professor Allen from Ohio University, and this is my wife, Jane. Welcome!" Annah was so grateful to these strangers that she wanted to lean her head on Jane's shoulder and weep, but she just stood, smiling. James shook the man's hand, grinning happily.

"It's great to meet you, Professor. This is my wife—"

"I'm Annah," she said loudly, holding out her hand. Even this friendly couple looked a little startled by the fervor of her interruption, but she knew James had been about to call her Frances. This was Toto's big, wonderful world, though, and in it she would be Annah. "These are our children, Gilbert and Ruby."

The following weeks were filled with many new adventures and joyful moments. After one night in a dorm room on campus, the family was moved into a furnished apartment in International Student Housing. The two-story, two-bedroom apartment felt like a castle to Annah. She still feared that they would be returned to Uganda, so she told herself not to get used to this, but she couldn't help just wandering from room to room, staring at all the open space in it.

Most remarkable, though, was the care they were given by the professors and graduate students in James's department. Almost every day, one of them would arrive to take the family shopping or sight-seeing. On their first day in the apartment, a professor picked them up and drove to an enormous store named Kroger. James and Annah entered behind the professor and stood there uncertainly as he pulled out a wheeled cart.

"We'll just push this around and fill it with what you need," he said kindly as he led them between two enormous shelves that reached almost to the ceiling and seemed to go on for miles. Annah looked closely at the items arrayed on the shelf in front of her in all colors of plastic bags, and she suddenly realized they were loaves of bread. She wondered how many loaves there must be—hundreds? thousands? Suddenly she found herself giggling.

"James, it's all bread!" she exclaimed.

"Shhh, Frances," James whispered. "Not in front of the professor." But he was grinning, too, and she knew he was as amazed by all this as she was. With a great deal of guidance from the professor, they finally managed to get up and down the aisles and buy the food they really needed, although the fresh vegetables seemed limp and uninviting.

They had two weeks before classes began, and each day was one of discovery and adjustment. It was the multitude of choices that Annah found most troublesome—even in Kampala, there simply weren't so many things to pick from. One night when a professor took them to Ponderosa for dinner, Annah just gave up and asked James to get her food for her. Gilbert's reaction to this new environment had been to become even more quiet and watchful, but he ate the American food with relish. While they all missed their native food, the Ugandan dishes that Annah cooked at home didn't taste real to any of them anymore.

When James began classes, Annah found herself alone with two small children for most of the day. He would leave around seven o'clock in the morning and often not return until midnight, after the library closed. Annah missed the days in Amuria when she could look forward to seeing him every day at lunchtime, and he missed being with her and the children, but they were both determined that he would earn his degrees quickly and with honors. Annah found a playground near the apartment, and she often walked the kids there to play. On the day she discovered it, she sat on a bench in the shade of a tall tree and watched as her children shrieked with joy over their impromptu sandbox game.

Annah looked up at the big tree that shaded her and was reminded of her childhood, sitting under a tree and holding Rebecca while Toto worked in the field. She had already noticed that the countryside in Ohio was somewhat similar to that in Teso, except for the lack of mud huts clustered under trees. As her mind flowed back to her childhood surroundings, Annah instinctively glanced all around the park, checking to be sure there were no soldiers. When she realized with a gasp that she would never have to worry about this in her new home, tears came to her eyes and she wished fervently that she could bring Toto and Papa here, to enjoy this carefree world with her.

Sometimes Annah thought she would wake up and find that this had all been a dream. How could her life have suddenly become so wonderful? Her days were filled with outings to the playground with the kids, or activities with other international wives—shopping, cooking dishes from home to share with each other, or trying out

American dishes together. There were many children in the international student community, so her two always had playmates, and Annah enjoyed getting to know so many different women. She was still making big adjustments. One afternoon, a friend who was visiting went into the kitchen for something.

"Annah, I don't smell anything. What are you cooking in this big pot?" she called. Annah went in and laughingly told her it was just the day's water, boiling so they could drink it.

"Oh, my friend," the woman laughed. "You don't have to boil the water here. You just drink it out of the faucet!" With that, she filled a glass from the tap and took a long drink of it.

Annah stopped boiling the water, but although she enjoyed the ease of getting clean drinking water in her new home, she and Gilbert seemed especially bothered by the taste of American water.

"It tastes like medicine, Mommy," Gilbert would always complain. She didn't fuss at him because she secretly agreed.

James was working hard and enjoying his classes thoroughly. He would complete his master's degree in a year and a half, then begin his PhD program. He also had a job as a teaching assistant for a professor of African Studies. Most nights he would come home too full of new ideas to go right to sleep, so they would sit in the kitchen while he told her all he was learning. As she took in his words and his excitement, Annah thought with a thrill how unlike a Ugandan man James had become. She had never seen Papa just sit and tell Toto what he was thinking, and she knew this was true in the vast majority of Ugandan families. How lucky she felt to have this man for her friend as well as for her husband.

Fall advanced and the family worked into a comfortable routine; Annah found that the wonderful quality of their time with James made up for the small quantity. Weekends were the best. The library closed early on Saturday, so James came home and then either cooked or took the family out for dinner, and on Sunday they all slept late and went to the Pentecostal church James had found. Everything seemed perfect, except that Annah seemed to be unable to adjust to the food she was eating. Instead of getting used to it, she was more frequently nauseated, especially by the smells emanating from the other international kitchens in the apartment complex. With the overwhelming number of changes she was handling constantly, she didn't think about any other reason for her sickness, besides her body's inability to adapt. She pushed herself through each day, even though she was tired all the time, and she knew she was getting thinner. Finally, worried about how emaciated she looked, James asked a friend to drive them to the hospital. Even though she felt quite weak, Annah couldn't stop looking around the exam room and marveling at the equipment and supplies there—they would have kept the Olio Hospital going for years!

After her exam, James was sent in to sit with Annah and then the doctor returned to tell them his findings. He was an older man, and he sat on a stool and looked at them for a few moments. Annah was comforted by his steady, kind eyes.

"Well, it looks like you two are having a baby," he said with a smile. "I'd say you're about three months along." Annah looked at James and realized they both were feeling intense joy. What else could go right for them in this wonderful land?

Annah's morning sickness continued for another month, but she took the vitamins that the Student Health Clinic gave her and quickly regained some strength. When James and Annah went to the clinic for her second checkup, the doctor asked if they would like to know the baby's sex.

"Maybe we should find out," James said with a chuckle. Annah was startled by his reaction: in their villages, as in all villages in Teso, there were older women who had finished bearing their children who were known to be able to foretell the sex of an expectant mother's baby. When a woman's belly was quite large and the baby's movements had been felt for many weeks, she would go to the hut of the "sex teller." There, she would lie on her back on a mat and the teller and her assistants—all women who were beyond child-bearing age—would break stalks of Atigo plants and rub the sap in their hands. The sap was a pungent, gooey substance that they would then massage into the woman's belly. Legend said that the sex teller would be able to determine the sex of the baby by how it reacted to the massage. Some people said that girls would kick and fight, while boys would just ignore the old women, as they would do when they had become men. But the sex tellers never revealed what exactly led them to pronounce that a baby was a girl or a boy. James and Annah were a modern young couple, and they had only laughed when anyone suggested they go to a sex teller when they were expecting Gilbert. "Only God can know the sex of this baby," James had said. "And that's the way we want it."

The doctor explained amniocentesis to Annah, and James clarified things when she looked confused. "Let's do this, Frances. We are in a modern new world and we should take advantage of the advances here." When she was told it would be a girl, Annah was thrilled. She had always wanted ten children, so she was pleased to have a baby sister coming for Ruby, and a good start on her five girls. Gilbert was disappointed it wasn't a brother, but he was happy at the prospect of another family member. At nearly four years old, Gilbert was clearly a serious child, and he was already protective of his little sister, so Annah knew he would be a good big brother to two girls.

In spite of the added warmth of pregnancy, Annah was constantly cold that fall and winter. A couple that James knew from the department had driven the family to a store to buy winter coats, and they had laughed when they arrived and saw that Annah and James were only wearing sweaters. The wife tried to show Annah how to layer clothing, but she hated carrying around the weight of the clothes. She ended up keeping the apartment so warm that their American friends were uncomfortable when they visited. Annah didn't venture out unless she had to, and since James did the shopping for the family, she was indoors most of the time. She used the time to teach Gilbert his ABCs and counting, and the three of them spent lots of time reading books.

Snow was the big topic in the minds of all the new international students from warm climates, and especially their children. One morning in November there was a knock on the door and Annah found the neighbor standing there with two snowballs and a big grin. He came in and handed the balls to James, who quickly tossed one to Annah and one to Gilbert. Annah held hers out for Ruby to inspect, but Gilbert immediately took a bite out of his. He let out a yelp and jumped up and down from the cold, but he happily took another bite before James could grab the ball away. By then Ruby had also tried a small bite, and they were all laughing as James opened the door and tossed the balls out into their strange, white yard. Fortunately, the children never tired of playing in the snow that winter, although Annah still hated the cold and stayed in behind the storm door to watch them when they went out to play. James didn't like the extra clothing he now needed to walk to school, and one day he slipped and sprained an ankle, so the adults in the family didn't relish the snow nearly as much as the kids did.

Sometimes, on those cold, cold days, Annah would glimpse her reflection in the glass door—sitting, hunched over, with her sweater buttoned up to her chin and a blanket wrapped around her legs— and she would gasp in surprise. Where was the lithe, free girl who had run miles to school each day? But then she would think of the soldiers—the random terrorizing, the looting, the killing—and she would thank God that her family was safe here in Ohio. She and James knew from news reports that Uganda was still not stable—Museveni continued to challenge Obote, who sounded less and less in control with each quote they read in the newspaper. There was good news from Uganda, though, in the letters that came from her sisters Rosemary and Rebecca and from James's mother, Lucy. In spite of the turmoil in Kampala, things were fairly quiet way up north in Teso District, and their families were tending their crops, repairing their huts, and telling stories by the fire at night. Annah was happy to know that life had eased for Toto and Papa, and she sent frequent letters to be read to them, filled with stories and pictures of her family.

The holidays were wonderful times for the family. They spent both Thanksgiving and Christmas at the homes of professors and were amazed by how they were welcomed into these families. At Christmas, Annah and her family were the only black people among the three families gathered, but no one seemed to notice, and the children all played and opened presents in a mad frenzy of torn paper and shouts of joy. Annah and James had never seen a Christmas tree, but the international students put one up together in their great room and they all helped hang decorations on it. One student, who had been there for a few Christmases, handed out song sheets and played carols on the piano. No one minded the cacophony of accents that filled the air as everyone sang as loudly as they could. Recalling her own childhood Christmases, Annah knew that her children would never forget their wild, extravagant yule seasons in America.

The winter quarter brought even more excitement for both James and Annah. James had suggested that Annah take some night classes, since she could do so without cost as a graduate student spouse, so Annah enrolled in English composition and math. She felt shy at first, but then she purely loved sitting in the fancy classrooms and doing her homework at the kitchen table. She quickly regained her skill at learning, and she was delighted that James was once again keeping his promise to see that she would become a modern, educated woman. On the nights when she had class, James took care of the children, bathing them and putting them to bed. Sometimes Annah would chuckle and wish that those women in Lucy's village, who had been so skeptical that a girl with an eighth-grade education could possibly be a suitable wife for James, could see their family now.

James was taking a course titled "Beyond Culture," in which he was learning that the vast difference between Ugandan and American cultures was replicated between societies all over the world. He told Annah about the course daily, and they shared their amazement at the diversity of the world. Annah loved watching his face as he told her about all the cultures he was discovering, and how important it is for all people to understand their place in the world. Many of his sentences began with, "When I am the minister of education, the children will learn . . . " She was reminded that it was this man's deep love of learning that had first endeared him to her, when they sat hiding under the bushes near Olio.

Sometimes that spring Annah felt wholly American—attending university classes, taking her children to the grocery, sitting at the table doing homework while James cooked dinner. But at other times she knew she was basically an African woman who could never fathom all of the customs of this new culture. She just stared when she saw a couple walking across campus together, holding hands. No couple in Uganda would think of such a display of affection. She and James were already defying their home culture in the way they shared domestic duties, but they never touched in public. Water was a continuing source of discomfort for Annah—the American ways of using it were so wasteful. In Masindi, where they had indoor taps and plumbing, they still got as much use as possible out of every drop of water. After doing the dishes or bathing, they would use the water again, to wash floors or to flush the toilet. Even though she was in America now, Annah couldn't bear to run a full bath just for herself, so she would often bathe the children and then use the water again for her bath. When she saw other women letting water run down the drain, she thought of those times Toto had gotten her up in the middle of the night to begin their trek to find a functioning well or stream, and she wanted to shout at them to turn it off.

But the medical care she was receiving for herself and her baby reminded her just how much she wanted these American luxuries. Her regular checkups were thorough and reassuring, and she realized she couldn't imagine how she had managed her pregnancies at home. In mid-March, when she was within a month of her time, they actually had her coming in once per week.

"James, I think we'd better get serious about this girl's name. I want to call her Diana," Annah said one day.

"*Diana* is perfect for a strong American girl," he responded, "but just to be sure she knows where her strength came from, she'll be Diana Atai, after your mother."

Annah didn't tell James that she had chosen the name because of Diana, Princess of Wales. She didn't consider *Diana* a British name; she just felt that a child born into the luxury of America would be a princess.

One Saturday afternoon, while James was at the library, Annah felt the familiar grip of labor. But the contractions were slow and erratic, so she knew nothing would happen for a good while. She packed her bag, made sure the kids' clothes were clean, and made supper for the family. James did the dishes and put the children to bed, as he had been doing most nights in these late weeks of her pregnancy. Then the two of them went to bed—James to sleep peacefully and Annah to plan her life with Diana.

She awoke James early to tell him it was time.

"Our daughter is coming on a Sunday," he exclaimed. "A double blessing." A neighbor drove them to the hospital, where Annah was immediately put in a wheelchair and taken to the labor room. The attendants helped her into a crisp, clean bed, and a nurse came and checked her pulse and blood pressure. James joined her, and the two of them worked through her contractions, doing the breathing exercises they had learned.

Diana Atai Emuge arrived at ten o'clock on Sunday, April 16, 1984, to meet her smiling parents. Holding the tiny child to her breast, Annah turned to her husband and said, "This barely hurt, James. It was fun!"

"You've come a long way from that trek across the school field, my wife," he laughed, holding them both in his strong arms. "And you, my American daughter, have a long way to go!"

Chapter 16

SOMETIMES DURING THAT SPRING, Annah felt almost as if she were still in her mud home in Olio. Neighbors, other graduate students' wives, and even professors' wives came by constantly to bring her food and to help with the children, just as their Ugandan neighbors and friends had when Gilbert was born. But when James came home she felt wholly American again. He loved to help with the house and the children, even changing Diana's diapers. With all this attention, Annah regained her strength quickly and Diana thrived. James led the family daily in Bible reading and prayers to God, and his prayers always began with thanks for their blessings and ended with a plea for continued protection of his family. Annah added her silent thanks as well, while she dreamed happily of bringing many more children into this loving environment.

Summer arrived with more good news: James's grades had been excellent, he needed to take only one course during the summer quarter, and he had gotten a summer job cleaning and prepping classrooms since teaching assistantships didn't run through the summer quarter. With so much extra time together, the family became a familiar sight on the streets between their apartment and the playground. Gilbert and Ruby rode their tricycles while James proudly pushed the baby carriage. Annah walked along, savoring the sun's warmth on her skin, and thought about how much her life had changed. She no longer had to worry about finding enough water in dry seasons, nursing along enough of a fire to cook their meals in rainy seasons, or finding enough food to last through all seasons. Sometimes, as she walked along the sidewalk on the Athens streets, she would pace out a rhythm by reciting all that she wanted never to do again: digging, planting, weeding, picking, pounding, grinding, making do with nothing. The lists would go on and on, but they always ended with hiding.

In midsummer, James announced that he had found an old but reliable car to buy from a graduate who was leaving the area.

"James, we don't know how to drive!" Annah exclaimed. "You had a driver in Masindi, and I certainly never learned."

"Oh, it can't be that hard, Frances," he laughed. "I'll have some friends from school show me."

About a week later, James arrived home one evening and told the family to come outside. They found a red Chevy Nova parked on the street.

"It's ours," James said. "Do you want to go for a ride?" The children began clapping and ran toward the car.

"It's too late tonight, children," Annah said immediately. "I have to get Diana into bed, and you should be there, too." Annah managed to avoid riding in the car for a few days, but when grocery-shopping day came, James announced that they would all go—in the car. Annah got Gilbert and Ruby settled in the backseat and reluctantly climbed into the front passenger's side with Diana. James started the car and then reached over and patted her leg.

"Calm down. I won't hurt you," he said gaily, but Annah held Diana tightly with one hand while the other gripped the armrest the whole way to and from the store. It was many weeks before she got the least bit comfortable riding with James, but the children begged to ride along whenever Daddy went somewhere.

The summer was almost perfect, except that communication from home lessened. Annah sent frequent letters to her family and to Lucy, always with photos of the children, but her eager check of the mailbox each day was fruitless more and more often as the days wore on. James and Annah were able to get some news of the political climate in Uganda, but it wasn't good: Obote continued to lose power, and the terrorizing of villagers, especially in the north, was on the rise. Their joy in their own situation was strained by worry about loved ones at home.

When the fall quarter arrived, James received the news that the university would only be able to grant him a part-time teaching assistantship. Then one day early in the semester, James came home and told Annah that his stipend hadn't arrived from Uganda. University officials had assured James that they would continue his scholarship for tuition, but they had also stressed that they couldn't provide living expenses. James's student visa could be revoked if he couldn't prove that he could support himself while attending college. At the urging of a counselor in the university's Immigration Department, James contacted the Ugandan Embassy in Washington, DC, and the ambassador there investigated the problem.

Finally, a month into the quarter, the ambassador sent money to them, but it was less than the previous year and they were already struggling to get by.

It soon became clear that they couldn't afford to stay in the International Student Housing. James found an arrangement that was basically a house rented by two students who were looking for a third to occupy an empty bedroom. Annah wasn't troubled by having to sleep in one room with the children—she had never pictured her life otherwise until they left Uganda—but sharing the cooking and living space with two more adults wasn't easy. By Thanksgiving, with the worry of a collapse in Uganda becoming more and more real, James had decided he needed to have a backup plan to take care of them if the stipend stopped completely. He traveled to Washington, DC, where he had learned that a friend from Uganda was living. The friend worked at the embassy, but there were no jobs there, and it soon became clear to James that he would have to take a menial job just to get by, even in this vast city. He returned home with the news that his friend had offered them a place to stay if they needed it, but Annah could see that the trip had depressed him.

"James, what is it?" she finally asked that evening in bed. "I can see you're worried."

"I looked at jobs while I was there, Frances," he told her quietly. "There's nothing at the embassy, and all that really seems possible is for me to work in a gas station or a restaurant, because of our status at immigration. The U.S. won't give me more than a three-month work permit, and no school or professional employer will take a chance that I'll be able to stay. Frances, I am a teacher!" Annah heard the desperation in his voice, so she hugged him tightly.

"James, you once said that we could face anything as long as we are together, and you were right. We will work it out, you and I." She could feel him relax a little and she rubbed his back until he was sleeping, but the worries stayed with both of them through that winter.

The family was fortunate to be able to spend Christmas Day with a professor's family, so the kids had presents to unwrap and toys to play with, but it was a sad holiday for Annah and James. The next day, James left for Columbus to see if he could find a job for the summer there, since there would be so many students looking for summer jobs in Athens. He came back to report that the immigration office there allowed him to apply for a summer work permit, and he thought he could get a menial job pretty easily.

James earned his master's degree at the end of the winter quarter, but neither of them saw much reason to celebrate. He began tackling his PhD course load that spring, and he and Annah continued to worry about money, and Uganda. The children were their main source of solace and strength. Each night, James would come in and kiss each child, even if they were already in bed. Annah continued taking one course each quarter, and James faithfully took care of the kids while she studied, but his eagerness to share his new knowledge with her waned, and she found herself missing the old James at times.

By summer, both James and Annah had been able to obtain summer work permits, but there were no jobs to be found. James finally went to work in a Subway sandwich shop in Columbus, so he would work for five days and then come home every weekend or two. Annah and the children were lonely during the week, and the weekends never seemed long enough, but they all coped as best they could. Now that they weren't living in the international student community, all of their neighbors were white, but the children always welcomed her two into their games, and Annah became friends with some of the mothers on their block.

One hot Saturday late in July, 1985, James and Annah were watching the news on television after supper while the children played outside in the yard. Suddenly, James sat up and turned up the volume. Amidst camera footage of black soldiers running and waving their weapons, the announcer was saying that Milton Obote had been overthrown by his military officers. Annah and James sat in disbelief as the announcer described the scene in Kampala: soldiers everywhere, citizens hiding in their homes, gunfire and looting going on.

"James, what will we do—your classes start in two weeks!" Annah cried.

"I don't know, Frances. I just don't know." They roused themselves and got the kids inside, washed, and to bed, and then the two of them lay down. Normally, Annah was comforted by the rhythmic breathing of the children who lay untroubled in their beds, but now that sound only frightened her more, as she fought off images of having to take them back to Uganda amidst all the turmoil there. A vision of the countryside around Olio came to her mind, and she suddenly felt some calming, as she thought of their first years of hiding, when James's strong voice beside her seemed to be a barrier between them and the soldiers and the mayhem they could bring.

"James, please pray to God for us," she whispered, just wanting to hear that voice.

"Lord, you have given us so much." He seemed tentative at first, but his voice strengthened as he spoke, and Annah felt the tension drain from her like an ebbing tide. This is the man who became the moon in my sky, she thought. He is my anchor to God, who will surely help us now.

In the weeks following the news that Obote had been overthrown, James and Annah tried without success to get word of their families. James began classes, and his advisor assured him the scholarship was still there, as long as he could get his living expenses from Uganda. After several frantic calls from James, the ambassador wrote a letter to the university stating that he wasn't sure how long the turmoil in Uganda would last, but that the payments would assuredly resume once peace reigned. The university accepted this answer, but for Annah and James, it felt like waiting for the gun at their backs to go off. When had Uganda ever recovered quickly from outbreaks of violence?

As the quarter went on, James stopped coming home for lunch, and then he began arriving later and later in the evenings. Annah was stretching the little money they had saved from the summer as best she could, but she began to recognize in her children the look she had seen in her sisters and brothers when the rains hadn't come yet and the stored grains were dwindling. On many nights she knew she put them to bed hungry, and all she could do was sing songs from her childhood until they fell into fitful sleep. She yearned to talk to James about their plight, but it was often 1:00 a.m. or later before he would tiptoe in and quickly climb into bed. Sometimes she waited, and when she felt the mattress sag under his weight she would reach a hand out to him, but his back was always toward her.

"James, what is it?" she asked on many nights, but he said nothing.

Somehow Annah managed to keep the family from getting sick in spite of their limited food, and the children were growing and happy. Gilbert had started school, so Annah spent her days with the girls and then walked them to the bus stop to greet their brother each afternoon. Dinners were quiet and the evening stretched longer and longer, but she played with the children and kept their spirits up.

"Where's Daddy?" Gilbert would often ask.

"He's working, Gilbert. He has to work very hard to take care of us," she would always answer, glad that he didn't understand the longing in her voice.

James became quieter as their money shrank and their worries increased, but somehow he managed to keep his grades at an excellent level. Their salvation that winter was that an immigration officer on campus had advised James that they should apply for political asylum, because of the strife in their homeland. That action would place them in a status that would qualify them for food stamps. They made it through the holidays, with help from the professors, and James took on the battle once again to convince the university that his stipend would arrive any time. The ambassador wrote that he concurred with this judgment, so James's scholarship was renewed.

Then, on a cold Wednesday in January, Annah heard on the news that the military junta leading Uganda's government had been overthrown by Yoweri Museveni. Her heart felt like lead as she dialed the phone to call James in his office. Luckily, he was there.

"What is it?" he asked sharply when he heard her trembling voice.

"Museveni," was all she managed to say.

"I'll be right home," he said, and she heard the phone click before she could even reply.

When James walked in the door, they just stood, clinging to each other. Annah could feel James's heart pounding, and she knew hers was answering it, beat for beat.

"James, our families," Annah finally said.

"I know, Frances. I know," he answered in a hoarse voice. Museveni, a Bantu, and his followers were from southern tribes, and they hated all the northern tribes—especially the Iteso. Christopher, Esther, Lucy—all of them were in mortal danger.

Over the next few days their fears were confirmed by the news reports. Hundreds of thousands of northern Ugandans were being killed or run from their homes. Villages were being burned to the ground. James found someone at the Red Cross and explained their concerns, and the person said she would investigate and let him know. He came home a few days later and told Annah that the woman had said they didn't have anyone on the ground in Agu or Amuria, but they had received reports that both villages, and the people in them, were gone. There were refugees running toward Gulu, in the west, she told him. "If they're strong, your family members could be headed there."

How strong were Lucy, Christopher, and Esther, Annah wondered. She recalled images of her mother—toiling in the fields, carrying water on her head with twins tied to her breast, beating the cassava into the family's meal of porridge—but how would Toto cope with being driven from her village, the only home she had ever known? Annah recalled the lost, extinguished look that Lucy had worn for more than a year after Jesse's death. Could this woman rally yet again from life's blows?

When Annah tried to voice her fears to James, he just shook his head and stopped talking to her. Soon, silence was what the whole family came to expect from him. He began staying later and later at school, but then one day just before the quarter's end he came home at lunchtime. He sat down with Annah in the kitchen, and she told the girls to play in the living room while she and Daddy talked.

"Frances, you know we haven't been paying all the rent," he began, and her blood ran cold. "The landlord said he wouldn't throw us out, but we have to either pay or move. I've talked to my advisor, and he says my scholarship will wait for me, if I leave for a while."

"Leave! But James, leave for where? What do you mean?" He held up a hand and she let him continue talking.

"With this quarter, I'm finishing my course work, so all I have left is to write my dissertation and take my orals. But we have no money, and you know there won't be any from Uganda. It's time for my backup plan. My friend in Washington said I can go and stay with him and find a job."

"But what do we do—the children and I?" she asked, waving weakly toward the living room and fighting to keep the panic out of her voice so the girls wouldn't hear.

"I need to earn enough money to pay our back rent and give us something to live on while I finish," he said. "Then I should be able to qualify for a permanent work visa and we'll be fine. But you can't stay here long—I'll go and make sure I can get work and then you'll join me." Annah felt strangely buoyed by this news. For a few crazy moments she had thought he was telling her he was leaving them entirely.

"James, we'll do whatever is needed. But we always said we would face these things together." He just stared at her for a few minutes, and she realized how old he looked, and worn out.

"I'll send for you soon, Frances. I will."

James left the day after his last final and called her from Washington that evening. Within a few days he reported that he had a job, at a 7-Eleven store, and so they planned that he would come to get the family in four weeks, after he had saved enough money for the gas and food. Annah packed up their most vital belongings and gave the rest away to student friends. When James arrived in the Nova, the things she had put together fit easily into the trunk. They drove out of Athens the next morning. James was patiently trying to answer the barrage of questions about their new home that came from the backseat. Annah stared out the window at the countryside that had reminded her of Uganda, wondering if she would ever see either place again.

Chapter 17

ONCE, WHEN THE RIVER NEAR Agu had dried to a shiny, cracked flat of mud, and all the nearby wells had run dry, Annah and her mother and sisters were walking through the breaking dawn with the jugs of precious water that they had found miles from home. Suddenly, Rebecca, who was about eight, sat down on the path.

"I can't go any farther," she announced flatly. "My legs won't do it." Without even thinking, Annah bent down to pick up Rebecca's jar. Toto walked over to them and pulled the little girl up onto her back. Rebecca clasped her arms around Toto's neck as Annah, Magdalene, and Toto resumed the journey.

"Annah, are you sure you can carry her jug? I don't need two of you who can't walk."

"Of course I can, Toto," Annah replied quickly. "I won't get tired. I have long legs and I'm strong from running to school every day." Toto looked at Annah with a kind smile and a gleam in her eye.

"It's more than just your legs that are strong, my girl," she said gently. "You have a strong spirit. You will do great things one day—I just know it." Annah had walked on in silence that day, feeling proud but a little scared. What could Toto have meant? What kind of greatness is asked of a girl from a tiny African village?

Annah thought about that morning from so long ago as she rode out of Ohio with her family. Her husband, one of the best teachers in all of Uganda, a man with an American master's degree in education, was taking them to Washington, DC, so he could work as a clerk in a convenience store. As the countryside rolled past the car window, Annah realized she was thankful that Toto couldn't see them now. This was certainly no longer the big, wonderful world that Toto had worked so hard to prepare her daughter for.

The late afternoon sun stayed mostly behind the tall buildings as James drove the family into Washington, making Annah feel more closed in with every new street they turned into. James's Ugandan friends Grace and Stephen welcomed them into their small home. Grace and her three children took Annah to the bedroom where the five of them would sleep, while Stephen sat with James in the living room. As Annah put away the few sets of clothes she had for the children, she could hear the low murmur of the men's voices, punctuated often by rumbling, relaxed laughter. Maybe this place will be good for him, she thought. Maybe this is what he has needed.

The very next day, after he had finished his shift at the 7-Eleven, James drove her to several fast-food places to apply for work. McDonald's called Annah the following day and she began work immediately. They arranged their schedules so that James could work during the day, then come home in the afternoon and drive Annah to work for her evening shift. She found the work easy—she started as a dishwasher but was quickly moved to food preparation. Annah was amused by her boss's pleasure at how fast she worked. Toto had taught her daughter well, she thought. She grinned proudly when she handed her first paycheck to James. Surely they would have enough money to return to Ohio soon, and all this would be behind them.

Soon after the family had arrived, Stephen had helped James and Annah connect with a free legal service for immigrants. A friendly woman lawyer took on their application for political asylum and began collecting the necessary information. Annah was perplexed by the lawyer's explanation that this would be a long process of filing forms, answering queries, and attending hearings. How could it be so complicated? She and James were Iteso; Museveni, a Bantu, was in power. No Ugandan would question the inherent risk in that equation. She wished she could take the lawyer back to their apartment in Kampala, when their being Iteso had been enough reason for the Bantu soldier to place a gun to the side of Annah's head.

In spite of her worries—about how, or if, their families were surviving in Uganda; about getting asylum so that James could get a real job; about getting them back to Ohio to fulfill their dreams—Annah enjoyed the family routine in Washington. She liked feeling productive and needed at work, and she loved how she would arrive home to find the kids sleeping peacefully, having been tucked in by their daddy. Her only regret was that both she and James had been hired based on their willingness to work on weekends. Neither of them realized that this meant they would work every weekend, so that the family couldn't attend church together. Annah continued to offer prayers to God, thanking him for her family and their safety, but she noticed that James spent almost no time reading the Bible, and God just didn't seem to enter into his thinking anymore.

One evening, Annah walked out with her boss as she locked the door to the McDonald's. They said good night and Annah stood on the sidewalk under the darkened golden arches, waiting for James to pick her up. She peered up into the sky, where she could barely make out the pale form of the half moon. She couldn't see any stars around it—the lights of the city formed a thick blanket between her and the sky. The moon seemed almost menacing as it hung there, aloof and alone. Annah was frightened at first when a strange car pulled up next to her, but she quickly realized it was Grace and Stephen's car. Puzzled, she got into the front, next to Stephen. James was sitting in the backseat, staring out the window on the other side of the car.

"Is our car broken?" she asked, turning to James. But he didn't answer her and Stephen remained silent. Neither spoke on the way home.

Once there, Annah waited for James to finish his shower so she could talk to him, but he went directly to bed and fell asleep. She didn't go in and try to make him talk to her for fear of waking the children. A few days later, Grace asked Annah to come out into the yard so they could talk away from the children.

"Annah," she said, "I think you need to know that Stephen had just picked James up from jail when they came to get you the other night."

"Jail—but why?" Annah's stomach tightened harder than it had since she'd lived in Uganda.

"You didn't smell the alcohol on him?" Grace sounded incredulous.

"No, I didn't," she said. "But how did that get him in jail?"

"He was pulled over for driving drunk, Annah. They towed the car."

Annah stared at Grace, but she couldn't say any of the things that were running through her mind: This can't be—our religion doesn't allow drinking. The man I married is too strong and too intelligent to become a drinker. James cares too much about our family to do this. We are supposed to face life's challenges together; how does he think *I* am surviving this? I've known for months that something was happening to him. James Emuge, my friend, my religious guide, my mentor, the father of my children, my husband—the moon in my sky—is a drinker.

Annah's realization that she was caught in a downward spiral with James didn't lessen the pain and shock of each new setback. Women in her world didn't question their husbands, but she finally got the courage to ask how their savings plan was going, only to have him walk out the door and refuse to speak to her for days. Thinking of the gourd full of money that Toto kept under the dirt in their hut, Annah began keeping her paychecks. She thought she was creating their savings for a new start at Ohio University, only to be told by Stephen and Grace that James hadn't been paying them for the family's share of groceries. Stephen looked uncomfortable discussing this with Annah, but then he cleared his throat and said that they should look for someplace else to live. James began looking for apartments to rent, but at each place he was told they didn't have enough income. Annah knew not to question James, but it was apparent now that he wasn't able to declare any income at all, that he was no longer working. No one would rent to them on her McDonald's salary.

When Grace gave them a week to pay what they owed or leave, James waited until a day when Stephen and Grace were at work and directed Annah to pack the family up so they could leave. Her face burning with shame, Annah put their things into the car and got the three kids settled in the backseat. James drove them around for several hours and ended up in Fairfax, Virginia, where he pulled into the littered parking lot of a dingy motel.

James went into the office and then came and told Annah and the kids to follow him and the motel manager. They entered a unit that had a main room with a kitchenette in one corner and a bedroom in the back.

"What are we doing here, James?" Annah asked warily.

"This is where we live," he said in a voice that told her she shouldn't argue. "There's no deposit, so just write a check for the first month's rent. It's $700." Annah was surprised that he knew she had an account, but she had only $800 in it, and they were now over forty-five minutes by car from her job at McDonald's. She opened her mouth to ask James how this could possibly work, but he cut her off tersely.

"Pay this man or we're in the street, Frances."

Annah made the best of their cramped home, fortunate not to know that this wouldn't be their worst situation in the coming years. The manager at her McDonald's had never complained that she had to update her work permit every three months, but Annah knew this could be a barrier to getting hired elsewhere. Her manager helped facilitate a transfer to a McDonald's just four miles from the motel so that she could walk to work on the days James failed to come home to give her a ride. She still worked evenings, so she would put out some bowls of food for dinner and leave the kids on the fold-out bed in the main room, watching television. A woman in a room down the way looked in on them regularly, and the kids got used to falling asleep in front of the TV. Annah carried them to their beds when she got in.

This was the beginning of the pattern that was to be their family routine: James became more distant and would be absent for days at a time. Annah overcame each obstacle, always keeping the family just above the surface of the water that seemed to be drowning James. Then a glimmer of hope would open when James would seem to come back to himself for a few weeks. This happened in the spring, when Annah's boss asked if she could recommend anyone who would work as hard as she, and she suggested that James go for an interview. He impressed the boss and was made a day manager, and for two months they were a family again. Annah's spirits lifted and she began to plan their return to Ohio, but then James disappeared again, got fired from his job, and became a distant occasional visitor who scared the children and demoralized her with his surly silences.

In late summer of that year, 1986, as Annah was working out how to get Gilbert to and from the school-bus stop, she realized she was pregnant. When she was able to tell James, on a rare day when he was home and seemed sober, he just stared at her and then left the motel in silence. Annah cried herself to sleep that night, thinking about how *he* had actually told *her* when she was pregnant with Gilbert, and how joyfully they had embraced that news.

Throughout the next six months, while a new person grew inside her, Annah faced the fact that the husband she knew and loved was slowly disappearing. Even when she found a church and convinced James to join the family in Sunday worship, she could see that he was there in body only. Where was the spirit of this wonderful, holy man? How could the man who brought Jesus Christ into Annah's heart sit like a stone in the house of their Lord?

As she entered her third trimester, Annah discovered that James had found her checkbook in the drawer and written himself checks, forging her name. When she attempted to pay the March rent, she learned that he had drained the account. Two weeks later, the family was evicted from the motel. They were able to stay in quarters that their church kept for visiting missionaries for a few days, and then they went into a government-run transitional housing shelter, where they would be allowed to live for ninety days. Annah was forced to confront the reality that her family had become homeless. Thinking about how her parents and she had helped the orphaned children when the family had barely enough food for themselves, Annah felt physical pain over her separation from her family in Uganda. "Toto, I need you," she would cry as she lay unsleeping on so many nights. But no letters had come from Uganda for over a year now, and newspapers continued to report the atrocities being inflicted on the Iteso people.

Annah had been unable to continue her job because of all the standing and walking, but James was now following the rules of the housing contract and looking for work. Their building contained several homeless families and was overseen by a social worker who assisted the residents in getting their lives together. The doors were kept locked and it was made clear that no resident would be admitted drunk, so James was staying sober more often. Sometimes he sat and read with the children before bed, but Annah was troubled by the lack of prayers in the household. When she asked James if he wanted to pray or read the Bible with them, he just changed the subject.

Brian was born on April 12, 1987. James was home when Annah went into labor, and he drove the whole family to the hospital and waited with the kids until Brian arrived. Annah had hoped to have a brother for Gilbert, so she was grateful for this second son. When the doctor held him up for her to see his tiny face, Annah took in a sharp breath. Those were James's eyes looking steadily at her. This tiny creature was the image of his father. Surely he would move James to return to his family once and for all.

But the pattern continued. James stayed for a week and then was gone again. Annah began looking for a job for herself, but the social worker in the building advised her that she would be better off staying with the children since she couldn't afford to pay for babysitters and she didn't qualify for food stamps or public assistance because of her continued lack of immigration status. There was truly nothing for her to do but stay in this shelter and hope that James could collect himself and support them. Sometimes Annah would begin to ache from the desire to just go home and then realize with a start that there was no home to go to. James, and maybe she, would be jailed immediately since he had been a favored official in Obote's education ministry, they had no villages to return to and no reason to think there would be family to take them in, and they had no money for travel. At times like these, Annah couldn't even think about how she was shaming Toto and Papa, who supported their family alone no matter what the hardships. But she took strength from the faces of her children—humiliation was the least of what she could endure for them.

As the time was running out on their ninety-day eligibility for housing, James had managed to keep a job at a restaurant for several weeks. He found them a small apartment in Fairfax and they settled in. Brian was a healthy, cheerful baby who seemed unaffected by the stresses the family endured, but Diana was a quiet, intense two-year-old who seemed to be able to feel Annah's emotions without any verbal communication. When they moved to each new place, she cried herself to sleep while Annah held her and whispered promises that Mommy would always be there, knowing she was leaving out what Diana and all the children really needed to hear.

Just after the move, their lawyer sent word that she had been able to submit the application for asylum. While this meant more waiting and uncertainty, it also meant that both she and James would now qualify for six-month work permits and that the family could receive food stamps. They had a summer of relative calm, with sunny days spent in the park, and James home on many weekend evenings, playing ball with the children. In the fall, Annah found a job cleaning medical office buildings, and James got work assisting with basic English and math training at a technical college for medical professions. Annah knew better than to hope, but still she often found herself smiling and humming as she prepared dinner and listened to James entertaining the children with stories.

Annah had two children to get ready for school that year, and she was able to get Brian and Diana into subsidized daycare. The children adapted to their schedules well, and the family got through the cold and other weather challenges of winter, but then in early spring James suddenly lost his job and became an erratic figure in their lives again. Annah developed a routine of taking a city bus to daycare with the little ones, returning home to get her older children to the bus stop, and then running the four miles to work, because no bus line ran to the office building. Her day began at 5:00 a.m., and she would arrive at work tired and stressed from all she had already accomplished. She was reminded of the days in Agu when she and her sisters and Toto would walk miles for water before making breakfast and then she would run to school. On rainy days, she was reminded even more strongly of her dashes to school, and ached for those carefree days. Still, she thanked God for her healthy family, and for her long, strong legs that never failed her.

Once, when James was home and fairly sober, she asked him to talk to her.

"James, I just don't understand why you drink," she told him, praying he wouldn't shut her out again. He looked at her for a long time and tears welled up in his eyes.

"Frances, I just can't stop thinking about all this failure," he whispered at last. "Failure to support my family, to take care of my mother at home, to get my PhD, to get us back to the life we dreamed of in Uganda—me as education minister and you working as a nurse and raising our children."

"But James, drinking doesn't help with any of this."

"No, but for a while it makes me forget."

"James, look at me," Annah said, tilting his face up. "We need you, the children and I. We need your strength, and your spirituality, and your wisdom. I will work three jobs if I have to, if you could just stop drinking. We need the real you."

"Oh, Frances!" he cried. "I can't bear to think of you working and running so hard. I don't know how you do it, but I can't be like you. I just can't. I get so lonely and depressed."

"James, I'm tired and frightened, too. But I always remember that we said the whole family would come here and face everything together. James, have you forgotten that? I need you."

"Frances, why don't you drink a little wine with me? You'll see—it helps. It really does." With a cold, hard stone in her stomach, Annah took James into her arms.

"I just can't do that, James. But I will keep trying to help you stop, and I will keep us together forever. We'll be OK, James. We will." Then Annah just held him, not expecting any promises from him in return.

One summer day, as Annah was running to work after getting the children to summer camp and daycare, she became aware of birds chirping in the trees overhead, and she began rejoicing in the beautiful day. James had been gone for a whole week this time, but now she only had thoughts for what she knew she could control. She thanked God for her children and for her health, and then she realized she now often left James out of her prayers of thanksgiving.

"God, how do I thank you for my husband, the head of my family, the father of my faith and my children, the moon in my sky, when he is a drunk and a derelict?" She began to weep the familiar, bitter tears over her situation, but then something stopped her. She looked up into the blue, cloudless sky, and her crying stopped.

"God," she prayed, "I am here in this country that is not mine and doesn't want me. All I have is James and my children. But James is gone and I am tired—tired and beat up. Giving up is not an option. So, God, please protect me. Be my husband; be the father to my children. You gave them to me, so now you must protect them." She wiped her tears and ran the rest of the way to work.

On her way home that day, Annah was enjoying the beautiful weather and smiling. Suddenly, she knew she must leave Virginia. God is telling me to return to Athens, she thought. He will help me do it. On that day she began planning and saving, determined to get James back to Ohio University and the family to Athens.

The next time James showed up at home, she managed to get him to talk to her.

"James, I want us to go back to Athens. It's just no good for us here."

"I've been thinking that, too, Frances."

"Good, then get a job to help us save and we'll go this fall." James contacted the university and was told his scholarship was still available, if he could support himself. He reported this to Annah, and they began to work toward their trip.

James didn't succeed in staying sober, but Annah never wavered. One day in August, when she felt she had enough money to get them started, she waited until James came home and told him they would leave the next day for Athens. He looked shocked, but then grinned at her.

"We will," he said. The next morning the family put their clothing into the car and James drove them out of Fairfax, heading west. They left everything else—dishes, books, their meager furniture, Annah's job—behind them. Annah prayed as they drove that they were leaving James's drinking behind them as well.

Chapter 18

ANNAH HAD NO BASIS for comprehending the devastation that James's alcoholism would wreak, on him and on their family. In Agu the men traditionally drank home-brewed beer in the evenings, and she and all the other children would beg their fathers for the one sip allowed them each night. There was a man in a nearby compound, Michael, who would sometimes get too drunk from the beer and go home and beat his wife. This behavior was abhorred by the community, and the following morning Michael's wife, Sarah, would come with her children to ask the village elders for justice. For much of Annah's childhood, her papa was the most revered elder, so she would see the family coming into the compound. Sarah and the children all looked sad and ashamed. Annah didn't know much about village justice, but the elders would then call Michael before them, and things would be quiet in his compound for several weeks before the incident repeated itself.

When Annah questioned Toto about the family, she was told to keep her nose out of other people's business. But frequently Toto would wrap some millet flour in a cloth and give it to Annah with a gourd filled with milk and instruct her to take it to Sarah's family.

"Don't give this to Michael—make sure Sarah gets it," she would tell Annah sternly, "and mind your manners." Annah's recollection of those days was that there were always several other women in the compound, helping Sarah with her chores and giving extra attention to the children while casting disapproving looks toward Michael whenever he dared to walk past them.

But as her family drove into Athens that day, Annah's mind was only on the joyful prospect of resuming their old life, with James at the university and her tending to their children. They stayed in university housing for a week before moving to an apartment, and James began his studies along with a new job as a teaching assistant in the African Studies Department. Annah reveled in her days then—walking the children to the bus stop, playing in the park with

Diana and Brian, and greeting James when he returned from his day's work. This time, it lasted almost three months, long enough for Annah to begin to believe that James had truly changed.

James's pay didn't cover the full rent, so their money dwindled rapidly. Annah couldn't find work at any fast-food restaurants, in spite of her references from Virginia. By October, James was coming home later and later, creeping silently to bed when he arrived. One day in late November, James hadn't come home yet and there was an unusually early snow falling outside. Annah worried about James driving in the snow, so she waited up. Around midnight, she went to look out the front door and found James lying in the grass, face down. Annah's heart seemed to stop, and then she was kneeling beside him, shouting his name and running her hands over his face and neck to see if he was alive. He was bruised and he smelled of alcohol and vomit, but he was breathing.

"No, James. No!" she was screaming as she dragged him into the apartment. With strength she didn't know she had, she pushed and rolled him onto their bed. After watching him for a moment, Annah went to the closet and pulled out an old, battered suitcase. She stuffed some of her clothes into it, snapped the latches shut, and strode out the door. When the cold air hit her, she paused and realized that the suitcase was too heavy for her to carry very far, so she left it on the porch and walked out into the night.

Annah had walked several blocks before she began to register what she was doing. She had just left her four children in that apartment. Suddenly, she was a child again, standing at the edge of the compound in Agu, searching the horizon for her toto, willing her to come back and make the family whole again. But she wasn't a child; she was the mother now, and she was utterly alone, in Athens, Ohio. In the still night she was sure she could hear her children calling to her.

"But I can't make my family whole," Annah said into the thick, snowy air. "Oh, Toto, can't you come to me now?"

"Annah, turn around. Go back to your children." The strong voice seemed to come from nowhere and everywhere. Annah knew it was God, and she obeyed, her heart heavy but determined. When she entered the house, her three older children were huddled on the bed next to James's sleeping form.

"Mommy, where were you? I was calling you," Gilbert said.

"I just went out to get a little air, Gilbert. Everything's fine, but you need to be asleep." She carried the children back to their beds and then she lay down beside her husband and slept, knowing that somehow God would lead her through this.

The next months followed what was becoming a familiar pattern for Annah. They ran out of money, James lost his teaching-assistant job and failed to progress with his PhD, Annah struggled to keep the kids in their routines of school and play without letting them see her worries. James went back to looking for fast-food restaurant jobs, but those were just nonexistent in such a small college town. James began contacting friends in Columbus about finding work, and the family moved there in midwinter. He went to work in a Subway and Annah found a job at a McDonald's. James continued drinking but managed to hold onto the job through April. One night, a man robbed the Subway, holding a gun on James. Annah couldn't imagine how awful it had been for him to face a gun here, in the country they had thought would protect them from violence. She waited for him to fall apart, but instead he came home one morning a few days later and told Annah they were moving to St. Louis, Missouri.

Once they were in the car, Annah asked him what was happening and he told her he had applied for a job at St. Louis University doing research in the same field as his PhD project, so he would be able to work there and complete his dissertation. She felt a painful tightening in her stomach and realized that it was simply a nugget of hope. How had her life changed so much that she was afraid to hope? She realized that it was James she no longer fully trusted, although she knew she could still trust God.

But then, James had come home clean and apparently sober this time, so maybe things would be different. The family settled in for the long drive, and she and James told the kids about the landscape features that reminded them of Uganda. Just after noon, they began crossing the enormous bridge across the Mississippi River. Annah looked down on the wide, placid body of brown water with amazement. It was nothing like what she had imagined as a school child when they studied "the mighty Mississippi." She had pictured white, sparkling rapids and enormous boats surging down a tree-lined river. The dark water beneath them just rolled steadily past banks filled with industrial buildings of all sizes and shapes. From their vantage point above the river, the boats at rest along the shore looked small and insignificant.

"Mommy, look at the silver rainbow!" one of the children shouted from the backseat. Annah looked and saw an enormous arch rising from the ground on the far bank of the river. Reflections of the sky's blue and the river's brown glimmered in its surface.

"I see it," she said. "James, is this St. Louis? What is that thing?"

"It is St. Louis," he answered, a note of pride in his voice. "I don't know what that is, but I'm sure we'll find out once we live here."

"We're going to live under a rainbow! We're going to live under a rainbow!" the three older children chanted while one-year-old Brian squealed. James steered the car off the highway and began driving down streets lined with brick and wood houses, many of which had boards across their windows and weeds in their tiny yards. It seemed to Annah that they had come to a place just like the worst areas of Washington, DC. James stopped the car outside a store and said he would be right back. Annah could see him inside, on a pay phone.

"James, where are we?" she asked when he returned.

"We were lost, but I know where to go now." He drove back through the grimy neighborhoods and she waited for the houses to begin looking better. But he stopped the car at an old, shabby three-story house that had a sign that read "Larry Rice Evangelistic Center" in front of it.

When they walked through the door, they entered a large room with chairs against the walls and a stained brown rug in the center. There were several men and a few families sitting there, and they all glanced listlessly toward the new arrivals and then away. The girls took hold of Annah's skirt, and Gilbert edged closer to her.

"James, what are we doing here?" she hissed. But a well-dressed man had just entered the room from a door in the back, and James stepped quickly to him and pulled him as far away from Annah as he could get while they spoke briefly. Then James went to the front door and motioned for the family to follow him back to the car. As soon as they were all in, Annah turned to James.

"Please tell me that my children and I are not sleeping in that place tonight. It looks like a homeless shelter."

"That man is going to find us a place, Frances. Just be patient." He began driving down the street, and Annah stared miserably out the window. The scenes they passed—men in filthy clothes loitering around shops or sitting dejectedly against buildings—made her think of Soroti and Olio during the reign of Idi Amin. The men all looked so sad and hopeless.

The family did end up in a shelter, but it was specifically for families and looked a little better than the one where they first stopped. When Annah asked James why he had brought them there, he replied that he knew she wouldn't have agreed to come to Missouri if she'd known he had no place for them to stay.

The routine began again: Annah got a job at a McDonald's and James went to work in a Subway. After a few weeks, they were able to move to an apartment near St. Louis University, but Annah could see immediately that the neighborhood was going to be a problem. It was a slum, just like the ones in Washington; as they drove down the streets, dejected-looking black people stared at them warily. When they had been there just a few days, Annah sent the older kids to play in the yard while she kept an eye on them from the window. Suddenly she heard shouting from the yard, and she looked out to see three boys punching and kicking Gilbert. His sisters were screaming as they watched from a few feet away. Gilbert was a tall nine-year-old, but these boys were bigger and clearly older. She raced down to the yard and was shocked to find two mothers from the building sitting in yard chairs watching the fight. She got Gilbert away from the boys and sent the kids upstairs.

"Why didn't you stop that?" she asked the two women. "They were hurting my son."

"Fucking Africans," one woman said, and she and her friend bent their heads together, laughing shrilly.

On the Fourth of July, there were children and adults setting off firecrackers in the apartment yard, so Annah and James kept the kids upstairs. Just after they had gone to bed, Annah and James awoke to the smell of smoke. James ran to open the door and caught a glimpse of two boys running down the stairs. He ran after them while Annah opened all the windows. A smoldering firecracker lay near the door, where it had been pushed in through a crack.

Outside, the children were already down the street, so James asked the neighbor women sitting on the front stoop what had happened.

"What do you mean, African?" they laughed.

James walked down the street and found a police car. When the policeman came to the apartment, Annah showed him the fire-cracker that she had put in the sink and extinguished.

"We'll keep an eye on things," the officer said. "Keep the doors locked." Annah and James just looked at each other. They watched from the window as the policeman stopped on the front stoop and asked the women there if they knew anything about the incident.

"I don't know what those crazy Africans are talking about," one woman said loudly. The women all laughed as the officer went back to his car. The police car remained in front of the apartment, and the women below complained loudly about the Africans getting them all in trouble.

James started his university work and studies in the fall, while the three oldest children attended the same school. Diana was in kindergarten, Ruby was in second grade, and Gilbert was in fourth grade. By that time, Annah and the children were in the habit of hiding in the apartment whenever they were home, and she and James arranged their schedules so that one of them always walked the children to and from school. When James couldn't stay with Brian, Annah found a neighbor who would watch him. This woman had five children of her own and was happy enough to get paid for babysitting, but Annah hated sending him there—the house was full of cigarette smoke and she knew Brian got almost no attention. Although Annah tried not to bother James so that he could concentrate on his work, she knew that he could see the strain of worry and fear in her and the children because of their apartment. James spoke to the landlord, who said that he owned other places and might be able to move them when an opening came up. Annah held onto this thought every day as she and the kids ran the gauntlet of the cackling, cussing women who seemed to spend all of their time on the front stoop.

As time went on and the taunts and threats continued, James became quieter and quieter at home. He always picked Annah up from her job and helped make sure the kids were home from school, but then he began going back out most nights and not returning until he could be sure she was asleep. Annah tried to talk to him, but even she had grown tired of hearing her constant litany: "James, why do you drink? Why can't you stay sober and help us? Why can't you stay at home?"

Finally, after a bad week of his leaving and her nagging, James wasn't there to pick her up after work one Thursday afternoon. Annah was panicked, knowing that the kids would be walking home alone. She ran all the way and when she arrived at the apartment, the kids were already there. At least no one had bothered or chased them. James didn't come home that night, so Annah called in sick to work the next morning. That evening, after she and the kids had eaten dinner, James came home. He sat on the sofa and began watching the television. Annah went over and turned it off.

"James, where have you been? Why didn't you pick me up at work? You know we have to get the children—it's not safe for them here. What were you thinking?" She had tried to talk to him calmly, but soon she was standing over him, shouting.

With a roar James got unsteadily to his feet.

"I never should have you brought you to this country!" he yelled. "Look at what you've made me into! I can't be a man in my own home! All you do is belittle me for the life I'm giving you. Well, fine. You don't have to take it anymore!" With that he strode into the kitchen and Annah heard the crash of a drawer being pulled out and emptied onto the floor.

"Daddy, no!" one of the children yelled from the kitchen. "He has a knife, Mommy, run! Run!" Annah took a step toward the kitchen to get her child away from this man, but he came through the doorway with the knife raised over his head.

"I'll cut your head off!" he yelled, lunging for her. She dashed through the front door, down the stairs, and out into the night, running as fast as she ever had. As she crossed the front yard, Annah could hear James's footsteps not far behind her, and then she realized that the kids were up in the apartment window, screaming and watching their parents. Annah ran down to the end of the block, crossed the intersection diagonally, and then veered down a side street. Just then a police car pulled up next to her, its lights flashing.

"We have the victim," the policeman said into his radio as she collapsed into the backseat. His partner turned and looked at Annah.

"Can you tell me what happened here, ma'am?"

"He has a knife. I . . . I think he wanted to kill me," she gasped, trying to regain her breath.

The partner got out of the car and walked toward James, his hand on his gun.

"Put the knife on the ground, please, sir," he called.

James held his hands up in the air. "I don't have a knife," he said. "It's OK."

The policeman walked over and ran his hands quickly over James's body. "Nothing," he yelled back to his partner. "Let's go."

The first policeman got out of the car and opened the door for Annah. "I need to take you over there now so we can all talk about this, ma'am." Annah followed him to where James and the other officer were standing, and then the four of them walked back to the apartment. Once inside, James immediately sat down on the sofa and Annah gathered the children, hugging them and drying their tears. She took them into the bedroom while the police talked to James. When she returned, one of the policemen took Annah into the kitchen.

"Ma'am, he says you tried to run away and he was just chasing after you, to get you to come home. He doesn't have a knife—we checked."

"But he did have it, and he was threatening me. Ask the children—they know."

"He says if you'll just stay, everything will be fine." Annah looked at the young white man in his police uniform. She could see how he had believed James. Everyone believes James when he speaks so firmly and eloquently, she thought. She considered telling the policeman she needed to leave, but she doubted he would help her, and he certainly wouldn't let her take the children. And anyway, where could she go? Annah sighed, and then knelt to pick up the utensils that had fallen all over the floor and put them back in the drawer.

The two policemen left and Annah went back into the living room. James just sat there, watching television and not looking at her. She went to the children's room and got them ready for bed. After tucking them all in, she went to her and James's room and went to bed herself. Just after she lay down, the door opened slowly and she could see James's outline against the hall light.

"Now, if I wanted to kill you, I could do it right here," he said in a low voice that seemed to tremble with anger. She heard him walk to the kitchen, and she got out of bed and closed the bedroom door and leaned against it. In a few minutes, she heard the front door open and close.

Annah cried all night. At first she thought she should pray, but then she became angry. "God, I've prayed to you to heal this man and look what you do. I've prayed to you to be my husband in his place, and look what you do. You let my children see their father threaten to kill their mother." She fell asleep near dawn and then awoke to the alarm clock's beeping, feeling exhausted and utterly alone.

James came back late at night a few days later. By that time, Annah had hidden all the knives in the house, so she lay silently as he undressed and stretched out in bed.

"I'm not going to hurt you, Frances," he muttered, and then he turned his back to her and was soon snoring. She turned away from him and let her tears fall silently onto the pillow. Over the next few days, they fell back into their routine: James helped with the kids, picked her up from work, and then went out, apparently to drink. He remained quiet when he was home, but the silence seemed less menacing to her than before. She felt sure that he was drinking less, and that of course he had never meant to hurt her.

It was January before the landlord made good on his promise to move them to another apartment, in a better neighborhood. The family relaxed almost immediately in the new place, and the winter months passed calmly for them. Like the last place, this apartment had no yard for the children to play in, but the neighbors were quiet and everyone spoke kindly to them when they passed on the street. James seemed to be going to the university more and actually getting some writing done. The three older children were in a different school, one where the other children were kinder to them, and Annah was able to arrange her hours so that she didn't need a babysitter for Brian. James was still drinking, but he said he could control it now. Annah asked why he didn't drink at home, so he began bringing his bottles in. He would sit in the living room and drink while Annah stayed with the children in their bedroom, helping with homework, reading to them, and then putting them to bed. Annah felt grateful to God that he had led her to find a routine that could sustain her family.

At McDonald's, Annah was being given increased responsibilities. In the spring her boss asked her to attend their week-long management-training program in a suburb of St. Louis. James managed to take care of the kids for the week, and Annah enjoyed her time of learning and making friends among the other management trainees. One fellow trainee in particular, Delores, became a good friend. When James came with the kids to pick her up, Annah introduced the family to Delores. She admired the children, asked questions about Uganda and their families, and then asked Annah and James if they were happy in their apartment. They answered "No!" in unison, and Delores said that her husband was a realtor and she thought he could find a small house for them to buy.

Annah returned home buoyed by her experiences at the training seminar. Her boss immediately gave her more responsibility, and a raise. She was able to pay for rent and food and still save some money. Through a coworker, Annah was able to locate a legal services organization for immigrants, and a new lawyer took over their asylum application. With things going this well, she began to wonder if they really might buy a house. In some ways, it felt like a step that would cut them off from Uganda and their families forever, and yet to be safe and warm in their own place sounded so good to her. Sometimes she went to sleep dreaming of a small, white house surrounded by a big yard where the children could play safely anytime they wanted. On those nights she always dreamed that Toto and Papa were here with them, playing with the children and laughing.

Chapter 19

WHEN ANNAH WAS A GROWING CHILD in Agu, she felt at one with the natural forces and cycles that carried her through her days, and her life. The sun, the moon, the rains, and the scorching heat all came with the same assurances: you are alive, you are strong, you are special. On most days now, she felt mocked by those same earthly rhythms. The sun and moon seemed locked in their own battles with the obscuring smog and city lights. Rain no longer poured out its thirst-quenching, plant-nourishing blessing upon her and the fields she ran through. Instead, passing cars splashed it into her face, leaving gritty smudges on her cheeks. And the few spindly trees that collected dust along the streets in her neighborhood provided no relief from the summer heat that simmered up from the pavement.

She tried to give her children a sense of the rhythms of nature that surely did still govern their lives, but she found that they, like her, felt controlled solely by the ebb and flow of James's sobriety. On the days when James was fairly sober, the younger kids wrestled with him and the older ones sought his help with homework—especially math. When James sat in the living room, silent and smelling of alcohol, Gilbert kept the girls in the bedroom playing quietly, and even Brian seemed to know to keep his distance from his father. That spring, with the apartment, school, and Annah's work going well, it seemed like they might be on an even keel. But then James's drinking increased and his behavior became more surly and aggressive, until one night in June, when Annah found herself once again running down the street from him as he brandished a knife.

"This can't be happening again," she cried to herself as she ran. She didn't even know what she had done to trigger his outrage this time. After running two blocks, she entered a store and asked the clerk to call the police. She kept watch for James, but a police car pulled up first. After she explained what had happened, the two officers took her back to the apartment. James was already there, and once again he denied having had a weapon and told them she had threatened to run away. Once again, the policemen accepted James's story and left. Annah sat up until James fell asleep on the sofa, and then she checked on the kids and went to lie in her bed, staring at the ceiling.

The next morning, Annah found Gilbert asleep on the living room floor with the television going while James still snored on the sofa. When she roused Gilbert and asked him what he was doing, he said he couldn't sleep so he came in to watch TV.

"Mommy, I found a man who can help Daddy," he said. "It was on TV, and his name is Reverend Tilton, and he said if we know someone who is drinking and tired and sad, he can pray for them and they'll get better. We have to make a pledge and pay a thousand dollars." Annah didn't know what to make of this, but when James finally woke up around noon, Gilbert told him all about it. "This man on TV will pray for you, Daddy, and you'll stop drinking. We just have to make a pledge and pay the money. I've written it all down on this paper."

Annah was on the evening shift at that time, so she was gone each day from midafternoon until nearly midnight. After the second incident with a knife, she and James avoided each other during the day, but he did stay with the kids while she worked. Annah prepared their dinner each afternoon, and she instructed Gilbert on how to heat it up. One night Annah got home to find that Gilbert and James were waiting for her.

"Mommy," Gilbert said as soon as she walked in, "we've been watching Reverend Tilton all week and praying, and Daddy wants to be healed. But we have to pledge to send him $1,000. Please, Mommy? Daddy says he'll work very hard." Gilbert's eyes were shining and he spoke very rapidly; Annah hadn't seen him that enthusiastic about anything for months—maybe even years.

"I can do it, Frances," James said quietly. "We can pay it in installments, a little at a time."

Annah sat on the sofa next to the two of them and studied their faces. Both looked determined but happy. "One thousand dollars is a lot of money," she said slowly, looking into James's eyes, "but I would do anything to have you back the way you were." James smiled at her and at Gilbert, who was clapping and cheering.

"Frances, Gilbert, I promise I will stop drinking right now, with Reverend Tilton's help—and with yours. Please pray for me," James said solemnly. "Frances, I don't have any money. Can you send it?" Annah was shocked to learn that he had no money. How had he been functioning? Obviously, he hadn't been working at the university for some time, but how was he buying the liquor? She decided not to ask and agreed that she would begin payments to the Tilton Ministry immediately. Thankfully, her pay as a manager could cover the new expense, if she was very frugal and seriously reduced the amount she was putting into the house savings fund.

All her life, Annah had lived by the belief that God would answer her prayers, and she knew he answered the prayers of children, so once she and the family began praying for James's sobriety, she was not surprised that he managed it. Throughout the following months, they joined a local church, watched Reverend Tilton regularly, sent in their money, and reveled in their new life with James. He returned to researching and writing his thesis at the university, came home early, helped around the house, played with the kids, and was gentle and respectful to Annah. James again became the spiritual head of the family. He read the Bible to the children, and he became friends with their pastor. Soon, he was helping with services there. He played the guitar during services, and he and the pastor had long discussions about scripture, with some of James's views ending up in the Sunday sermons. The younger children had never seen their daddy like this, and they were happy and proud. Annah thanked God—and Gilbert—for leading them to Robert Tilton and giving her back the James she had fallen in love with.

It took Annah almost seven months to pay the full $1,000, and she had to go back to her old ways of scrimping and saving every penny, but she did it with joy. God was answering their prayers, and she and James and the children were growing stronger in their love for him every day. James's sobriety continued after the money had been paid, and Annah began to believe that they might finally become the family that she and James had promised each other ten years earlier in Kampala.

Soon after they had paid off their pledge, the family got together and decided to ask Reverend Tilton to pray for further blessings for the family, in return for another $1,000 pledge. James called a family meeting one Sunday afternoon, and they all discussed what they truly wanted from God, while Annah wrote the list. Their first priority was news from Uganda, and Annah said they should ask God to help them find a way to stay in communication with Toto, Papa, and Lucy once they located them.

"We should go visit them," Gilbert announced. James and Annah exchanged worried looks.

"You know, Gilbert," James said, "it's still pretty unsafe over there."

But the children kept insisting that Grandpa Christopher and Grandma Esther would take care of them and make sure they didn't get hurt.

"Alright, my dear ones," Annah said. "We will see if we can visit, but first we have to have God's help to find them. I'm listing next that we want God to help Daddy stay healthy." The children all became quiet and stole glances at first her face and then James's.

"Yes, list that." James pressed his lips together and looked down at his lap.

"What else do we want God to help us with?" he asked Diana, who had been quiet during the discussion of Uganda.

"A bigger car!" she immediately answered. James gave a deep chuckle and Annah realized that he had noticed how the older kids always made their five-year-old sister sit squeezed between them in the backseat.

"I agree, Diana, but maybe we should ask for a house first?" she suggested. "We might be able to get one with enough bedrooms that you wouldn't have to sleep in the same room with your brothers and sister."

"Yes! Yes! A house!" the three children shouted, and even Brian began clapping his hands and chanting with them.

"I want it to be near a school!"

"A school with really nice children!"

"It should be a house in the country, with lots of grass and trees, too," Gilbert added, making Annah wonder if he somehow recalled their home in Amuria, nestled among the meadows where Lucy's cattle had grazed.

"Well, then, I think we better ask for more money, too," Annah laughed. "We need two good jobs, for Mommy and Daddy," she added, looking steadily at James. He met her eyes briefly and then looked away.

Annah copied over their list of desired blessings—contact with their Ugandan family, continued healing of James, a house of their own, a bigger car, and more income—and then the family watched solemnly while James put it in the envelope addressed to Reverend Tilton with their pledge form. It would be two years before Annah would read in the news that Tilton had been accused of gaining money fraudulently because he never even opened the petitions of the hopeful whose checks he cashed. She truly didn't care. God himself had said, "Pay thy vows unto the Most High: Call upon me in the day of trouble: I will deliver thee." Tilton had been the messenger who convinced James and the family to call upon God, and she never regretted having sent money to a con artist.

On the Monday after they sent their second pledge, Annah called her contact at the Red Cross to ask about news from Agu and Amuria. As always, the woman didn't chastise Annah for her frequent calls there and again promised to look into the situation. She called back that afternoon to say that there was nothing new, that the villages no longer existed and the residents were unaccounted for. She promised Annah she would call if she heard any news, but Annah could hear the lack of hope in the woman's voice. You will be calling us, Annah thought: my whole family is praying for this, it will happen.

Her next call was to the immigration attorney, who also reported no progress. Their application for asylum was still held up. Annah asked if more information was needed, and she added that she had just received confirmation from the Red Cross that their families in northern Uganda were still considered missing and probably dead. The attorney said no, she didn't think more evidence was needed; it was just that these things take a long time for processing. She reminded Annah that, because their application had been officially accepted, at least they both were eligible for six-month work permits.

A few days later, Annah came home from work to find that James and the kids had gone through the Sunday paper and cut out a picture of a house they'd like to own. It was a white, two-story house with a shady front porch and flowers growing along the edge of a big, grassy yard. Gilbert had taped the picture to the wall above the kitchen table, where they sat to pray each day.

"This way God knows just what we want," he told Annah solemnly.

Once, when Annah was just learning in her village school about how God answers all prayers, she had sat down in the middle of a row of cassava that she had been helping her mother hoe.

"Toto, why don't we just ask God to make the weeds go away?" she had demanded with exasperation.

"Foolish girl," Toto scolded, "God doesn't give you what you can work for yourself. He gave you strong arms and legs so you could hoe the weeds—that's how he answered that prayer. Now back to work, miss!"

Annah thought about Toto's words on that hot day long ago and decided she wasn't using what God had already given her. So while she was at work the next day she called Delores, the realtor's wife whom she had met more than a year earlier in management training. Delores said of course she remembered Annah and of course she and her husband could still help them find a house. Annah decided not to tell the family about her contact yet, so she and Delores met at McDonald's one evening during Annah's break. Annah showed her the picture that she had carefully removed from the wall that afternoon, and Delores said she would get to work on it.

A few days later, Annah told James that Delores and her husband were coming the next day to take them to see some houses for sale. His eyes widened, but he didn't even ask her how this had all come about. On Tuesday morning, they got the kids dressed and fed, and the family went to meet Delores and Edward. Annah and James walked silently through the first house they showed them. It was brick, but it had a nice yard and all the rooms they needed. When she dared to look at James, she could see in his eyes that he was feeling just what she was—can this really work for us? Could this become our own home? After four more houses, Annah's head was swimming. They returned home and Delores and Edward helped them draw up an offer and a bank loan application for the one they had liked best.

Delores came to McDonald's the next evening to tell Annah their loan had been denied by the bank.

"Now, don't get discouraged," she said. "That just means we need to find a less expensive house. I'm thinking that we should look for houses over in St. Charles. It's just across the river, and the houses there are less expensive."

"I'm not discouraged, Delores," Annah answered. "God will put us where we belong."

Annah and James rode with Delores the next morning across the bridge over the Missouri River into St. Charles. She drove them through the downtown area, and also through the historic section that had cobblestone streets and small, old-fashioned shops. Then she drove north into an area that had large farm fields dotted with subdivisions. Annah couldn't believe that fate had brought them here.

They fell in love with the second house they saw: a white, one-story house with three bedrooms and a fenced-in backyard where children could play all day without a care. Within a week they had been approved to buy it, and Annah began packing their things. Three weeks later, on a sunny Saturday in October 1990, friends from church brought pickup trucks and helped move them. Some members of the congregation had given them used bicycles for the older children and a tricycle for Brian, and the kids were riding happily up and down the cul-de-sac before the trucks were unloaded. Once all the boxes and furniture had been carried in, the congregants gathered in the living room and the pastor led them in prayers of blessings for the family and their new home. Then everyone shared a potluck meal and helped set up the beds, putting James and Annah in the larger bedroom, the girls in the one down the hall, and the boys in the room nearest to their parents.

The next morning, James drove Brian to Head Start preschool for the morning and Annah waited at the top of their street with the older kids for the school bus. Once she and James were back home, they walked hand in hand through the rooms, grinning at each other. They looked out the window over the sink in the kitchen, at the apple and plum trees in the backyard. James was murmuring prayers of thanksgiving, and Annah was supplying the appropriate responses. For a moment she felt as if she'd been transported back to Olio, where they had prayed together just like this in their first home.

During their first month there, James dropped Annah off at the McDonald's in the city on his way to St. Louis University to work on his thesis, but in November she asked her boss if she could transfer to the restaurant in St. Charles. She went to meet the manager of the new location, who seemed eager to hire her. When he asked her what she made as a shift manager at her old McDonald's and she gave him her answer, the man's eyes widened. "Well, here we start shift managers at about one-and-a-half times that figure. Are you sure that's all you made there?"

Annah couldn't wait until she could go home and tell James and the kids about her new job and big raise. As she waited for James to pick her up, she ticked off the items on their list: James seemed to be doing well, they had their own house, and now they would have lots more money. "Only two more, God, she thought as she stood on the sidewalk—we need a bigger car and we need to hear from Toto and Papa." She thought about telling God to hurry up, but it felt ungrateful, so she just prayed her thanks.

That fall, Annah felt that her life had become just about perfect.

She had more time now, and every Friday evening and Saturday the family worked together in their yard. James mowed the lawn and trimmed the bushes, with Gilbert always at his side helping and asking how to perform every task. Annah and the girls weeded the garden and raked leaves together. She couldn't believe the joy she felt, working her own land. They had a big Thanksgiving meal, including a turkey that turned out perfectly for the first time, thanks to the good oven in the kitchen. As the family stood around the dining room table, their hands joined for prayer, James began praying his thanks to God for all their blessings. His prayer went on and on, and even Annah stole a couple looks at him to see if he was aware of how long he was taking. Finally, when he paused to take a breath, one of the children shouted "Amen!" and they all sat down, laughing.

In January, James was offered a management position at Head Start, and he eagerly took on the work of overseeing the teaching curricula there. After a few weeks, they felt they could afford a new car, so they all went to a car lot and purchased a used minivan. As they drove it home, Diana was giggling with delight that she was in a seat by herself. Finally not in his mother's lap, Brian stretched out his arms and legs and fell asleep. Once again, Annah ticked off the list: James's sobriety, the house, more income, and now the car. Together, she and James could accomplish anything!

The family thrived during that winter and spring. The new school was completely different from the inner-city schools the kids had attended. The girls and Gilbert came home every day with a new story about praise from a teacher or a friendship forged on the playground. Brian was a quick-witted, playful boy who won the hearts of all the teachers and staff at Head Start, and James seemed to truly enjoy his work, both at the university and at Head Start. Annah's job went well and she made some friends in the neighborhood who shared gardening tips and even seedlings with her when the weather turned warm. Annah couldn't wait to show the kids how to weed the garden and harvest their homegrown vegetables.

James's job ended in May, when school ended, so he was home with the kids more while Annah was working. By early June, the kids were full of stories about their new adventures on their bikes and where Daddy had taken them in the van. James had found a road nearby that had a canopy of overhanging trees that gave it shade. He told the kids it reminded him of the shady groves in his boyhood home in Amuria, and whenever they were out driving together, they asked if they could go "through Uganda" to go home. On many evenings, Annah came home from work to find that James had cooked dinner and gotten the children ready for bed. As she walked through the door, she would be greeted by the sweet sounds of her husband and children singing hymns of praise to God while James played the guitar.

As the month progressed, Annah noticed that James was a little quieter when she came home, and she worried that he felt bad about her working when he wasn't. But he had been asked to return to Head Start in the fall, so it was just a summer vacation. She made sure to tell him how glad she was that he was there to take care of the kids while she worked. In recent months James's involvement in their church had increased, and the pastor contacted him at the end of June to ask if he would be the guest preacher when he went on vacation in a few weeks. James agreed, and Annah was thrilled to think that James Emuge would once again be speaking from a pulpit.

On the Saturday night before James's first sermon, he said prayers with the kids and helped get them to bed, and then he told Annah he would stay up a while to work on his sermon in the living room. She kissed him good night and went to bed. She awoke around midnight, surprised that he wasn't in bed yet. He must have been inspired to change his sermon, she thought, and went back to sleep thinking about that deep, gentle voice that had taught her how to truly accept God's love into her heart.

At 3:00 a.m., Annah awoke and leapt out of bed when she realized James still wasn't there. When she found the living room empty, she went to the window, her heart pounding. The van was gone. She went back to bed and tried to calm herself. "God, please bring my husband home," she prayed over and over. When the kids awoke her on Sunday morning, Gilbert immediately asked where his Dad was.

"I'm not sure, Gilbert. I . . . I think he probably went to church early, so he could get ready."

"Then how will we get there to hear him preach, Mom?"

"Well, if he has time I'm sure he'll come back and get us."

Gilbert gave her a serious, questioning look, but she just busied herself making breakfast. She sent the kids out to play in the backyard after the meal, and then she paced back and forth in the living room.

At ten minutes after ten, the phone rang and she jumped up to answer it.

"Annah," the voice said urgently, and her heart dropped. It was the assistant pastor. "Where is James? Everyone is here and we're ready to start the service. Where is he?"

"I don't know," she said softly. "I don't think you should count on him." Annah gently replaced the phone in its cradle and just sat there.

Chapter 20

ANNAH HAD NEITHER the strength nor the will to try to lie to the kids when she called them in for lunch and they asked where their daddy was.

"I don't know. He didn't make it to church, so I guess he just needed to be by himself today," she told them wearily.

"No, Mom!" Gilbert shouted. "He'll get drunk! We have to find him!" Gilbert began to weep as if James had died. The girls tried to comfort him, while Brian began to whimper, looking from Gilbert's face to his mother's.

"But I have no idea where to look for him, Gilbert. I think he'll be OK. We just have to pray to God to protect him." The last thing Annah thought she could do at that point was to pray for James, but she led the kids in a prayer, silently adding her own admonishment to God that she thought their bargain had been clearer. She felt so let down by James, and yet she knew that somehow God would send her the strength to handle this.

The rest of Sunday and all of Monday passed slowly for the sad, anxious family. On Tuesday morning, just after breakfast, Annah heard the kitchen door opening and looked up from the sink to see James standing there, filthy and dazed-looking.

"Don't start with me, Frances," he mumbled and walked past her to the living room. She heard him sit heavily on the sofa just as Gilbert came dashing down the hall. She stepped to the doorway to stop her son, but he had already seen James.

"Daddy, no! Oh, Daddy, please don't do this again!" James flinched, as if he'd been stabbed, but then he just turned away from Gilbert and stared out the window.

The pattern began again: James would be gone for days, only to return late one night and remain silent and menacing during the next day. Annah felt sad at first, but then she became angry. If this was to be her life, then she would count on James for nothing. Annah got switched to the day shift when the kids returned to

188

school, and she walked to work or sometimes took taxis to get home in time to meet the kids when they got off the school bus. One afternoon, as the taxi brought her to the driveway, she noticed that a neighbor down the street had a car for sale. She already had a learner's permit. She had needed some form of ID, so she had studied the book of laws and James had driven her to the testing station so that she could take the written test. She felt that having passed the written test for the permit gave her some preparation for learning to drive, although it would be illegal to drive by herself without a license. But she certainly had watched James drive enough to know the basics. Once she had settled the kids with snacks, Annah walked up the street and asked the neighbor how much he wanted for the car. The price was within her means, so she said she would buy it.

"Don't you want to test-drive it?" the man asked, surprised.

"No, it looks fine, and I know I can come to you if I have problems with it." Annah wrote out the check and the man handed her the keys. She sat in the driver's seat, ran her hands over the steering wheel, and then got out.

"Is something wrong?" The neighbor walked back down his driveway toward her.

"No, not at all. But would you mind driving it over to my driveway?"

"Can't you drive?" he asked, looking more closely at her.

"Sure I can, but I, um, I'm not wearing my glasses."

Once the car was parked in the driveway, Annah got some rags and wiped down the seats and the dashboard, and then she sat in the driver's seat looking at all the knobs and switches, carefully comparing them to the owner's manual. Something caught her eye, and she looked out the side window to see her four children all standing in the yard, their mouths open. She got out and said, "Well, how do you like my car?"

"Mommy, you can't drive!" they shouted.

Annah just laughed and told them she was sure she could learn. The kids played outside for the rest of the afternoon, but Annah noticed that they stayed far away from the car, as if it were an alien being. That night, after she had put Brian to bed, Annah told the older kids to stay in the house while she went out to drive the car. Over Gilbert's worried protests, she settled them in the living room and went out and turned the key in the ignition. The engine roared and she eased into the street, put the car in drive, and turned the steering wheel. Just before accelerating, she noticed the faces of her three children pressed against the front windowpane. She gave them a cheery wave and drove slowly up the street, starting and stopping as she went. Her hands were sweaty and her heart was pounding, but she managed to drive the eight miles to her McDonald's. She pulled into the parking lot and resisted the urge to let out a triumphant whoop. She could do this! When she got back to the house, the kids were still peering out the window, and she was sure they hadn't moved. As she walked in the front door, Diana burst into tears and Gilbert chided, "Mom, we thought you would get in an accident and die."

The next day, Annah left two hours early and drove—tight-lipped and terrified—to work. "God, I am sick and tired of James controlling my life when I can't count on him," she prayed as she sat in the car. "I know I'm breaking the law, but is there any way you can just protect me while I do this?"

Over the next week, Annah managed to learn to drive to and from work without sweating so much that she had to stand outside in the cool air to dry off before entering McDonald's. She stayed off the highway, and the narrow streets with parked cars on both sides terrified her, but she refused to be afraid to continue driving.

Her next hurdle came when she realized she needed to put gas in the car. She pulled in at a gas station on the way home from work and drove up beside the pumps, as she had seen James do. She got out and located the gas-tank door, but she couldn't figure out how to get the pump going. She read everything written on the pump, but it left her no closer to seeing how to do this. Finally, she drove home and asked Gilbert if he would like to come with her to the gas station so she could buy him some candy.

Once they pulled up to the pump, Annah casually asked Gilbert to pump the gas as he did with his dad sometimes. Gilbert got out and effortlessly negotiated the operation of the pump, while Annah studied his every move. When they went in to pay for the gas, she happily bought him a soda and a candy bar.

By the time James returned home, Annah was feeling competent and in control. He asked about the car, but she didn't answer him. That afternoon, she just walked out of the house, got in her car, and drove off to work, aware that he was staring out the front window at her. When she got home, he began again to ask where she had gotten the car, and she still refused to answer.

"Frances, how did you learn to drive? How did you get your driver's license? You better be careful, taking my children out when you can't really drive." He pushed further and further, but it only made Annah angrier and more determined not to speak. How dare he question what she did with the children? That night, she went into the bedroom and locked the door before going to sleep. From then on, James slept on a mattress in the basement when he was home.

The car became the place where Annah talked to God. She noticed that she no longer asked things of him; she would just say something like, "God, there is a policeman behind me. You know I don't have a license and I can't pay a big fine. Make him go away now." It seemed that, on most days, God did what she told him to do.

James continued his downward spiral, showing up drunk and then disappearing for days or sometimes weeks. Annah was able to handle the day-to-day challenges, but sometimes she stepped out into her backyard on a clear night and searched the sky for answers to her dilemma. There the lights of the city were far enough away that the night sky seemed at least a pale imitation of Uganda's glorious heavens, but this display just seemed to mock her. James was as unreadable as the placid moon that hung over her, and her toto as unreachable as the stars.

After six months of driving only when necessary, always looking over her shoulder for policemen and taking back roads, Annah decided she needed to get a driver's license. She drove to the licensing office where she'd gotten her permit, her heart in her throat as she approached and saw the police cars parked at the side of the building. She went there several times and discovered that she could watch the testing routine: at the beginning of each driver's test, a policeman came out and stood on the curb directing the applicant to turn on various lights and honk the horn, and then the officer got into the passenger's seat and they drove away. After Annah had learned this routine, she followed the car one day as a woman took her test. She memorized the route, and then she returned several nights over the next two weeks to practice every turn and stop.

Finally, Annah decided she was ready to take the test. She drove to the license office and parked on the far side of the parking lot so that the people inside wouldn't see her getting out of the driver's side of the car. She walked nonchalantly into the building and signed in. After twenty tense minutes, an officer walked into the room holding some papers.

"Emuge?" he called. "Annah Emuge?"

"That's me." Annah stood and looked him directly in the eye.

"OK, Ms. Emuge, I'm Officer Williams and I'll be doing your test today. Let's go out to your car and I'll have you get in the driver's seat and turn on lights as I ask you to." Annah almost giggled as she thought how she could do this whole procedure without his prompting. When Officer Williams got into the car, he told her she had done everything perfectly and asked her to pull out into the street after looking both ways. While Annah drove the familiar route, the officer took notes on his clipboard.

"Alright, Ms. Emuge. Now I'll have you pull up to those poles and parallel park, please." Annah knew she would fail this part; she hadn't been able to practice parking on a street because she was afraid of being caught without a license. She had just hoped that she might able to have a license if she performed perfectly on the rest of the driving test. Within seconds, she had knocked down both of the poles.

"That's fine," Officer Williams said, writing on his clipboard. "Drive up the road to the office. Pull into that parking place, please." Annah saw with horror that he was having her park directly in front of the building—how could she drive away after failing the test?

"Well, your driving is very good, Ms. Emuge," Officer Williams said, "so you just need to practice parallel parking and come back tomorrow."

"Thank you, sir," Annah said weakly as he got out of her car. She sat there for a few minutes, wondering how she could get away, and then she got out and stood under a tree down the sidewalk a few yards. After about fifteen minutes, Officer Williams came out with another driver, took that driver through the lights-and-horn routine, and then got in the car. Annah remained where she was until the car went down the road and disappeared after the first turn. Trying to look nonchalant, Annah walked over to her car, got in, and drove away, her hands shaking so hard she could barely steer.

That night, when the street was quiet, she went out and put two rocks on the road to mark a parking space. She tried for almost two hours, but on each attempt the tires crunched infuriatingly over one rock or the other. She just didn't get this.

At eight o'clock the next morning, Annah drove carefully to the license office. This time, she got a female officer. She went through the full routine, driving once again the route she knew so well, and then pulled up to the posts for the parking test. Annah made several attempts, and she never knocked over a pole, but she never got both ends of the car into the space. Finally the officer told her to pull out and park at the office.

"You're a good driver, Annah," she said, "so I'm going to pass you, but you need to practice parallel parking, OK?"

"Yes, ma'am. Thank you," Annah said, thinking, "Thank you, Jesus!"

"You're all done. Just come inside with these papers and the clerk will give you your license." Annah could barely believe those words. As soon as she entered the building she began sweating and shaking from the tension. For the next two years she carried around a driver's license bearing the image of her shocked, exhausted face. It took several more months before the kids agreed to ride in the car with Annah driving, and when they did, Diana threw up from anxiety as Annah turned off their street.

That fall, in 1992, Brian entered kindergarten, so Annah had all the kids in school all day. James was home and staying fairly sober for the last two weeks in August, and he had arranged to return to St. Louis University to work on his thesis. He had lost his driver's license because of the number of times he had been pulled over drunk, so Annah drove him to and from campus on the days he could go in. He was often silent on the rides home, and Annah realized that his alcoholism was taking a toll on him, both physically and mentally. He seemed to be having trouble picking up the threads of his research, and it was difficult for him to articulate what he was learning.

It wasn't long before James was coming home only sporadically, and when he was home, he was silent and miserable. Annah ached to see him deteriorating before her eyes, but she had no idea how to help him. They spoke little, and often it was now James who begged her to talk him—a strange reversal from all those years when she had endured his stony silences. Once, in the middle of the night, Annah heard sounds and went out to find James kneeling and sobbing in front of the TV. An evangelist was shouting about God's forgiveness, and James seemed to be mumbling a prayer as he cried. She watched for a few seconds, and then tiptoed back into the bedroom. Sometimes after that night James would ask the family to pray with him, but Gilbert would just say, "No, Dad," with a pained expression, and the other children would look away.

Just before Christmas, Annah got a call from the attorney who was handling their immigration case.

"We have a court date for your asylum hearing," she said breathlessly. "It's in early January, so I need to meet with you right after the holidays to prepare for it." The family celebrated Christmas with cautious hope that year, praying that this time they would actually make it to refugee status.

James and Annah spent two hours going over with the attorney the issues they would need to emphasize: the continuing civil war and genocide in Uganda, their parents' ethnic origins in the Iteso tribe—the ones being killed by soldiers and other tribes—and the reports from the Red Cross that their villages had been destroyed and their families' whereabouts were unknown. It was painful to go over and over these facts, but they knew how vital to their survival as a family it was.

On the day of the hearing, Annah kept the kids out of school and they all put on Sunday clothes and went to the federal courthouse in St. Louis. They sat on a long wooden bench outside the courtroom, waiting for their case to be called. When the attorney joined them, Gilbert immediately told her he knew they would win today.

"How do you know that?" she asked with a smile.

"Because we have prayed so hard for this. We need it so much, and it just has to happen!" Gilbert's earnest fervor made Annah's heart ache.

"Well, I think we should have you tell that to the judge," the attorney said. When they all went in and the judge called their case, the attorney had James and Annah supply the information just as they had rehearsed. Then she said, "Your Honor, I'd like to ask if Gilbert Emuge could address the court?" She indicated Gilbert, who was sitting with his siblings.

"All right, counselor," the judge replied, and the lawyer motioned for Gilbert to come up to the witness chair.

"Please tell us your name and how old you are, Gilbert," the attorney said.

"Gilbert Jesse Emuge," he answered in a quiet but firm voice. "I am thirteen years old."

"All right, young man," the judge said, "what is it you wanted to tell me?"

"Sir, my family really needs this. My parents need to be able to get better jobs so we won't be so poor, and we've prayed to God every day that you will give us refugee status."

The judge thanked Gilbert and then turned to address Annah and James.

"I will grant you asylum today, based on the evidence you've provided of the threat to your safety in your home country of Uganda. I am actually retiring today, so yours is my last case. Counselor, I will also grant permanent resident status to this couple, so that their fine young son can concentrate on school and stop worrying about his family so much. You've raised an impressive young man." The judge extended his hand, and the whole family went forward to shake it and thank him.

They followed their attorney out of the courtroom, and she stood with them in the hallway while they thanked her and she explained the process.

"You'll get what we call 'green cards' in a few days, which will identify you as permanent residents. You'll never need work permits again!" she announced, clearly proud of the news she was delivering. Annah looked at James, who was smiling but looking tired and worn out from this long struggle. They had begun their petition for asylum seven years earlier, and during all that time he had been yearning to simply stand in front of his own classroom, addressing his own class again, but he couldn't, in spite of his vast talents and advanced degrees. But there was no way this man had the strength or clarity of mind to teach now. Annah thanked the attorney and they left the courthouse.

The family decided to celebrate by going to McDonald's for lunch. After they ordered, they sat talking with the kids about the hearing, and Annah was explaining to the younger ones what their new status meant for them.

"It means now Dad can get a good job, and we'll be rich!" Gilbert added. James just looked at him, and Annah hurried to change the subject.

In the next week, Annah realized that she needed to put into place the plan she had held in her heart for a long time: she would return to school and earn her bachelor's degree. After long thought, she had decided that she would major in business administration. She couldn't imagine going back to hospitals like Olio, after she had seen all the advanced medical care that was available to people in this country. Besides, why should she stop at nursing, a typically "female" profession in Uganda, when she could return to her country fully qualified to enter the business world there? She knew how Toto would answer that question.

Now that she had her green card, Annah would qualify for financial assistance. She received her acceptance for admission to

St. Louis University for the fall 1993 semester, and then went to the Financial Aid Office and learned that she could get a partial grant, but that she would also have to take out a student loan to cover the costs. It was terrifying for her to take on more debt, even though payments would be deferred until after she had her degree, but James encouraged her to do this when she finally spoke to him about it. For just one painful moment, he seemed like the man who had promised he would honor her pledge to Toto to become as educated as she could. She signed the papers and enrolled in three classes.

While the new status gave Annah new energy, it seemed to have the opposite effect on James. He began the semester going with Annah to the university sometimes, so that he could work on his thesis, but his erratic behavior returned and he stopped going in to school at all after a few weeks. Annah kept her focus through the year, earning A's in all of her classes in both the fall and spring semesters, but James's behavior became more and more unpredictable. In May, he disappeared completely for what would end up being over a year. When he didn't return after the summer, Annah realized that she had actually begun to relax, and the children seemed less tense, too. Gilbert was thirteen and in the seventh grade, and he had become kind of a surrogate father to the other children. When Annah was at work or at class, it was Gilbert who made sure the kids were obeying the rules and getting their homework done. It seemed to Annah that all the children had a strong sense of how vital it was for them to be helpful and make their fragile family life work, but it was Gilbert who got the others back in line when they slacked off on homework or tried to stay up late. They all knew that Gilbert would call Mom at work if they weren't behaving.

In many ways, Diana resembled Gilbert, and so she had become a close mentor and nurturer to Brian. Even as a first-grader, Brian couldn't go to sleep until Diana read him a story. Sometimes Annah worried that she was the only one in the family who still felt there was an empty space when James was gone, but then one of the kids would have a problem figuring out math homework and he or she would proclaim, "I need Daddy to explain this math to me." When James was sporadically home again after that year, the kids were careful to catch him when he was there and in a good mood, to help them with their math. On those evenings, Annah listened to him patiently explaining the lesson, and she remembered all the evenings in Olio and Amuria, when she had sat with her new husband and he had shared his wisdom with her.

By this time, Annah had managed to develop a strong support system so that the family could function well. A couple across the street, who had twin sons Gilbert's age, checked in on the kids when Annah wasn't there and took them to church on the Sundays when Annah was working. The mother of one of the children's friends frequently invited all the kids over to play, and Annah's church community checked in with her and the kids regularly.

It was early in the summer of 1994 when James returned to the family. After he had been home for just over a month, in July, Annah noticed that he was not eating and that he was very weak. One morning, he came upstairs from the basement looking so pale that Annah decided to take him to the hospital. They admitted him and kept him there for a whole week to run a battery of tests, and then the doctor called Annah to come in for a consultation with James. She arrived at his room and sat beside his bed, waiting for the doctor. Finally he came in and introduced himself. He took out a thick chart, leafed through a few pages, and then looked at James.

"Well, James, we've talked about this before, but I need to emphasize it again. You simply have to stop drinking, or this will kill you." James just looked at him and said nothing. Annah's mind reeled as the doctor told them that James's liver was badly damaged, and that basically a quarter of it was destroyed. The doctor cleared his throat and continued. "The tests also show that you have type 2 diabetes, so we'll need to get you set up with insulin for that and you'll have to come to my office for instructions on controlling your blood sugar levels."

"No. I'm not taking medicine," James said. Annah looked at him, surprised, but when she saw the look in his eyes, she knew it wouldn't happen. He wasn't defiant so much as defeated. "I just won't do that."

"Mrs. Emuge, perhaps you could talk to your husband. This is very serious. James, I'll release you to go home now and expect to see you in my office in a week. You'll need to call for an appointment." The doctor nodded to Annah and left. James got dressed, and then the nurse came in to give him his paperwork.

The drinking began again within a few days of his coming home, but James seemed to be keeping it at a controlled level. After she tried several times to talk to him about what the doctor had said, Annah realized she needed to leave him alone to come to his own decisions. He never mentioned the diabetes at all, but one night he came home and told Annah he had learned of a Christian detox facil-

ity in St. Louis city where he could work with the pastor and coun-
selors and overcome his drinking. With great hope, Annah drove
him to the center. It was in a severely run-down neighborhood,
with gutted buildings lining the streets and equally vacant-looking
men sitting on the sidewalks or leaning on signposts. The building
itself was an old brick house with a huge, locked fence surround-
ing it. Once inside, James had to agree to be locked in for sixty days,
with no outside contact for the first month, and then he would be
allowed to attend church services with his family there on Sundays
during the second month.

By the time Annah and the children saw him in church at the
center, James was physically diminished but seemed stronger mentally than Annah had seen him in years. She and the children began
looking forward to seeing him on Sundays, and they all went over
to pick him up when his sixty days ended. James asked each of the
children how they were doing, and they gave him reserved but
friendly reports of their lives. When the family got home and she
and the kids were in the kitchen preparing dinner, Annah realized
that once again they had all come together to try to get James past
the demons that haunted him. She said a brief prayer that it would
truly happen this time.

Over the next few months, James became physically stronger
and said he was going to try again at the university. He rode there
with Annah and while she was in class, he went off to speak with his
former professors. That evening he told her he was going to resume
work on his PhD thesis. For a few weeks he seemed to be working there, but then she began to notice that he smelled of alcohol
when he got in the car to ride home with her. She asked him about
it, but he refused to answer her. His drinking seemed to be worsen-
ing over the next several weeks, and she and the children just natu-
rally adapted their lives to not having him home or to avoiding him
when he was there.

One weekend evening, when he had been gone for a few days,
Annah was in the kitchen making spaghetti for supper. Suddenly,
James was standing in the back doorway with a twelve-inch hack-
saw from their garage. He had it raised over his head, and he was
staring at her. Annah screamed, and she could hear the kids running to the kitchen. Before she could warn them away, she heard
one of them scream.

Gilbert stepped forward and grabbed the others, urging them to
get out by the front door.

"I'm gonna kill you today, woman!" James shouted. He sliced the saw downward, ripping through the side of the garbage can. "Why do you lock me out of your room? You're sleeping with other men, aren't you?" He approached her and raised the saw over her head, and Annah moved her hand toward the pot of boiling water, getting ready to throw it at him. Just then a voice told her not to do it. She looked into James's eyes and he dropped the saw and crumpled onto his knees.

"Why are you sleeping with other men and not me?" he sobbed. "Why, Frances?" Annah looked down at him, and then she turned off the stove and walked outside. By then a police car had pulled up and two officers were standing with Gilbert in the driveway.

"Ma'am, your son told us what happened," one of them said. "Where is your husband now?"

"He's in the kitchen."

"Does he have a gun?"

"No. He had a saw, but he dropped it." The two men went into the house and Annah walked in after a few minutes. James was speaking quietly to them, and then one officer gave him a court summons and the two of them left. James went downstairs, and when Annah went down after eating sandwiches with the kids, he was asleep.

Annah watched him for a few minutes to be sure he was sleeping and then went back upstairs and settled the kids in their beds. She kissed each one good night and then walked to her room. Closing the door, she leaned her back against it and let the sobs escape from her throat.

1995 to 2004

WHEN THE THREATS FROM Joseph Kony's Lord's Resistance Army against the citizens of northern Uganda lessened late in the 1990s, the government began encouraging residents of the refugee camps to return to their communities. Knowing that their homes had been burned down, many families took down the ten-foot-diameter huts they had occupied in the camps and carried home as many mud bricks as they could, along with the clothing and few possessions they owned. Once they located where their homes had been, they staked out approximations of the land they had owned and established their compounds out of nothing. They rebuilt huts, planted crops, and began to raise goats and chickens. Cattle, which had once been a primary source of food and income for Iteso farmers, were scarce. With the return of the families to rural villages, educational and health systems also had to be reestablished. Since some citizens had been members of the Lord's Resistance Army, what once had been peaceful communities were now villages in which neighbors had to come to terms with their history of atrocities committed by one family against another.

Uganda was one of the first sub-Saharan African countries to undergo an epidemic of HIV/AIDS, with the peak of the infection rate coming in 1993. By 1996, President Museveni had launched a rigorous education program that lessened the disease's impact over the next eight years, but its effects were felt in every village, refugee camp, and city. By the early 2000s, there were over two million orphans in Uganda, with nearly half of them having lost one or both parents to AIDS. In addition to his efforts to stem the spread of HIV/AIDS, Museveni launched the Universal Primary Education Program in 1997. This program allowed each Ugandan family to send up to four children to primary school without paying tuition. However, only 25 percent of primary-school graduates were able to continue to secondary school, and this group was largely skewed toward male students.

The average life expectancy in Uganda in the early 2000s was fifty, more than half of the population's income fell below the international poverty line of US$1.25 per day, and fewer than half of the people in rural areas had access to clean water or sanitation.

Chapter 21

ALL THAT NIGHT AFTER James threatened her with the saw, while he slept below her in the basement, Annah thought about Oprah Winfrey. A few months earlier, on an afternoon off from work and school, Annah had turned on the television when Oprah was doing a show about spousal abuse. She had watched uncomfortably as woman after woman told of the terror and pain her husband had inflicted. Most of these stories seemed much worse to Annah than the times James had threatened and even chased her with a knife. After all, she had thought then, he's never actually hurt me. At the end of the program, the camera went in close on Oprah's face and she pointed directly at the viewers.

"If you are in an abusive relationship, I have just one thing to say. Woman, get up, grab your children, and run. Don't look back. Don't say, 'But I have nowhere to go.' Just run!"

Oprah's message kept coming back to Annah that night. She thought about what she would do if James did hurt one of the kids. She thought about what would happen to the children if James did kill her. By morning, Annah knew she would not go anywhere with the kids, but she also knew what she had to do. After she got the children off to school, Annah awoke James and told him they needed to talk. He came to the living room and sat on the sofa, so she walked to a chair across the room from him. She was nervous, but she knew she had to remain calm and not resort to yelling at him out of her hurt and frustration.

"James, do you remember what happened last night?"

"Some of it."

Annah showed him the court summons, where it said, "threatened wife with a deadly weapon." His shoulders sagged, but she didn't soften.

"James, I pay all the bills. I take care of the children and the house. You disappear whenever you want. You come back whenever you want. And now you want to hurt me. This has to stop today. You have a choice. Walk through that door and never come back; or stay here, but if you do, you must turn around completely and never drink again. James, if you go out and drink, don't come back here or you'll be in jail."

Annah went to the kitchen and began cleaning up the breakfast dishes. In a few minutes she could hear James walking around the house. He had always paced when he had important things to think about, so she felt certain that she had made him hear her. She went about her chores, thinking about how she had finally realized that she had to choose between the children and James, that she couldn't have both the way things were. Of course she had chosen the children — their children.

James was still in the house when Annah left for work that afternoon, but when she got home that night he was gone. The kids were in bed asleep, so she didn't know if they had seen him, but it seemed that he had tidied up downstairs and left deliberately. Annah was surprised by the sense of loss that swept over her. Why should I feel this now, she thought. He's really been gone for years already.

James showed up again one day about a month later, but Annah met him at the door and saw that he had been drinking. He was thin and dirty, and she almost let him in out of her old habit of accommodating his needs. But then she recalled the knives and the saw, and her children, and Oprah, and she told him he couldn't come in. She shut the door firmly.

That was a dark time for Annah. She never changed the locks, and she was aware that James did come into the house sometimes when she wasn't there, but she decided that was OK as long as she didn't have to see him. On the few occasions when she did see him, it was obvious that he was continuing to deteriorate, but she also recognized that it was just too painful for the children, and for her, to have to watch him decay. He had told her many times that drinking was the only way for him to numb the pain of all that had gone wrong in his life. She wished fervently for some medicine to take away the pain she and her children felt each day. If I don't keep him away from me, I will die sooner than he will, Annah thought. She struggled to come to terms with this realization, while still handling her job, her classes, and the kids' need for a stable, loving home. Almost a year after she had told him to leave, James asked her to take him to a Christian detox facility again, but he called her one midnight after only a few weeks there, needing her to pick him up because he had gotten into a fight with the director.

It was not long after that incident that Annah's ability to approach God simply dried up. Her being angry at James also waned, since it just felt so futile. One night, on the way home from work, she began to ask God why he was punishing her husband in this way, even though James was trying to pray. "He is a loving, caring man, God. Why aren't you helping him? Why is my husband rotting away?" All the anger welled up in her and she said, "God, you are lucky you are up there, because if you were here I would break your legs and tie you up and lock you in the closet until you put things right for me—for us. How can you do this to us?" After that Annah stopped praying, and she yelled at God when things got to be too much for her. She stopped going to church, and she no longer led the children in prayers at bedtime. James's sporadic presence at the house when she wasn't there continued, and Annah just got herself through one day at a time.

After several months, Annah went to bed one night particularly drained and sad. She lay there feeling empty, and then she suddenly began to pray to God. She told him she was sorry she had wanted to break his legs and promised that she and the children would return to regular church attendance. That night, in a dream, she found herself in Uganda, but she was hovering over it as if she were being held up in large arms. Annah looked down and saw Toto and Papa, in a strange cluster of many small huts. There were many of her brothers and sisters there, too, and they were all thin and looked very tired. Suddenly, she heard a voice say, "Annah, your parents are safe. Remember you asked me to protect them, and I have." She saw a shallow, unkempt grave beside a path, and she somehow knew that it was her sister Rebecca's. Four young children that she realized were her nieces and nephews were crouched on the path, waiting for their mother to get up from her grave. Then her vision shifted back to Toto and Papa. Annah looked up at God and said, "All these years, God, why didn't you tell me?" He smiled and seemed to be saying "Annah, Annah, Annah" when she awoke. She sat up and thanked God, knowing now that most of her family had survived.

James arrived home one summer day in such bad shape that she immediately took him to the hospital in St. Charles. He was stumbling and delirious, and he smelled of liquor and urine. He was placed in a detox unit, where they maintained him on drugs that kept him barely conscious. He couldn't feed himself, so Annah went often to help give him meals when she wasn't working. The doctors told her they didn't know when—or if—he might recover some of his senses, but they warned her that James would never be able to function completely again. She became a fixture at the hospital, feeding him, changing his soiled sheets, and just holding his hand. After a few weeks he improved a little, although he was still confused about who she was and where he was. She wondered if he even knew *who* he was.

She never let the kids visit him, although Gilbert asked to, more than once. "He is just too sick, Gilbert," she told him, "and you don't want to bring in any germs that might make him sicker." Her son eyed her steadily for a few moments. At fifteen, he had such grown-up mannerisms, and yet she could still see the hurt child in him.

"Just take care of him for us, then, Mom," he said quietly.

One evening when Annah had just returned home from the hospital, the phone rang. When she answered it, a man's voice on the other end spoke to her in the Ateso language: "Hello, Frances! How are you guys doing?" Annah was so stunned she could only gasp.

"Frances, I'm sorry I have startled you. This is Dr. Odayet— James's friend and professor from Kampala. I'm here, in Ohio, so I thought I would call you."

"Oh, Dr. Odayet—yes, of course. But how did you get our number?"

"They have it here at Ohio University—I understand James has kept in touch with the professors in the Department of African Studies. I'd like to speak to him. Is he at home?"

"Well, James is ill and he is in the hospital right now. I just came from there."

"Oh, I am so sorry to hear that. When he gets out, Frances, will you have him call me?"

"Certainly, but, please, do you know anything about our families in Agu and Amuria?"

"Why, yes; aren't you in touch with them? Oh, I guess not. Well, I know your parents and James's mother are all alive, but they are very, very poor. They are in a refugee camp far to the west of Agu, and the conditions are so bad there. But they are OK. For a while, we were burying people like we were planting potatoes, but both of your families all made it, as far as I know. I understand that your parents plan to return to Agu soon." Just hearing him utter the word *Agu*, as if going there were such a simple occurrence, made Annah's knees feel weak.

"Do you know how I might contact them?" she managed to ask in a fairly even voice.

"Hmm, let me see. Oh, sure; your nephew, George, is a student at Makerere University in Kampala. I'll have my wife locate him and give him your address."

"Oh, thank you, Dr. Odayet. Thank you!" Annah hung up the phone and stood there, not sure she believed what had just happened. The feeling of tears running down her cheeks surprised her, and she realized she was crying from joy.

The next day she excitedly went to James's hospital room. When she arrived, she saw that he had been tied to the bed and the nurse's aide was feeding him. She told Annah that he had been combative, so they had restrained him. Annah sat beside him and said, "James, our families are alive. Toto, Papa, and your mother—they've all survived!" But he just stared at her. It was like talking to a small baby— he seemed to like that she was talking to him, but there was no comprehension. She had only her children to share the news with, and they were excited about having grandparents and aunties and uncles, but they really couldn't understand the depth of her relief and joy. And then George's letter arrived. How wonderful to read his news of the family! George was Rosemary's son, whom Annah had helped care for when she attended secondary school in Soroti. When she left Uganda he would have been about Brian's current age—nine—but now he was a college student!

The letter confirmed that her sister Rebecca had died when the family fled from the soldiers destroying Agu. She was pregnant with her fifth child when she died, and she was buried in an unmarked grave somewhere in northwestern Uganda. All of Annah's other brothers and sisters were alive, as well as Toto, Papa, Lucy, and James's three brothers. James's sisters Rose and Phoebe and their husbands all had died. Annah read the words hungrily, as if she would lose them if she didn't devour them immediately. George referred to her parents as Grandfather Christopher and Tata Esther, and she had to remind herself that he was truly speaking of her papa and toto.

And then George wrote what he had learned of her parents' experience when the soldiers came through burning the huts of Agu Village. The villagers had received word that there were soldiers coming, so Christopher told Esther and all the family to flee while he gathered a few things. Before he could leave their compound, the soldiers arrived in town and found him. The soldiers' practice was that when they found villagers, they beat them, tied them to a tree, lit their huts on fire, and shot them. Christopher endured a brutal beating with clubs and rifle butts, and then he was tied to the mango tree in the center of the family compound. The soldiers tossed burning sticks into the huts and then ran on to find more victims, and one soldier turned back to shoot Christopher. When he fired his gun, however, it was out of bullets. The soldier looked at it, shrugged, and ran to catch up with the others. After about ten minutes, Esther, who had seen everything from the brush near the compound where she had hidden to make sure Christopher got out, stepped into the compound. Fearlessly, she walked to the tree, cut her husband down, and half-carried, half-dragged him into the brush. Esther nursed his wounds for two days and then helped him make his painful way to the refugee camp. It took them weeks to reach the camp, and they had to travel mostly at night and hide in the daytime to avoid being killed or captured.

George explained that Annah's parents had just left the refugee camp, after over thirteen years there—among more than 200,000 people living eight and ten to a hut, with just a few feet between the huts. Most of James's surviving family members were still living there. George described how hard life was in the camp, with little food or space and no way to grow their own vegetables or raise animals. The camp was surrounded by soldiers as protection, but of course that made the refugees prisoners in their huts. George also spoke of how Toto and Papa had searched through the camp for people who might know what had happened to her and James, and they had found no one. Toto and Papa assumed that she and James had returned to Uganda when government support was no longer available, and that they had been living in the Kampala area when the Bantus took over. As Itesos, they couldn't have survived in Kampala, so the family had mourned the deaths of Annah, James, and their three small children. George said that Christopher had been inconsolable about losing "his Frances." Now, Toto and Papa were trying to rebuild their life in Agu. They, like all of the hundreds of thousands of refugees who were finally returning to their homes, had come back to nothing except vaguely familiar landmarks like a scraggly tree or an area whose low brush suggested it had once been cleared. It would take them months to rebuild their huts, plant some crops, and then begin to acquire a few animals.

For several days, Annah could barely concentrate on anything because she was playing the scenes George had described over and over in her head. Always, she ended with an image of Toto and Papa back in Agu, standing in front of their hut in a new compound that looked exactly like the one where she had grown up. She immediately wrote a six-page letter to George, telling him everything about her family, except for James's drinking, and asked him to get it to Toto and Papa as soon as possible. She found herself grinning often at the thought of Toto's face when she learned that her Annah was not only alive but raising four children and getting her bachelor's degree.

James had recovered somewhat and was released from the hospital after two weeks, and Annah nursed him constantly after she brought him home, in spite of her vow not to try to help him again. With her new knowledge that Toto and Papa were alive, Annah wanted James near her, to share her joy. He was gaining some weight, and his head was clear most of the time. Finally, after a few more weeks, she felt he was well enough to hear the news. She told him that their parents were alive in Uganda, and he just sat, staring at her.

"Frances, are you sure about this?" he finally asked.

"Yes, James; your mother, my mother, and my father are all alive. Here, let me get Dr. Odayet on the phone for you—he'll reassure you."

Annah could hear Dr. Odayet shouting "yoganoi" (hello) as she handed the phone to her husband. James sat up and his face creased in a big smile as he listened to his old friend and mentor, and soon he was talking rapidly in Ateso. James seemed to decide at that moment to go ahead and work to get better.

Little changed in their family situation over the next several months, except that Annah faced her struggles with a renewed sense of closeness to God and a very new sense of peacefulness. George wrote to tell her that Toto and Papa had been speechless when he told them the news that she, James, and the four children were alive. Finally, after he repeated several times the story of how they had stayed in the United States, her parents accepted his news. Through their tears of joy, George said, Toto stated that if anyone could have survived, it would be her Annah. Papa just sat there, saying, "My Frances is alive," over and over.

George said her parents had asked for photographs, "just to be sure," so she and the family posed in front of their house while a neighbor took several pictures of them. Annah imagined how Toto would scrutinize each face when she received the photos, and she made sure to send the ones in which the kids were smiling broadly. She was beaming in all of them.

As Annah entered her final year of classes, there were some required courses left that she couldn't work into her McDonald's schedule, so she had to quit and take a job in a factory, doing a 7:00 p.m. to 7:00 a.m. shift, seven nights out of every two weeks. The hours were brutal, but they left time for class. After a month she also got a part-time job as a clerk at a nearby Amoco station because the pay from her one job wasn't enough. The one relief was that Gilbert turned sixteen and got his driver's license that December. He was a studious high school sophomore then, and on the varsity football team, so his time was limited, too. But the other children knew they could ask Gilbert to drive them someplace or help them in any way, and he would drop whatever he was doing for them.

James recovered from his weakness, but as his strength returned, so did his desire for alcohol. His drinking bouts were a little less frequent, and there were occasional periods of several days when he joined the family for dinner and conversed with the kids about their lives and studies. He continued to sleep in the basement, and he would sneak into the house after drinking sprees and then emerge after he had slept them off and cleaned himself up.

In May 1997, Annah received her bachelor's degree from St. Louis University. James and the children all attended her graduation ceremony, but Annah barely heard their cheers when she walked onto the stage to receive her diploma. She only heard Toto's voice telling her she could do anything she wanted, as long as she set her mind to it. After the ceremony, the kids came running across the lawn to her, and all four of them threw their arms around her in a huge hug. After they had stepped back, James walked a little tentatively to her. Then his arms were around her and she leaned her head on his shoulder, feeling for a moment like her nineteen-year-old self nestled in her new husband's arms.

"Don't stop here, Frances," he whispered in her ear. "Get an MBA—that's what really successful people have." Startled, she pulled back and looked into his eyes and saw love and hope there.

"I will, James. I will."

Chapter 22

AFTER FINDING OUT THAT most of her family members were still alive, it took Annah eight years—until 2004—to find a way to visit her beloved Uganda. She faced so many hurdles: she was raising the children, handling James's illness, and trying to earn money, and she knew she couldn't return to Uganda with anything less than full U.S. citizenship status, to ensure that she would be able to leave again. She had also decided to pursue a master's degree, now knowing that she was fulfilling both Toto's and James's dreams for her to become an educated woman.

In spite of all her worries and responsibilities, these were mostly joyful years for Annah. She was able to send and receive regular letters from Toto and her sisters, through George. After sending the photos of her own family, and hearing how Toto had pored over each face and declared Diana to be Annah reborn, she asked if George might be able to arrange photos of Toto and Papa for her. She had to wait several months, but at last a thick envelope arrived. She sat down at the kitchen table, carefully tore open the edge, and pulled out George's letter and two photos, one of Papa and one of Toto and Rosemary.

There, in her hand, were her mother and father. Toto was dressed in a traditional Iteso dress, made of a silky orange material with full sleeves and a wide sash around her waist. She stood in front of Rosemary's house, looking slightly away from the camera with a small smile on her lips. This was her toto: tall, strong, and proud, even in the unusual circumstance of being photographed. Toto looked older, but her shoulders were just as square and her head held just as high as Annah remembered. She gasped when she looked at Papa's photo. He also stood in front of the house, but she barely recognized him. The man in the picture was wearing a light blue, Western-style sport jacket, and he was painfully thin and a little stooped. Could this old man really be her papa? But the man looked steadily into the camera, and she saw her father's firm, unwavering gaze in the slightly clouded brown eyes.

"Oh, Papa," she cried to herself, "you didn't have to dress up for me!" But she knew that this proud man would have wanted to look modern and prosperous for his daughter in America. She knew he had borrowed the jacket, probably from George, and she ached to tell him he was perfect the way he always was, that she couldn't love him more if he were in a king's robes.

Annah felt invigorated by her contact with her family, and she immediately enrolled in Lindenwood University to earn an MBA. Shortly after she began classes, she attended a job fair on campus and was hired as an assistant manager of a Walgreens drugstore. Her salary was more than the income of her other two jobs combined, and her manager there gave her flexibility to arrange her work schedule around her classes. For the first time in her life, Annah had health insurance and experienced the freedom of knowing she could take her children to the doctor any time she wanted. She thought about Toto carrying her the twelve miles to the Fredika Hospital, and then having to pay cash before anyone would even look at her daughter's foot. If only Toto could see this!

During these years the children continued to amaze Annah, and she was proud to be able to tell Toto about her accomplished grandchildren. Brian thrived through middle school and entered high school as a confident, talented young man. He tried football, did well at soccer, and then found he had a talent for track. Annah admired his discipline and commitment to a demanding, rigorous sport. Brian continued to resemble his father, in looks and demeanor. He had taken up the guitar and became more accomplished at it than James was, and nothing settled Annah at the end of a long day like sitting on the sofa listening to Brian playing softly.

Toto had been right about Diana looking like Annah. She grew into a tall, lithe young woman just as Annah had, and she played basketball and took voice lessons. She graduated from high school with honors and received scholarships to attend St. Louis University, where she studied business administration and marketing. She remained a nurturing, sweet sister to Brian. Annah was surprised by her choice of university, and she was disconcerted when Diana reported occasional glimpses of her father wandering the campus there. Diana admitted that sometimes she had to run to the restroom to cry after she had caught sight of a graying older man, dressed in a threadbare suit and walking hesitantly across the campus, only to realize who he was.

Ruby enrolled in college with dreams of continuing with an MFA in the arts. She was a lovely young woman with a strong, agile body. Annah was continually amazed by her creativity.

Gilbert remained the father figure to his siblings and entered Missouri State University to work on a dual major in graphic arts and computer technology. He was a humble, gentle young man who made deep, lasting friendships. He had gone the farthest away from home, but he managed to stay so close by phone that he always knew exactly where his mother was and what she needed.

In the early 2000s, Annah wasn't the least bit surprised to learn that God was calling in her debt: once they resettled on most of their old land in Agu, Toto and Papa took in fifteen children from the Agu area who had been orphaned either by the tribal conflicts or by the newer epidemic of AIDS. Annah's sister Rosemary managed to get a cell phone that worked in Agu, and Annah heard her parents' voices for the first time in more than eighteen years. She could recognize the fatigue in both of their voices, but their joy at hearing hers was obvious, and they spoke about the new brood of children they were raising as if they had never imagined doing anything else. Annah set up two savings accounts: one for plane fare to get to Agu and see for herself that her parents were alright, and one to provide the support she owed to these orphans that God had sent to her through Toto and Papa.

Woven through the joyful tapestry that was now her life was the black thread of James's deterioration. He continued to have a few weeks or occasionally a month where he was home and fairly lucid, but his years were mainly spent drinking and wandering. Once, while he was gone for over a year, the family received a crudely scrawled postcard from Canada that they were fairly sure was from him. When he was in St. Louis, he sometimes called the house looking for help. There were nights when Annah would come home from work around midnight and learn that Gilbert and one of the girls had been driving around the seedy street corners of the city, trying to locate him from his garbled description of his whereabouts. When Gilbert was away at school, he often called and asked Annah to drive downtown and see if she could find James. She never did find him, but sometimes she would find someone who knew him so she could report to Gilbert that he was still out there, somewhere.

On the few occasions when Annah let James sleep in the basement in those later years, he was haggard and weak. She watched achingly as the older children tried to help him, with grim looks of acceptance and pity on their faces. Gilbert seemed to feel some responsibility for James's condition, and she knew that he was torn by his unwillingness to give up on his father while knowing at the same time that by helping him he was making his father more dependent on him. Brian, who had never really known him as the vital, intellectual James Emuge, withdrew from contact with this shabby man whose features so clearly mirrored his own.

In 2002, the family had a glorious month when George stayed with them on his way to study at Ohio University. He had been accepted into the master's/PhD program there, so he had decided to spend August in St. Louis before going on to school. A gangly, cheerful young man, he liked to grab his "Auntie Frances" around the waist for a big hug when she came home from work, and he often stayed up half the night debating with his newfound cousins about life philosophies and current music trends. Even James stayed home during that month, eager to talk with George about Ugandan politics and to share his amazement that Museveni was still the president after all that time. Annah loved to hear the cadence of their discussions, their utterances punctuated with Ateso expressions and deep, rumbling laughter. On the night before George was to leave for Ohio, the family took him shopping for warm clothes and then out to dinner, and they couldn't wait for his return for Thanksgiving and then Christmas.

Annah was awarded her MBA, with an emphasis in marketing, from Lindenwood University in December 2003, and then she took up what would be the most important studies of her life: preparation for American citizenship. She eagerly studied the Constitution and U.S. history, with plenty of coaching from her kids. She felt frustrated as she learned how painstakingly the American leaders had constructed a government of, by, and for the people, and how U.S. presidents had resisted the temptation to hold onto the power given them, even before term limits became law. Why hadn't there been such visionary leaders in her own country? It also pained her to learn the words engraved on the Statue of Liberty since she and James struggled for so long, yearning for nothing more than the freedom to work at a permanent, appropriate job and to raise their children safely, before receiving official status in this country that claimed to welcome all people.

On January 23, 2004, Annah stood in the St. Louis federal courthouse, raised her right hand, and swore allegiance to the United States of America, forsaking all other states, principalities, or sovereignties.

Once the forty immigrants in the courthouse that day had officially been granted citizenship, the judge asked them each to stand when he read out the name of their native country, to recognize the origins of the very newest citizens of the United States. Uganda was at the end of the alphabetical list, and Annah felt a rush of conflicting emotions when it was finally her turn to rise. The officials holding this ceremony clearly believed she was happily turning her back on Uganda, and yet she was doing all this just to get there. She wondered why Uganda, where her toto and papa were, felt so foreign and yet the United States, home to her children, felt no less alien. Then she realized with a pang that, ever since she had moved into the little house in Olio, it was James's strong presence that had made a place feel like home to her.

James had not contacted the family since just before Christmas, and when she told him then that she was applying for citizenship he had not answered her. She didn't mention to him that she was doing it to clear the way so she could visit Uganda—he had not been a consideration in her plans for a long time. With the certificate of naturalization in hand, she immediately went to the post office to apply for a U.S. passport. This was recommended for all new citizens so that they would have proof of citizenship without having to carry the certificate with them. For Annah, though, it was the next of many steps.

Once she received her passport, she studied her bank accounts and made her plans. She went to a travel agent and, with shaking hands, wrote out a check and accepted a round-trip ticket to Entebbe Airport, leaving on May 16 and returning three weeks later. She wondered if this would be enough time to even begin to reconnect all the bonds she had thought were broken and gone for fifteen years, but it was the best she could manage.

Annah and the kids talked incessantly about her upcoming trip. They wished they could be with her, but they were completely supportive that she must go soon to see her family and to help Toto and Papa with the orphans. With three of them working or in college and Brian a senior in high school, she knew they would be fine without her. Both girls lived at home, so Brian was assured of more attention than he probably wanted, and home-cooked meals. Gilbert took Annah aside a few times to make her promise to be careful. He never questioned her ability to cope with adversity, he just wanted reassurance that she would stay out of its way as much as possible.

Annah wrote joyful letters to Toto, telling her when she would arrive and that George, who had returned to Uganda, had agreed to drive her up to Agu as soon as she arrived. She got back equally joyful letters telling her about all the people who would be there to see her—her sisters and brothers, nieces, nephews, aunties, uncles. Through all of this, Annah wanted desperately to let James know she was going, but he never showed up at the house. On several evenings, she and at least one of the kids drove through the streets of the St. Louis slums, peering at the men leaning against buildings, but they never found him.

Finally, in April, she took on the task she had avoided for so long: she wrote to James's brother Benjamin, who was living in Kampala, to tell him that she would be there. She asked Benjamin to pass this news along to James's other brothers and to Lucy. And she told him that she was coming alone because James had been in and out of their lives for some time, and that she didn't know his whereabouts at all. She mailed it with trepidation, knowing that they would see no honorable explanation for a woman to have to admit that she couldn't locate her husband.

Annah gave her boss the exact dates that she would be off work, and then she went to the human resources office and applied for a cash-out of her retirement plan. The assistant there tried to talk her out of it, pointing out how much she would need this money when she was older, but Annah just smiled and insisted on receiving the $5,000 that was available to her. When she got home, she told the kids that she was taking this money to build a house for Toto, Papa, and the orphans, and they all immediately agreed with her plan.

During the week before her flight, Annah collected all the clothing—mostly for children—that she could stuff into her two allotted suitcases, along with some basic first-aid items. She packed barely anything for herself, knowing how quickly clothing dried in the Ugandan sun after being washed in the river. She emailed George with her flight arrival time, and he replied that he would be there to pick her up. "Your mother will be with me," he wrote. "She says she must see the machine that brings her child from America." Annah could imagine how he had tried to convince Toto not to make such an arduous bus journey when he would bring Annah to Agu immediately, and she knew exactly how Toto had looked at him and then informed him that her mind was made up.

At last, May 16 arrived. Gilbert came home that weekend, and all the kids went to see her off at the airport, full of last-minute advice and admonitions. As she settled into the seat on the plane, she recalled the last time she had flown, so full of hope and expectation, with James and their two small children. She watched St. Louis shrink below the plane as they took off, trying to put thoughts of the past out of her mind.

The trip took her first to New York to change planes and then to Rome, so she was tired and a little disoriented by the time she got on the plane to Ethiopia. Annah watched the map in the front of the plane, and as soon as the little airplane icon arced over Africa, she began to cry. Passengers near her and the flight attendants asked if she was OK, and she kept reassuring them she was just emotional about going home. Soon a large portion of the plane knew some of her story—that she would see her parents for the first time in twenty-two years—so people constantly stopped to congratulate her and wish her a happy reunion.

This flight was at night, but out the window she could see the lights of cities in Egypt and Sudan, and then those of Addis Ababa, Ethiopia. The passengers going on to other destinations were taken by bus to a hotel to rest, but Annah just paced the little room they gave her until it was time to board the plane for Entebbe. This flight was just over an hour, and Annah spent the whole time peering down at the landscape below. She caught sight of the Nile River several times, and she felt certain that they flew very close to Agu, but it was all just a brown and green blur.

The plane bumped down on the runway and Annah watched the airport getting closer, thinking it looked exactly the same as in 1983, when she had watched it receding and held her breath until she was out of Uganda. This time, she wanted to kneel and kiss the ground that she had fled from the last time she touched it. In the customs area, some people looked at her with curiosity when she got in the line for foreign passports instead of the one for Ugandan citizens. She tried not to show how her heart was pounding as she handed her passport to the official, whose uniform brought waves of nauseating, terrifying memories to her. He barely looked at her, stamped the page, and handed the passport back, mumbling, "Enjoy your stay in Uganda," as she took it and walked through the gate. Baggage lay on the large expanse of the concrete floor, and she quickly picked up her two large suitcases and dragged them to the door. A few porters were eagerly pushing carts up to the few white passengers, who had been in the passport line with her just minutes ago, but they all acted like she was invisible. Annah walked through the gate, past families and individuals lined up with welcoming smiles and signs. She scanned the crowd eagerly, but George was not there. She made her way out into the midday heat and stood near the taxis, searching the road for George.

After half an hour, a car pulled up just across the road from her and she saw George step out. Then Toto got out on the far side of the car, and Annah ran toward her. Toto ran, too, and they met in each other's arms behind the car. Annah was vaguely aware that George had sprinted toward her bags, and she realized how risky it was to leave bags here even for a second, but it didn't matter because she was hugging her mother and Toto's strong arms were around her again.

"Let me see," Toto was saying after several moments. "I must see your eyes. Yes, that's my baby," she said, holding Annah's face in her hands. "Don't cry anymore, my girl. I'm here, I'm here." Annah felt cradled and safe at last. How she had longed for just this moment.

George put the suitcases into the trunk and came to the two women. "I have my cell phone. We're supposed to call your father right now," he said, dialing it. "Hello, Grandfather," he said. "Yes, your daughter from America is here." He handed the phone to Annah, and she whispered, "Papa, Papa, it's me." "It's you," his voice came back strong and joyful. "I know that voice: it's my Frances. I am happy now. I'll see you tomorrow."

Just as they were about to get in the car, a soldier with a machine gun began walking quickly toward them. Annah looked around her in terror, but, seeing no escape route, she grabbed George's arm. He said something to the soldier in Swahili, and then the soldier answered. Noticing Annah's expression, George explained in Ateso, "Auntie, this is my old high school mate." She couldn't contain her trembling as George introduced them and she shook the soldier's hand. "Things are different now, Auntie. It's safe here; these aren't Idi Amin's soldiers," George told her as they settled in the car. Still, she watched behind them to be sure they weren't being followed.

They spent the night in George's apartment in Kampala, because the drive to Agu would take most of the next day. Annah and Toto talked and talked, even into the night after they lay in bed in George's spare room. Finally, they said their prayers together and quieted. Toto fell asleep first, and Annah just lay there, listening to her mother's familiar breathing. She awoke several times during the night and happily drifted back to sleep with the gentle sound in her ears.

They got up early the next day to begin the long drive to Agu, and Annah found that she suddenly had no patience for the six-hour ride ahead. But as they crossed the border into Teso District, she knew she must put off her arrival for one important errand. Annah asked George to take her to a market in Kumi so she could buy some staples like salt, cornmeal, and paraffin for the family. Toto clucked her tongue over the amount of food Annah bought, but Annah could see joy and relief when she looked in her mother's eyes. They drove down the dusty road that would take them through Ngora to Agu, and Annah began to cry as she looked at the familiar fields and huts. Toto reached up from the backseat and patted Annah's shoulder. "Shhh, my girl, this is a joyous time. Here you are with us when we thought you were dead." The tears kept falling, and finally George whispered, "Auntie, you have to stop crying. You're upsetting your mother. Please don't do this." It took all of Annah's willpower, but she ceased her crying. When they got to the small track that branched off the road past the primary school, there were dozens of people running to catch a glimpse of Annah—the returning American. Women and children were standing along the track, singing songs of welcome and dancing. "Should we stop and talk to them?" Annah asked, amazed that she was creating such a stir.

"No, no," Toto said. "If we stop we'll never be able to get started again—they'll surround the car." George drove slowly on toward their compound. He stopped the car in an open area, and Annah looked ahead to see why they were stopped. About a third of a mile away she could see a cluster of huts around a big mango tree, and then she saw the man standing in the road just outside the compound. He was tall, dressed in orange-patterned robes in the local tradition, and he leaned on a cane as he peered toward them. Suddenly, he saw the car and began to walk toward them. He raised his arms, waving the cane in the air as he limped forward. Annah climbed out of the car and ran toward her papa, tears streaming down her face. When she got to him she saw his tears, and then she was being pressed against his chest and he was crying so loud he seemed to be howling. "My Frances is alive! My Frances is alive!" he kept shouting, clutching her to him.

Annah let the feeling of being engulfed in his strength wash over her, and then she struggled back just a bit.

"Papa," she laughed, "I can't breathe." She took her handkerchief out of her pocket and wiped his face gently, but his tears kept falling. Finally, he took her hand and said, "Come on, my Frances, I will show you our huts and then you must see the graves of your brother and his family."

Chapter 23

ANNAH STOOD HOLDING her father's hand as they gazed down at the slab of concrete that rose a few inches out of the dirt in a corner of the compound, under some low trees. There were just the names of George, his wife, and their twin daughters, but her father was staring at the slab steadily as if it might provide him with an answer as to why he stood above while his son and grandchildren lay below. Annah realized that he must have stood there on many days in the past mourning her and her family as well, and Rebecca and her unborn child, wishing at least for this crude symbol of their having existed. How hard this had all been on him, she thought. No wonder he looked so careworn.

After surviving the refugee camp, helping Papa and Toto bring the family back to their land, working with them to build huts and plant crops, and helping to earn enough money to buy two goats to begin a herd, her brother George had caught the strange new disease that was sweeping the country, and infected his wife and their children. George weakened quickly and died within a year of first showing signs of being ill, and his wife and children died soon after him. In all of northern Uganda, no one's body had any defenses at all in these desperate times. It wasn't until a few years later that Annah's sister Rosemary was able to tell the family that he had probably died from pneumonia because his system had been weakened by AIDS. As a public nurse, Rosemary spent all of her time in those years tending the young adults who were succumbing in droves to the AIDS epidemic. Annah stood quietly at the grave with her papa, and he began naming all of the people from their village who had died: basically her entire generation had been wiped out, leaving orphans everywhere.

As they walked back through the compound, Annah was overcome by the poverty and illness she saw all around her. There were so many children, each one thinner than the last. While there were still only fifteen orphans living in the compound, there were dozens who slept in the village with elderly grandparents who couldn't feed them, so Toto was feeding and caring for many more children during the day. The children looked at her with dark-rimmed eyes, and she realized she would always be haunted by these gaunt little faces. Most of them were naked—they didn't even have a piece of cloth to cover their thin bodies. Many of them cried softly, and she knew from their swollen bellies that they weren't getting enough to eat. The older ones listlessly carried the little ones. None of them smiled or made any attempt to play.

Papa went to speak with other men from the village, and Annah walked over to the open fire where her mother was working with some of the older orphans preparing dinner. She asked to help, but Toto insisted that she sit on a small wooden stool that one of the children brought out. The smaller children became bolder, and they began to come and stand near her, watching her with their large eyes.

"Come, sit on my lap," she said, drawing a little girl to her. The child weighed practically nothing, and Annah could feel each rib as she settled her arms around the girl's waist. Soon, other children were sitting with Annah, leaning their heads on her knees or resting one hand someplace on her body. When it was time to eat, the older girls led the children to a shady area at the edge of the compound, where they all sat in the dirt holding out small blue plastic bowls to receive their portions of rice and beans.

Annah helped Toto carry the dishes for their dinner to a rickety table that had been set up under the big mango tree near her parents' hut. They put out bowls of rice, vegetables, and groundnut soup, and the family and some of the village elders sat down on crude chairs in a circle around the table. As Annah savored the wonderful tastes of her childhood, she stole frequent looks at the children. She ached to give them her food, but she understood why she must eat it: Papa would feel shame if the family didn't welcome Annah with a feast. She also recognized Toto's wise management of the food. Keeping the children's meals consistent helped them not to overeat when times were better and then suffer more in lean times. She knew that Toto would stretch the provisions that Annah had purchased to ensure steady, if meager, nourishment for the children, and that an occasion such as this dictated a better meal for the family. Still, the joy that such a homecoming meal could have sparked was lost to Annah. She answered the many questions about her life and family, but as soon as the meal was over, she excused herself and walked around the compound.

She looked for the bush that she had crouched under as a child, praying to God to keep her parents safe, but it was gone. A short way down the path to the river, she stepped into a cluster of trees and knelt.

"God, help me to help these children," she prayed, just as fervently as she had on that first occasion. "I will keep my promise to you, but they need so much. Please send me strength."

Darkness was descending as Annah emerged from the brush, and she saw Toto and the older girls rounding the children up for bed. There were just four small huts in the compound now, and Annah knew one was for her parents, so she watched to see where all the orphans would sleep. Toto was shooing the girls into one of the huts, and the boys filed into another.

"How can they all sleep in there, Toto?" Annah asked as she approached her mother.

"Oh, they fit just fine. You'll sleep over there, in that one," she answered, pointing to a fourth hut. Annah peered past Toto into the doorway and saw the girls stretching out, side by side on the dirt floor. They wore whatever clothing they had been playing in, so most were naked or barely covered. They seemed to have favorite spots in the tangle of bodies, and it took a few minutes for them all to settle in the tiny space available and get quiet.

"Good night, Auntie Frances," some of the girls called, and soon all of them chimed in, wishing her a good rest. Similar wishes rose from the boys' quarters, so she stopped at their doorway to say good night. There was more tussling going on in this hut, which was equally crowded.

Annah's suitcases had been placed in her hut, and there was a woven mat on the ground with a thin blanket folded at the bottom of it. She said good night to Toto and Papa, and then she stretched out in her clothes on the mat. She lay there, marveling at how truly dark it was without city lights, and listened to the sound of the wind stirring the thatch of the roof. As her body began to relax, she suddenly found herself transported to her childhood and teenage years. It was the time of Idi Amin, when she often went to sleep wondering if she would be killed in the night by his roaming soldiers. Her eyes flew open and she stared at the streaks of moonlight that glimmered through openings in the straw over her head, her heart jumping each time a bird shrieked in the distance. Finally, she got up and walked across the compound to her parents' hut.

"Toto, could I sleep in here with you?" she asked. "It's scaring me to be alone."

"No, my daughter," Papa answered, coming out to stand with her. "I'll get one of the older boys to sleep at your door. You'll be fine."

Annah felt bad for the boy who curled up near her doorway, but he fell asleep quickly, and she was comforted by the sound of his breathing filling the space between her and the open countryside. At last, she fell into a sleep filled with dreams of her sisters and parents from long ago. She awoke to the shouts of the children gathering outside and had to sit on the mat for several minutes to recall that she was grown up now and just visiting.

When she stepped out into the compound, Annah found Toto spooning cassava porridge into bowls for the children. She had already taken some girls to the river to fetch the day's water and the fire was smoldering under the big cooking pot. Annah ate a mango while she watched her mother's familiar movement through her daily routines.

"Toto, I want to talk to you and Papa this morning. I have some plans for you." Esther eyed her daughter quizzically, but she asked no questions. When the children had finished eating, she sent one of them to fetch Papa Christopher while she called the older girls over to clean up the breakfast dishes.

In a few minutes, Annah, Papa, and Toto were sitting on the chairs under the mango tree. Annah looked at her aging parents and felt overwhelmed by the years that had come between them. They could never understand all that she had endured, and yet it was her belief in their strength and in the power of the God they had given her that allowed her to be there that day. She knew that God had brought her there to remind her of her promise.

"Papa, Toto, I have brought some money with me, and I want to build a house for you." Annah had calculated how many Ugandan shillings her $5,000 would be, and she told them she wanted them to have a real house, with a concrete floor to withstand the rain and keep snakes and scorpions out of their beds, concrete-brick walls painted white to deflect the heat of the sun, and a metal roof that wouldn't leak. "I was meant to help these children, but it hurts me to see how hard you have to work to care for them. I will give you a house, and I will send all the money I can collect to help feed them and send them to school." Toto had looked stunned when Annah began, and now she sat with her fingers pressed to her lips, tears in the corners of her eyes.

"Oh, Annah, a house!" Annah could see that Toto was already imagining the luxury of this. "There are so many children, and I am too old to keep cutting straw for the roof. I knew that you would come to help me." Toto and Papa began discussing how many rooms this money would buy—bedrooms for them, the boys, and the girls; a living and eating area; a kitchen so that food could be stored and preparations done in cool shade. Annah listened happily, thinking that there had been few times in her life when her parents sounded so hopeful.

Papa had just sent one of the older boys to Soroti to find a builder who would come and plan the house with them when another child came to say there was a visitor for Annah. He pointed to the edge of the compound, and Annah saw a tall man about her age who looked vaguely familiar. She and Papa went to greet him, and Annah realized that he was one of James's brothers. He introduced himself as Samson, and Annah recalled that he was about ten years younger than James. She had known him as a young man when she and James lived near Amuria. He had aged well; although he bore the same thinness that everyone in northern Uganda had these days, he was a handsome man with a firm handshake and a frank gaze. She shuddered when she thought how he compared to James: the last time she had seen her husband, he had been gaunt and unable to look her in the eye.

Papa led Samson to the chairs under the tree, and he sat down with them. Annah was glad for her father's presence; he might have left her alone to deal with her in-law, but he seemed to sense a need to stay close to her. After answering Papa's questions—he lived in Soroti now; he was the youngest of James's surviving brothers; Lucy was frail but living contentedly in Kampala with his older brother, Benjamin—Samson turned purposefully toward Annah, asking politely but firmly how she could not know the whereabouts of her own husband. Annah told him the whole story, of the loss of government funding and James's inability to remain at the university or to find work as a teacher; of their moves to Washington, DC, back to Ohio, and then to St. Louis; and finally of James's descent into alcoholism and ill health. When she finished, Samson sat looking at her for several minutes.

"My brother, my brother, how could this happen?" he said softly, and Annah laid a hand on his arm. "Samson, do you know if James ever had trouble with alcohol here?" she asked. His eyes clouded for a moment, and then he sagged, as if accepting a blow.

"Yes," he said slowly. "I was very young, and he was in high school. Of course he drank beer—all fifteen-year-olds did, out in the brush where their parents wouldn't catch them. But James—James had been so sad and distant after our father died. One time, he was just gone, for about two weeks, and then he was home but he was throwing up a lot and seemed to be sick. I didn't know what was happening, but later I realized that he had been drunk for those two weeks and our mother had searched until she could find him and bring him home." He looked at Annah and then seemed to plead, "But he never did it again. He could control his drinking after that, and then of course he became an Evangelical and never touched alcohol." Annah looked into his eyes and realized that she was seeing her own pain— of knowing the better James and yet not knowing how to bring him back. As he rose to go back to Soroti, Samson asked Annah if she would make time on her return trip to meet with him and his brothers and mother in Benjamin's home in Kampala.

"We must find a way to bring James to Uganda," he said. "He could heal here." Annah felt a strong ache, realizing that Samson didn't truly understand the depth of James's fall, but she agreed to meet with them. She watched as Papa led the man back to his motor scooter and shook hands with him. How had she failed so as the wife of this man's brother? Why wasn't her love enough for James to overcome their challenges, as so many had done here in Uganda?

She was startled to feel Papa's hand on her shoulder. He sat in the chair next to hers and looked directly into her eyes.

"You are a courageous woman, Frances. You know, we always talk of how important sons are for an Iteso man, because they will always be there in his old age to help him, but you, my daughter, are the moon in my sky." He held his hand out to her, and she took it and stood up with him.

"Come now, Frances, we'll walk to the field and I'll show you my fine herd of goats."

Epilogue

ON A BLISTERINGLY HOT December morning in 2009, Christopher sat under the huge mango tree in the center of his compound, watching the southern horizon as heat rippled from the brown earth. It had taken a great deal of time and effort for the tall, gaunt man to get his weakened legs to carry him from the small concrete-brick house where he now lived to his chair, so he dozed off and on while the children played nearby. They knew not to bother Papa Christopher when he was resting, but occasionally a thin, tiny child would walk close to him and peer into his face, just to make sure he was alright. There were fifty-four orphans living with him and his wife now, and they all clung to their Tata Esther and Papa Christopher with the fierce determination that comes from loss and terror.

Finally, in the early afternoon, a cloud of dust signaled the arrival of George's car. Christopher's lined face creased into a smile as he watched the car approach and confirmed that it bore his American daughter. Annah opened her door before the car had stopped completely and rushed to him.

"Oh, my papa," she cried as she knelt in front of him. They took each other's hands and Annah held his to her cheeks, wetting them with her tears.

"My Frances, you are here," Christopher said. He pulled her arms wide apart to study her closely, just as he had done when she was a little girl. With pride he noted that his tall, strong daughter's arms were nearly as long as his.

"You look so good, my child. I thank God that I have lived to see you again."

"I've brought some Americans with me, Papa, the ones who will help us build a bigger home for all these children." Over the next week, Christopher watched quietly while his daughter and her friends surveyed land, drew building designs, and met with elders

227

and experts to make their plans for the large orphanage. The children were in a frenzy to hold the Americans' hands and play with the soccer balls and books that these strange people had brought to them.

When Annah's visit ended, she knelt once again to say good-bye to her father. "Papa, the people will be here to drill the well in April, and then we will raise money and build a bigger home that will give all the children a place to sleep. And I will come back just as soon as I can."

"My Frances, I may not be alive to see you here again. But I am a happy man. I know that your mother and all of my dear little children—here and in America—will be taken care of. And it is all because of you, my daughter." Annah kissed his hands, and Christopher watched her walk slowly to the car.

Christopher lived to see the 240-foot well dug near the edge of his compound in 2010. The well has the capacity to serve over two thousand people, so he invited the villagers of Agu to share in his good fortune. He laughed with the other adults when the children at first refused to drink this strange-looking water that had no smell and wasn't brown, and he rejoiced with Esther and the other care-givers as they realized how much time and work was saved by having the water source just fifty steps from the compound kitchen.

In March of 2011, Christopher didn't awake one morning, and Esther and Rosemary had to phone Annah to tell her that this strong, loving patriarch was gone. Annah got up at four in the morning in Missouri to attend her father's funeral by cell phone, and she listened and prayed as Christopher was buried in the compound, surrounded by three sons, their wives and children, and five orphans—all of whom died far too young, from the ravages of life in Uganda. Christopher died just a month short of his eighty-third birthday.

Today, there are still over fifty children living in the orphanage, and at mealtimes almost double that number line up to receive a bowl of meager sustenance. The additional children are orphans from nearby compounds, where they may have an elderly relative to live with, but there is inadequate food. Although it is a constant struggle to obtain sufficient funds to support the children, the dozens who live there do have at least one meal per day, and their health has improved with the availability of clean water. All of the young Atai orphans attend primary school, and most of the older ones are able to go to secondary school. They have outgrown the house that

Annah built, and fundraising is not yet complete for the large build-ing that is planned, so all but the most frail are again sleeping on the dirt floors of mud huts.

In the United States, Annah's own family has grown and pros-pered. Her four children are talented, successful adults. Annah has two wonderful grandsons, who bring light to her life. The three older children have traveled to Uganda to meet their grandparents and their cousins, the orphans of Atai. Annah's grandsons have vis-ited twice; they lived at the orphanage with Annah during the sum-mer of 2011. James was never able to return to his homeland, and he died from the ravages of his illness in June of 2009.

Annah divides her love and support between her two families in such distant countries. And yet, there are still times when she aches to have James Emuge at her side, and she realizes that nei-ther Uganda nor the United States feels entirely like home to her. But she has learned that some people are meant to be the moon in others' skies, and she is content, knowing that this was God's plan for her, all along.

Although the orphanage children miss their Papa Christopher, they still have their Tata Esther, who rises every morning to tend to their needs and tucks them all into bed at night. And, if you ask any of the orphans if they have a mother, they reply, "Oh yes, my Mama Frances is in America. She loves me very much."

Note on Sources

The descriptions of Ugandan history and culture in the book chapters are Annah Emuge's impressions of her surroundings, recalled from her youth, as well as what she understood to be happening while she was in the United States. I wrote the brief reports on Uganda at the beginning of each section to provide the reader with basic background on the broader events occurring during the different parts of Annah's life, and I used several types of sources to ensure that these sections give accurate, known information.

I obtained considerable insight into Uganda's history and culture from conversations with Godfrey G. Mukalazi of Kampala, Uganda, a graduate of the Rotary International World Peace and Conflict Resolution master's program at the University of Queensland, Australia, and currently the Programme Officer for Peace Building and Conflict Transformation for the Uganda Joint Christian Council. Godfrey was my generous and knowledgeable host during my travels in Uganda in 2009. Robert Opira of Gulu, Uganda, also a graduate of the Rotary peace program at Queensland, showed me the remnants of a refugee camp and explained what life was like there for those who escaped the tribal conflicts and attacks by the Lord's Resistance Army in the 1990s and 2000s.

A number of secondary sources were also useful to me in gathering this information. Good sources of basic demographic information were the Uganda section of the *CIA World Factbook* (https://www.cia.gov/library/publications/the-world-factbook/geos/ug.html), the United States Census Bureau International Data Base (https://www.census.gov/population/international/data/idb/informationGateway.php), and the Library of Congress's "Country Studies" (Federal Research Division, lcweb2.loc.gov/frd/cs/ugtoc.html).

The section on Uganda in *Africana: The Encyclopedia of the African and African-American Experience*, edited by Kwame Anthony Appiah and Henry Louis Gates Jr. (New York: Basic Civitas, 1999), pp. 1907–

11, and the Library of Congress's "Country Studies" provided valuable basic information on Ugandan history.

I found several good sources of information about the presidencies of Milton Obote and Idi Amin, including *Uganda since Independence: A Story of Unfulfilled Hopes,* by Phares Mutibwa (Trenton, NJ: Africa World Press, 1992), and *War in Uganda: The Legacy of Idi Amin,* by Tony Avirgan and Martha Honey (Dar es Salaam, Tanzania: Tanzania Publishing, 1983). Several articles provided interesting information on the two men as well. These include "Uganda—Lurching towards Obote," by Tony Avirgan (*Nation* 230, no. 13 [1980]: 397–98); "Uganda: What Was the Legacy of Milton Obote?" by Timothy Kalyegira (*Daily Monitor,* Kampala, Uganda, October 12, 2005); "A Peaceful Uganda Celebrates" (*New African,* no. 521 [October 2012]: 3-4); and Patrick Keatley's obituary of Idi Amin (*Guardian,* London, August 17, 2003).

While historians seem to agree that Idi Amin's presidency was that of a brutal dictator who brought ruin to his country, there are widely divergent viewpoints concerning Milton Obote and his legacy in Uganda. Although it is considered a fact that hundreds of thousands of people were killed during his regime, writings after his death still praised him for his early accomplishments in establishing a sound infrastructure. An interesting collection of those opposing views is contained in *Apollo Milton Obote: What Others Say,* edited by Omongole R. Anguria (Kampala, Uganda: Fountain Publishers, 2006).

Excellent sources regarding the divisions between northern and southern tribes and the atrocities of the Lord's Resistance Army include the aforementioned *Africana* and *War in Uganda* and articles by Mahmood Mamdani, especially "Kony: What Jason Did Not Tell the Invisible Children" (*Aljazeera,* March 13, 2012, www.aljazeera .com/indepth/opinion/ 2012/03/20123138139642455.html). Olara A. Otunno's "The Secret Genocide" (*Foreign Policy,* no. 155 [July–August 2006]: 44–46) was a valuable source as well.

While the full legacy of Yoweri Museveni, who has been Uganda's president since 1986, is yet to be determined, his actions during his early years in power, including efforts to fight the HIV/AIDS epidemic and to improve educational opportunities for his citizens, are well documented. Good sources for this information include "Uganda's Full School Benches," by Dan Elwana (*UNESCO Courier* 53, no. 3 [March 2000]: 22–23), and "The Lost Generation: How the Government and Non-Government Organizations Are Protecting the Rights of Orphans—Uganda," by Jeanne Caruso and Kevin Cope (*Human Rights Review* 7, no. 2 [January–March 2006]: 98–114).